WISDEN
The Laws *of* Cricket

Wisden: The Laws of Cricket sets out in full the text of the new laws of cricket, 42 in number (with permission of the MCC which own the copyright in them). For each law it provides a commentary, covering the reasons for any changes, explaining the background, and highlighting how they are likely to affect the way the game is played at every level. Full discussion is devoted to the major contentious issues, such as the introduction of penalty runs for various misdemeanours, and the revisions to the 'no ball' law. Don Oslear, the distinguished umpire, has been intimately involved over several years in the process of drafting the new laws, and explains why they needed changing, what views his committee received from the governing bodies of all the cricketing nations and from players, spectators and the media, how these were resolved, and what effect they are expected to have on the future of the game. No one who plays cricket, or is seriously interested in the game, can afford to miss this book.

WISDEN
The Laws *of* Cricket

Don Oslear

EBURY PRESS
LONDON

First published in Great Britain in 2000

1 3 5 7 9 10 8 6 4 2

Copyright © Don Oslear 2000

Don Oslear has asserted his right under the Copyright, Designs and Patents Act 1988 to be identified as the author of this work.

All rights reserved. No part of this publication may be reproduced, stored in a retrieval system, or transmitted in any form or by any means, electronic, mechanical, photocopying, recording or otherwise, without prior permission from the copyright owners.

Ebury Press
Random House · 20 Vauxhall Bridge Road · London SW1V 2SA

Random House Australia Pty Limited
20 Alfred Street · Milsons Point · Sydney · New South Wales 2061 · Australia

Random House New Zealand Limited
18 Poland Road · Glenfield · Auckland 10 · New Zealand

Random House (Pty) Limited
Endulini · 5A Jubilee Road · Parktown 2193 · South Africa

The Random House Group Limited Reg. No. 954009

www.randomhouse.co.uk

Papers used by Ebury Press are natural, recyclable products made from wood grown in sustainable forests.

A CIP catalogue record for this book is available from the British Library.

ISBN 0 091 87790 3

Designed by Lovelock & Co.

Printed and bound in Great Britain by Mackays of Chatham plc · Chatham · Kent

CONTENTS

	Foreword	7
	Introduction	9
	The Preamble – The Spirit of Cricket	12
Law 1	The players	14
Law 2	Substitutes and runners; batsman or fielder leaving the field; batsman retiring; batsman commencing innings	16
Law 3	The umpires	24
Law 4	The scorers	32
Law 5	The ball	35
Law 6	The bat	38
Law 7	The pitch	41
Law 8	The wickets	43
Law 9	The bowling, popping and return creases	46
Law 10	Preparation and maintenance of the playing area	49
Law 11	Covering the pitch	55
Law 12	Innings	58
Law 13	The follow-on	61
Law 14	Declaration and forfeiture	63
Law 15	Intervals	65
Law 16	Start of play; cessation of play	72
Law 17	Practice on the field	77

Law 18	Scoring runs	79
Law 19	Boundaries	86
Law 20	Lost ball	94
Law 21	The result	97
Law 22	The over	103
Law 23	Dead ball	106
Law 24	No ball	110
Law 25	Wide ball	117
Law 26	Bye and Leg bye	121
Law 27	Appeals	124
Law 28	The wicket is down	127
Law 29	Batsman out of his ground	131
Law 30	Bowled	133
Law 31	Timed out	135
Law 32	Caught	137
Law 33	Handled the ball	142
Law 34	Hit the ball twice	144
Law 35	Hit wicket	150
Law 36	Leg before wicket	152
Law 37	Obstructing the field	155
Law 38	Run out	158
Law 39	Stumped	162
Law 40	The wicket-keeper	165
Law 41	The fielder	170
Law 42	Fair and unfair play	176
	Appendices	202

FOREWORD

Since its formation in 1787 the Marylebone Cricket Club (MCC) has been recognised as the sole authority for drawing up the code and all subsequent amendments to the laws of cricket. Now in 2000 MCC has revised and rewritten the laws for the new millennium. In this code, the major innovation is the introduction of the 'Spirit of Cricket' as a preamble to the laws. An attempt has also been made to incorporate the notes into the wording of the laws.

I am pleased to have been invited to write the foreword to this study of the laws. *The Wisden Book of Cricket Laws* was first published in 1993 by the same author. Don Oslear was a member of the working party asked by MCC to undertake the work, and also a most energetic and meticulous member of the drafting group, which spent countless hours checking the wording and eliminating any ambiguities in the new code. Don has always been a student of the laws. As a first-class umpire he never missed a chance to air his knowledge, sometimes to the frustration of players, who would really have preferred not to be told that they were wrong, although accepting his authority and knowing deep down that he was right. He is a forthright man of principle, a stickler for discipline, who holds strong views which are not easily changed. He will not necessarily agree with all the final decisions of the working party, but he, like the other members, will have argued his case and will now take collective responsibility for the final version of the laws.

It was my pleasure to play as captain in a number of games in which Don stood as umpire. As a player, and especially as a captain, it was helpful to have conversations with Don, when we occasionally had a drink after a day's play. Current players often only have a sketchy understanding of the laws. Our conversations led to a good relationship between captain and umpire, which is very important for the conduct of the game. The first part of the preamble to this code reminds us that the captain is responsible for ensuring that play is conducted within the spirit of the game.. The umpires are the sole judges of fair play, but it is the captains' responsibility to take action where required. The relationship and respect between captains and umpires is an integral part of cricket and one of the reasons for the game's success over the years.

I have also seen him in operation as tournament referee in some of the European Cricket Council competitions. He has had to deal with a number of difficult incidents, and he has never shirked what he has seen as his duty. I, and others involved in European cricket, have enjoyed his company, enjoyed lengthy discussions with him about the intricacies of the laws, and appreciated his respect for the game of cricket and the spirit in which it should be played. Many people, not only in Europe but also elsewhere in the world, have benefited from Don's patient explanations and teaching on the laws. His slide shows are extremely clear and informative, and he speaks authoritatively.

This book will give the reader an insight into some of the deliberations of the working party. It will also help umpires to understand the new code and the reasons behind some of the changes. I hope that readers will dip into the pages and enjoy the experience and anecdotes of a man who has seen cricket at the top level from behind the stumps. I look forward to spending more time reading this excellent book.

ROGER KNIGHT
SECRETARY, MCC
JULY 2000

INTRODUCTION

In 1998 I received a letter from John Jameson, assistant secretary (cricket) of Marylebone Cricket Club. It was an invitation to me to serve not only as a full member of the laws working party but also to act as one of the five members of the drafting working party who would put together the 2000 code of The Laws of Cricket.

I naturally felt this to be an honour and privilege to sit on a committee containing so many high-profile names from the game of cricket, both past and present. In my letter of acceptance I stated that my main aim in the drafting of the new code would be to try to ensure that the game of cricket would be made safer and fairer for all those who take part in it at all levels.

The full committee was chaired by Lord Griffiths, one of the most eminent law lords in the land. The West Indies delegation included Sir Clyde Walcott, chairman of the ICC's cricket committee, and Steve Bucknor, one of the leading international umpires. The Australian party consisted of Bob Simpson, one of the country's most respected players and former captains, along with Tony Crafter, who for many years was one of their top umpires and is now in charge of all umpiring matters on behalf of the Australian Cricket Board. From India there was Srinivasaraghavan Venkataraghavan, a former captain of the national team. He is one of the leading present-day umpires and a member of the National Grid International Panel of Umpires. The name of Brian Basson may not spring readily to mind but he was the representative of the United Cricket Board of South Africa and contributed greatly in putting forward his board's views. He was one of the umpires who missed out because of the apartheid problems in his country.

Added to these names, along with my own, was that of Nigel Plews, a top-class international umpire for many years and one of the original selections for the ICC's international panel. Sheila Hill and Robbie Robins, two members of the Association of Cricket Umpires and Scorers, and John Jameson completed the panel. The experience that John brought to the meetings was enormous. He had seen the game from every angle and, in fact, I had seen him occupy all of these angles in my career. I saw him as a batsman with Warwickshire, as a first-class umpire – we stood together many times – as a coach with Sussex and in recent years as an MCC administrator.

Sheila and Robbie were mainly responsible for the wording of the draft of the new laws and brought to the meetings the thoughts of their ACU&S members. Nigel and I were largely responsible for the clarification aspect of the new code and worked closely together, as did Sheila and Robbie.

Nigel and I brought to our meetings the thoughts of the umpiring bodies of the many countries we had visited in the previous two years. I had made 19 visits to 12 countries, from as far away as Tonga to as close as Northern Ireland. Nigel made ten visits to seven countries including all seven states of Australia in nine days. John collated the comments he received from the four of us, along with those from the various cricket boards around the world. He was greatly assisted by his very efficient secretary, Rachel Lee.

Readers of this book will deduce that I am happy with 98 per cent of the new code but distinctly unhappy with a couple of aspects, notably Law 42.6 (b) and the action taken by the umpire in Law 42.14. They are law now, though, and I have to apply them, perhaps with slightly different clarifications to others. Also, I find some of the wording lengthy, particularly in respect of some of the titles of parts of certain laws.

This publication is not in itself a law book and I never intended it to be. The study of the Laws of Cricket can be very dull so I have endeavoured to bring to the readers' attention the changes that have been made from the 1980 code that are now included in the 2000 code. Some laws I have gone into in great detail, while others that have not been changed, apart from the wording, I have left alone. I have delved into the origins of some of the laws, and I have tried to show how they have evolved over two and a half centuries. I have related incidents from my 25 years of umpiring professional cricket that relate to the laws.

The meetings of the working party and the deliberations have been lengthy. We have met for a total of 33 days, hours of play 9am to 6pm, and on top of this there have been many hours of study by all of us of the various texts of the proposed drafts of the new laws.

I have to thank the other members of the working party for their understanding when I have tried to press a point with which they may not have totally agreed. We have spent much time in each other's company and I think that matters are just as amicable as they were at the start of our endeavours. Finally, I would like to thank those authors whose works have helped with my research, and MCC for granting permission to reproduce the laws.

THE LAWS OF CRICKET

THE PREAMBLE
– The Spirit of Cricket

Cricket is a game that owes much of its unique appeal to the fact that it should be played not only within its Laws but also within the Spirit of the Game. Any action which is seen to abuse this spirit causes injury to the game itself. The major responsibility for ensuring the spirit of fair play rests with the captains.

1. There are two Laws which place the responsibility for the team's conduct firmly on the captain.

Responsibility of captains
The captains are responsible at all times for ensuring that play is conducted within the Spirit of the Game as well as within the Laws.

Player's conduct
In the event of a player failing to comply with instructions by an umpire, or criticising by word or action the decisions of an umpire, or showing dissent, or generally behaving in a manner which might bring the game into disrepute, the umpire concerned shall in the first place report the matter to the other umpire and to the player's captain, and instruct the latter to take action.

2. Fair and unfair play
According to the Laws the umpires are the sole judges of fair and unfair play.
The umpires may intervene at any time and it is the responsibility of the captain to take action where required.

3. The umpires are authorised to intervene in cases of:
Time wasting
Damaging the pitch
Dangerous or unfair bowling
Tampering with the ball
Any other action that they consider to be unfair

4. The Spirit of the Game involves RESPECT for:
Your opponents
Your own captain and team
The role of the umpires
The game's traditional values

5. It is against the Spirit of the Game:
To dispute an umpire's decision by word, action or gesture
To direct abusive language towards an opponent or umpire
To indulge in cheating or any sharp practice, for instance:
a) to appeal knowing that the batsman is not out
b) to advance towards an umpire in an aggressive manner when appealing
c) to seek to distract an opponent either verbally or by harassment with persistent clapping or unnecessary noise under the guise of enthusiasm and motivation of one's own side

6. Violence
There is no place for any act of violence on the field of play.

7. Players
Captains and umpires together set the tone for the conduct of a cricket match. Every player is expected to make an important contribution to this.

The players, umpires and scorers in a game of cricket may be of either gender and the Laws apply equally to both. The use, throughout the text, of pronouns indicating the male gender is purely for brevity. Except where specifically stated otherwise, every provision of the Laws is to be read as applying to women and girls equally as to men and boys.

LAW 1
The Players

1. Number of players
A match is played between two sides, each of eleven players, one of whom shall be captain.
By agreement a match may be played between sides of more or less than eleven players, but not more than eleven players may field at any time.

2. Nomination of players
Each captain shall nominate his players in writing to one of the umpires before the toss. No player may be changed after the nomination without the consent of the opposing captain.

3. Captain
If at any time the captain is not available, a deputy shall act for him.
(a) If a captain is not available during the period in which the toss is to take place, then the deputy must be responsible for the nomination of the players, if this has not already been done, and for the toss. See 2 above and Law 12.4 (The toss).
(b) At any time after the toss, the deputy must be one of the nominated players

4. Responsibility of captains
The captains are responsible at all times for ensuring that play is conducted within the spirit and traditions of the game as well as within the Laws. See The Preamble – The Spirit of Cricket and Law 42.1 (Fair and unfair play - responsibility of captains).

This first law in the new code shows no real change but there are one or two significant points which must be noted. In the first book I wrote on the laws of cricket, I made mention of the fact that umpires may well have been remiss in the past in not making themselves aware of the "nominated sides". This comment was made in *The Wisden Book of Cricket Laws*, first published in 1993, and the matter has now been addressed in Law 1.2 of the the 2000 Code, "Nomination of players".

Law 1.2 now states that not only has each captain to nominate his side, but that this shall be in written form and the document must be presented to one of the umpires on the day of the match and prior to the toss for innings.

I have known captains, on a lovely summer's evening, walk out of the clubhouse and onto the field of play, with pints of beer in hand, and toss a coin into the evening sky. Upon their return to the bar the information would be dispensed as to which side would bat or field the following day. It will be seen that this practice can no longer take place, unless, of course, the drinking session is still taking place after midnight. As long as it is after midnight, then it is legal to nominate a side under Law 1.

While the reasons for this may not be immediately clear, it certainly is if you look under the definitions for before the match and before the toss. However, I do not see any point in this action taking place for, as stated, it is not legal to toss for innings at that time. This now has to be undertaken in an exact time-span of 15 minutes, as laid down in Law 12.4.

One of the reasons the working party recommended this change was that it is essential umpires know who is going to take part in a match, should there be cause at a later hour to allow a change in the nominated side. Also, if rain has fallen overnight after the toss, the nominated side may well be vastly different the following day to that envisaged when the toss took place.

Law 1.3 (a) requires that if a captain is not available in the 15-minute time-span during which the toss must be made, a deputy must be responsible for not only the toss but the nomination of the side, if it has not been already made.

Law 1.3 (b) makes the point that "at any time after the toss, the deputy must be one of the nominated side". However, it fails to state whether or not the deputy can be changed at any time during the match. I wonder if this hould be considered for the future, bearing in mind the Yorkshire League match I wrote about in the 1993 edition of this book. On that occasion, the away side, because of a traffic jam, had only three players ready at the time for play to start. The home captain insisted that the toss took place, and when he won it he put the visitors into bat. Before the other players arrived, two wickets fell and therefore the innings was at an end.

I endeavoured for the new law to state that a minimum number of players should be present before a game could commence. I did not persist for very long along these lines, however, as it was pointed out by other members of the working party that this position had been well covered in the 1980 code and is still well covered in the 2000 code. The number is 11 and always has been, unless agreement to the contrary is arrived at before the match starts or, umpires please note, there are special regulations stating otherwise. Should the captain of the home team in the match referred to above still be engaged in a similar capacity, I suggest that he studies and digests "The Spirit of Cricket" at the beginning of this book.

LAW 2

Substitutes and Runners; Batsman or Fielder Leaving the Field; Batsman Retiring; Batsman Commencing Innings

1. Substitutes and runners
(a) If the umpires are satisfied that a player has been injured or become ill after the nomination of the players, they shall allow that player to have
    (i)   a substitute acting instead of him in the field.
    (ii)   a runner when batting.
Any injury or illness that occurs at any time after the nomination of the players until the conclusion of the match shall be allowable, irrespective of whether play is in progress or not.
(b) The umpires shall have discretion, for other wholly acceptable reasons, to allow a substitute for a fielder, or a runner for a batsman, at the start of the match or at any subsequent time.
(c) A player wishing to change his shirt, boots, etc. must leave the field to do so. No substitute shall be allowed for him.

2. Objection to substitutes
The opposing captain shall have no right of objection to any player acting as a substitute on the field, nor as to where the substitute shall field. However, no substitute shall act as wicket-keeper. See 3 below.

3. Restrictions on the role of substitutes
A substitute shall not be allowed to bat or bowl nor to act as wicket-keeper or as captain on the field of play.

4. A player for whom a substitute has acted
A player is allowed to bat, bowl or field even though a substitute has previously acted for him.

5. Fielder absent or leaving the field

If a fielder fails to take the field with his side at the start of the match or at any later time, or leaves the field during a session of play

(a) the umpire shall be informed of the reason for his absence.

(b) he shall not thereafter come on to the field during a session of play without the consent of the umpire. See 6 below. The umpire shall give such consent as soon as is practicable.

(c) if he is absent for 15 minutes or longer, he shall not be permitted to bowl thereafter, subject to (i), (ii) or (iii) below, until he has been on the field for at least that length of playing time for which he was absent.

    (i)   Absence or penalty for time absent shall not be carried over into a new day's play.

    (ii)   If, in the case of a follow-on or forfeiture, a side fields for two consecutive innings, this restriction shall, subject to (i) above, continue as necessary into the second innings but shall not otherwise be carried over into a new innings.

    (iii)   The time lost for an unscheduled break in play shall be counted as time on the field for any fielder who comes on to the field at the resumption of play. See Law 15.1 (An interval).

6. Player returning without permission

If a player comes on to the field of play in contravention of 5(b) above and comes into contact with the ball while it is in play

    (i)   the ball shall immediately become dead and the umpire shall award 5 penalty runs to the batting side. See Law 42.17 (Penalty runs).

    (ii)   the umpire shall inform the other umpire, the captain of the fielding side, the batsmen and, as soon as practicable, the captain of the batting side, of the reason for this action.

    (iii)   the umpires together shall report the occurrence as soon as possible to the Executive of the fielding side and any Governing Body responsible for the match, who shall take such action as is considered appropriate against the captain and player concerned.

7. Runner

The player acting as a runner for a batsman shall be a member of the batting side and shall, if possible, have already batted in that innings. The runner shall wear external protective equipment equivalent to that worn by the batsman for whom he runs and shall carry a bat.

8. Transgression of the Laws by a batsman who has a runner

(a) A batsman's runner is subject to the Laws. He will be regarded as a batsman except where there are specific provisions for his role as a runner. See 7 above and Law 29.2 (Which is a batsman's ground).

(b) A batsman with a runner will suffer the penalty for any infringement of the Laws by his runner as though he had been himself responsible for the infringement. In particular he will be out if his runner is out under any of Laws 33 (Handled the ball), 37 (Obstructing the field) or 38 (Run out).

(c) When a batsman with a runner is striker he remains himself subject to the Laws and will be liable to the penalties that any infringement of them demands.

Additionally, if he is out of his ground when the wicket is put down at the wicket-keeper's end, he will be out in the circumstances of Law 38 (Run out) or Law 39 (Stumped) irrespective of the position of the non-striker or of the runner. If he is thus dismissed, runs completed by the runner and the other batsman before the dismissal shall not be scored. However, the penalty for a No ball or a Wide shall stand, together with any penalties to either side that may be awarded when the ball is dead. See Law 42.17 (Penalty runs).

(d) When a batsman with a runner is not the striker

   (i)   he remains subject to Laws 33 (Handled the ball) and 37 (Obstructing the field) but is otherwise out of the game.

   (ii)   he shall stand where directed by the striker's end umpire so as not to interfere with play.

   (iii)   he will be liable, notwithstanding (i) above, to the penalty demanded by the Laws should he commit any act of unfair play.

9. Batsman leaving the field or retiring

A batsman may retire at any time during his innings. The umpires, before allowing play to proceed, shall be informed of the reason for a batsman retiring.

(a) If a batsman retires because of illness, injury or any other unavoidable cause, he is entitled to resume his innings subject to (c) below. If for any reason he does not do so, his innings is to be recorded as 'Retired – not out'.

(b) If a batsman retires for any reason other than as in (a) above, he may only resume his innings with the consent of the opposing captain. If for any reason he does not resume his innings it is to be recorded as 'Retired – out'.

(c) If after retiring a batsman resumes his innings, it shall be only at the fall of a wicket or the retirement of another batsman.

10. Commencement of a batsman's innings
Except at the start of a side's innings, a batsman shall be considered to have commenced his innings when he first steps on to the field of play, provided Time has not been called. The innings of the opening batsmen, and that of any new batsman at the resumption of play after a call of Time, shall commence at the call of Play.

Over the years there have been many provisions embodied within the laws of cricket, to allow, or otherwise, the use of a substitute. These provisions have been in respect of both teams, either while batting or acting as fielders. These changes are numerous and in setting them down it can be seen how this law has evolved over the years since 1744.

Nothing in regard to the number of players is laid down in this early code, although it is known that in the Grand Matches each side consisted of 11 players. There was, though, a law which stated "no fresh men were allowed to act as substitutes on any account".

In a code of laws dated 1755 there is a lovely descriptive piece under Laws for Umpires and it reads, "they are the sole judges of all hurts, whether real or pretend". This law then carries on to say: "in case of a real hurt to a striker they are to allow another to come in and the person hurt to come in again but are not to allow a fresh man to play on either side on any account". No mention is made in this code of allowing the use of a substitute for a player while fielding.

It is not until 1774 that we first see a mention of a substitute for a player while fielding. The law is rather vague but it appears probable that they were allowed by consent. 1798 saw a law for a substitute fielder without any restriction as to where he may field, and some time prior to 1823 this law contained matters which bear some relation to that which has existed for many years, parts of which still exist today. "Substitutes are not to bowl, keep wicket, field at point, middle wicket or long stop (to a fast bowler) except by agreement."

In 1835 the wording of the law is slightly confusing in one aspect. "Substitutes, even with consent, may not bowl, keep wicket, field at point, cover point or long stop and in the last named position this applies to any type of bowling." It is the first four words that I find confusing. Did it mean that some time prior to 1835 a substitute could be used without consent? I feel that a further change in this law in 1854 throws some light on the matter. It reads, "the consent of the opposite side is required to the particular player required to act as a fielding substitute and to the place in which he may field".

Also in this law it is stated "that an injured striker along with the injured striker's runner were liable to be run out, if either were out of their ground whilst the ball was in play". It was not until 1884 that an injured striker would be out for any infringement of the laws by his runner. Previously, only run-out applied.

The 1947 code allowed a batting captain to say in which positions the substitute may not field. Previously, he was required to state where he may field. Also, with consent, a substitute could keep wicket. This law was changed again in respect of the wicketkeeper when England, in one Test match, had four players fill that position at various times, two of whom were virtually dragged out of the crowd. This change was made on 1 April 1989, and it applied to all classes of cricket, again reading that a substitute may not keep wicket.

So much for the evolution of the law in regard to a substitute. Now to the 2000 code, and how it may have changed from the previous one of 1980.

Law 2.1 (a) sets down, in a much clearer manner, situations in which a substitute can be used by right. It will not matter if the indisposition takes place while his side are actually on the field of play or not. Neither will it matter if the individual is at the ground where the match is being played or away from the ground when his indisposition occurs - nor even whether it happens during the hours of daylight or during the depths of the night. It matters not if the injury be by contact of a nasty hard ball upon a part of the player's anatomy or should his illness be acquired by the consumption of too much good ale in the team's hotel at night.

The duration of the match is from the time of the nomination of a side on the first morning of a match, prior to the toss for innings, until a result is achieved or "time" is called at the conclusion of the match. You can say that every second counts, even though the duration may vary. Most limited-overs cricket starts some time after noon and finishes between 7pm and 8pm the same day. That will be the duration for that match. There are also matches that start at 11am on a Thursday and finish at 6pm the following Tuesday. These are five-day Test matches, even though they cover six days. For the purposes of this law, even the Sunday, the rest day, will count.

The duration of a match can be even longer, as in the following example. I umpired Premier League cricket in New Zealand during the 1980-81 season and these matches are played on consecutive Saturdays, with the hours of play from 10am until 6pm, if I remember correctly. After play had been concluded on the first Saturday, there were rest days, six of them to be exact, before the match was completed the following Saturday. What a lovely way to play a game of cricket.

One Wednesday evening, in the "middle" of such a match, four young men returning to Christchurch by car from their labours on an outlying farm had an accident. It was not serious. The car slid off the "dirt" and into a gully. All of them had minor cuts and bruises and the following Saturday all four employed the use of a substitute as of right. This was quite legitimate because their injuries were incurred during the match, which had begun with the nomination of the sides on the first Saturday and was to end at close of play seven days later.

Law 2.1 (b) shows one important omission from the 1980 code. It is in regard to the situation of a substitute being required for a player through a situation other than illness or injury. Previously, in exceptional circumstances, the opposing captain had to give consent to his opposite number before a substitute could be allowed. Now, in the 2000 code, this matter is left entirely in the hands of the umpires. It is at their discretion whether they should allow one or not, for either side, not only during the match, but also at the start of it.

Laws 2.2 and 2.3 make it crystal clear that a substitute may not act as a wicketkeeper. Much time was spent by the working party discussing this point. We felt at one time that perhaps we should allow a substitute for a wicketkeeper, as it is looked upon as a specialist position. A novice from the remaining ten players may leave himself open to injury should he be asked by his captain to deputise. In the end we decided against any change, for it might not stop there. A slip fielder is certainly looked upon as a specialist fielding position, along with that of a bat-pad fielder. Law 2.3 also specifies that a substitute may not act as captain. I am not sure that this really matters, as most sides now appear to have at least eight captains on the field. What difference would one more make?

Law 2.5 contains one subtle change, which umpires must observe closely. In part (c) the time of absence by a fielder is stated as "15 minutes or longer". In the previous code, for a fielder to commit himself to have to serve penalty time, he had to be off the field for "longer than 15 minutes". I know that we are only talking about seconds here, but do note the change.

Law 2.5 (c) (i) covers the second part of a situation that I have fought hard to have altered. I felt that penalty time should be carried over into the following day. However, in the end it was agreed not to make a change from the 1980 code. The other part, which I was successful in having changed a number of years ago, was in regard to a member of the fielding side. Previously, he could arrive as late as he desired after play had started on any day, come on to the field and bowl immediately. I felt that this was unfair. As I say, this has been changed for a number of years now. I have won half the battle and live to fight another day for the rest. I will settle for that.

Law 2.5 (c) (ii) has been clarified as a direct result of a situation that was presented to my good friend and colleague Nigel Plews. It occurred on my own club ground at Cleethorpes in a Minor Counties match. I do not remember the exact timing details but the gist of events was as follows. A side batted on the first day and made a fair total but when their opponents started their innings it was a disaster and by the close they had lost most of their wickets for not many runs. On the second morning the opening bowler, after a few deliveries, left the field of play as he was unwell and he did not return until 20 minutes before the close of his opponents' innings. He had been off the field of play for 50 minutes and when the innings closed he still had 30 minutes of penalty time to serve under ordinary circumstances. The unusual aspect of this situation was that, as the batting side had been dismissed for such a low score, they could be asked to follow on. The fielding captain took advantage of this situation and, after the interval between innings, led his side out again to field.

The thought had already passed through Nigel's mind that an unusual situation could arise. When the captain handed the ball to the player who had been back on the field for only those last 20 minutes of play during the first innings, Nigel and his colleague approached the captain and informed him that his player would not be allowed to bowl until he had completed his penance. While such a situation was not fully covered in the 1980 code, that was the decision that Nigel and his colleague made at the time, fully supported by the MCC Laws Committee.

Nigel, a former detective standing 6ft 9in in his socks and weighing 18 stone, was one of the best umpires in the world and players seldom argued with his decisions. Being one of the members of the working party, Nigel raised the above point and it has now been incorporated into Law 2.5 (c) (ii).

Law 2.5 (c) (iii) now includes an important point that has been inserted in regard to what I can only refer to as penance time being discounted. Here are a couple of examples. A fielder leaves the field injured and has been off for 50 minutes when all of the other players leave the field because of rain. This is an unscheduled break as opposed to an interval. After 30 minutes the umpires order a resumption of play and the injured player returns to the field with the rest of his team. In such a situation his penance time ceases from that point and he may eliminate from the 50 minutes whatever time has elapsed for the unscheduled break, in this case 30 minutes. He will then only have 20 minutes of penance time to serve until he is able to bowl again.

In the 1980 code the player had to be back on the field for the length of time which he was absent, if it were more than 15 minutes. There was no allowing for a reduction of this time if he was joined by his team-mates because of an unscheduled break in play. It would still have been 50 minutes, even if he had returned with the rest of his side after this break in play.

Under the 2000 code, if the break had lasted 60 minutes, the player can return with the rest of his team and bowl immediately. Please remember that we are talking about an unscheduled break in play and that none of the intervals contained in Law 15.1 will apply. Again, under the new code, if the absent player fails to return with his team after the unscheduled break and he still has penalty time to serve, then this is added onto any other time which he may be absent from the field after the call of "play". We felt the law to be much fairer as now written. The injured player is gaining no advantage over any other player while everyone is off the field.

Law 2.7 has one very small addition but could well have had another. The addition is "and shall carry a bat". I know that it would appear inconceivable that a runner would not avail himself of this advantage and I am sure that an umpire would not allow a runner to take part in the proceedings without one. The law previously has never made this statement.

The change which we considered for some time in respect of a runner's equipment was that a runner must wear "similar protective equipment as the batsman for whom he was running". This had great dangers, for to ascertain this, the umpire might be accused of interfering with the runner's person. Heaven help us if he were officiating in a ladies' match.

Another suggestion was that the word "external" should be replaced by the word "visible". The word "visible" was disregarded because we felt that some umpires may feel that a large thigh pad worn under fairly tight trousers is visible. They might have a point, although in no way could it be classed as external. After a deal of discussion we decided that it would be best to stay with "external".

The important point of change in Law 2.8 (c) is that no runs will be scored if an injured striker with a runner is dismissed run out at his end while batting. Runs that will be added to his side's total can come from the delivery of a no ball or wide, or now from Law 42.17, "Penalty runs". This is fully covered in Law 18, as well as Law 42.17.

Law 2.10 covers the commencement of a batsman's innings. In the 1980 code this was as stupid as any law could possibly have been. I think that we all were agreed on this point. Take this example. A batsman sitting in the pavilion observes that his colleague has been dismissed and immediately walks out and onto the field of play. Looking up he is met by 13 players and two umpires leaving the field because the umpires had called "time". A further example. The opening batsmen walk out and one of them is preparing to receive the first delivery of the match. Suddenly there is a downpour and everyone flees the field. By the wording of the law, those three innings had started. Ridiculous.

Now I feel that this part of Law 2 in the 2000 code is well thought out and well laid down. I believe that this should be the policy and function of any working party. What the law points out is that a batsman has not started his innings if he enters the field of play after "time" has been called. In the case of the opening batsmen, they shall have started their innings once "play" has been called, and not until. Other incoming batsmen will have started their innings once they have set foot on the field of play after "play" has been called and as long as "time" has not been reached. Any fresh batsman starting his innings after an interval, scheduled or otherwise, will only have started his innings once "play" has been called.

LAW 3

The Umpires

1. Appointment and attendance
Before the match, two umpires shall be appointed, one for each end, to control the game as required by the Laws, with absolute impartiality. The umpires shall be present on the ground and report to the Executive of the ground at least 45 minutes before the scheduled start of each day's play.

2. Change of umpire
An umpire shall not be changed during the match, other than in exceptional circumstances, unless he is injured or ill. If there has to be a change of umpire, the replacement shall act only as the striker's end umpire unless the captains agree that he should take full responsibility as an umpire.

3. Agreement with captains
Before the toss the umpires shall
(a) ascertain the hours of play and agree with the captains
   - (i) the balls to be used during the match. See Law 5 (The ball).
   - (ii) times and durations of intervals for meals and times for drinks intervals. See Law 15 (Intervals).
   - (iii) the boundary of the field of play and allowances for boundaries. See Law 19 (Boundaries).
   - (iv) any special conditions of play affecting the conduct of the match.

(b) inform the scorers of the agreements in (ii), (iii) and (iv) above.

4. To inform captains and scorers
Before the toss the umpires shall agree between themselves and inform both captains and both scorers which clock or watch and back-up time piece is to be used during the match.

whether or not any obstacle within the field of play is to be regarded as a boundary. See Law 19 (Boundaries).

5. The wickets, creases and boundaries

Before the toss and during the match, the umpires shall satisfy themselves that

- (i) the wickets are properly pitched. See Law 8 (The wickets).
- (ii) the creases are correctly marked. See Law 9 (The bowling, popping and return creases).
- (iii) the boundary of the field of play complies with the requirements of Law 19.2 (Defining the boundary – boundary marking).

6. Conduct of the game, implements and equipment

Before the toss and during the match, the umpires shall satisfy themselves that

(a) the conduct of the game is strictly in accordance with the Laws.

(b) the implements of the game conform to the requirements of Laws 5 (The ball) and 6 (The bat), together with either Laws 8.2 (Size of stumps) and 8.3 (The bails) or, if appropriate, Law 8.4 (Junior cricket).

(c) (i) no player uses equipment other than that permitted. See Appendix D.
- (ii) the wicket-keeper's gloves comply with the requirements of Law 40.2 (Gloves).

7. Fair and unfair play

The umpires shall be the sole judges of fair and unfair play.

8. Fitness of ground, weather and light

The umpires shall be the final judges of the fitness of the ground, weather and light for play. See 9 below and Law 7.2 (Fitness of the pitch for play).

9. Suspension of play for adverse conditions of ground, weather or light

(a) (i) All references to ground include the pitch. See Law 7.1 (Area of pitch).
- (ii) For the purpose of this Law and Law 15.9(b)(ii) (Intervals

for drinks) only, the batsmen at the wicket may deputise for their captain at any appropriate time.

(b) If at any time the umpires together agree that the condition of the ground, weather or light is not suitable for play, they shall inform the captains and, unless

 (i) in unsuitable ground or weather conditions both captains agree to continue, or to commence, or to restart play,

or (ii) in unsuitable light the batting side wish to continue, or to commence, or to restart play, they shall suspend play, or not allow play to commence or to restart.

(c) (i) After agreeing to play in unsuitable ground or weather conditions, either captain may appeal against the conditions to the umpires before the next call of Time. The umpires shall uphold the appeal only if, in their opinion, the factors taken into account when making their previous decision are the same or the conditions have further deteriorated.

 (ii) After deciding to play in unsuitable light, the captain of the batting side may appeal against the light to the umpires before the next call of Time. The umpires shall uphold the appeal only if, in their opinion, the factors taken into account when making their previous decision are the same or the condition of the light has further deteriorated.

(d) If at any time the umpires together agree that the conditions of ground, weather or light are so bad that there is obvious and foreseeable risk to the safety of any player or umpire, so that it would be unreasonable or dangerous for play to take place, then notwithstanding the provisions of (b)(i) and (b)(ii) above, they shall immediately suspend play, or not allow play to commence or to restart. The decision as to whether conditions are so bad as to warrant such action is one for the umpires alone to make.

The fact that the grass and the ball are wet and slippery does not warrant the ground conditions being regarded as unreasonable or dangerous. If the umpires consider the ground is so wet or slippery as to deprive the bowler of a reasonable foothold, the fielders of the power of free movement, or the batsmen of the ability to play their strokes or to run between the wickets, then these conditions shall be regarded as so bad that it would be unreasonable for play to take place.

(e) When there is a suspension of play it is the responsibility of the umpires to monitor the conditions. They shall make inspections as often as appropriate, unaccompanied by any of the players or officials. Immediately the umpires together agree that conditions are suitable for play they shall call upon the players to resume the game.

(f) If play is in progress up to the start of an agreed interval then it will resume after the interval unless the umpires together agree that conditions are or have become unsuitable or dangerous. If they do so agree, then they shall implement the procedure in (b) or (d) above, as appropriate, whether or not there had been any decision by the captains to continue, or any appeal against the conditions by either captain, prior to the commencement of the interval.

10. Exceptional circumstances

The umpires shall have the discretion to implement the procedures of 9 above for reasons other than ground, weather or light if they consider that exceptional circumstances warrant it.

11. Position of umpires

The umpires shall stand where they can best see any act upon which their decision may be required.

Subject to this over-riding consideration the umpire at the bowler's end shall stand where he does not interfere with either the bowler's run up or the striker's view.

The umpire at the striker's end may elect to stand on the off side instead of the on side of the pitch, provided he informs the captain of the fielding side, the striker and the other umpire of his intention to do so.

12. Umpires changing ends

The umpires shall change ends after each side has had one completed innings. See Law 14.2 (Forfeiture of an innings).

13. Consultation between umpires

All disputes shall be determined by the umpires. The umpires shall consult with each other whenever necessary. See also Law 27.6 (Consultation by umpires).

14. Signals
(a) The following code of signals shall be used by umpires.
    (i)   Signals made while the ball is in play

Dead ball	- by crossing and re-crossing the wrists below the waist.
No ball	- by extending one arm horizontally.
Out	- by raising an index finger above the head. (If not out the umpire shall call Not out.)
Wide	- by extending both arms horizontally.

    (ii)   When the ball is dead, the signals above, with the exception of the signal for Out, shall be repeated to the scorers. The signals listed below shall be made to the scorers only when the ball is dead.

Boundary 4	- by waving an arm from side to side finishing with the arm across the chest.
Boundary 6	- by raising both arms above the head.
Bye	- by raising an open hand above the head.
Commencement of last hour	- by pointing to a raised wrist with the other hand.
Five penalty runs awarded to the batting side	- by repeated tapping of one shoulder with the opposite hand.
Five penalty runs awarded to the fielding side	- by placing one hand on the opposite shoulder.
Leg bye	- by touching a raised knee with the hand.
New ball	- by holding the ball above the head.
Revoke last signal	- by touching both shoulders, each with the opposite hand.
Short run	- by bending one arm upwards and touching the nearer shoulder with the tips of the fingers.

(b) The umpires shall wait until each signal to the scorers has been separately acknowledged by a scorer before allowing play to proceed.

14. Correctness of scores
Consultation between umpires and scorers on doubtful points is essential. The umpires shall satisfy themselves as to the correctness of the number of runs scored, the wickets that have fallen and, where

appropriate, the number of overs bowled. They shall agree these with the scorers at least at every interval, other than a drinks interval, and at the conclusion of the match. See Laws 4.2 (Correctness of scores), 21.8 (Correctness of result) and 21.10 (Result not to be changed).

Although Law 3 is one of the longest, it has not changed a great deal since the 1980 code, when it came into being. Previously, it was mainly contained in Law 45 of the 1947 code. The 2000 code contains even more words and definitions in relation to the duties of the umpires, both before and during a match, which I think to be no bad thing.

Law 3.1 states that umpires now "shall" (a mandatory word) be present at least 45 minutes before the start of a day's play. In the past this wording of the law was only found in a note to Law 3 and the word "should" was used. This is what I call a take-it-or-leave-it word. It can be seen why Law 3.1 has been worded in this fashion when we cross-reference with Laws 10.1 (d), 10.3 (b) and 12.4.

If an umpire wishes to attire himself in the correct manner and to complete all of his pre-match duties, he needs to arrive at the ground at least 45 minutes before the match. My wife now often travels with me to matches and she is always telling our friends that I arrive at a ground before the groundsman has risen from his bed. My response is: "I see nothing wrong in that." I think what she really means is that I arrive before the shops are open.

Law 3.2 sets down the procedure that applies when a change is required for an umpire who is injured or is taken ill during a match. It is a situation with which I am familiar, having had to replace a colleague nine times in my career as a first-class umpire, for one reason or another. Such a situation bothers me, as I have always felt it derogatory to the replacement to be allowed to umpire only at the striker's end. If, of course, that is the wish of the replacement and a condition which he himself stipulates, that is a different matter.

In first-class cricket, if a replacement is required and there is no first-class umpire available, the replacement is only allowed to umpire at the striker's end. What must be borne in mind, and I am sure rarely is, is that the umpire in such a position may have to answer far more appeals than his colleague. These are: Law 38, "Run out"; Law 39, "Stumped"; and Law 35, "Hit wicket. There are many other matters which he has to observe and take action on. For instance, the limitation of on-side fielders, as in Law 41.5, and a bowler's action, legal or otherwise, as in Law 24.2. He must also observe if a batsman, in running, makes good the ground at the striker's end. He may have to take care of all of this, while the umpire at the bowling wicket may only have to count to six legal deliveries and call "over". It is no good anyone saying, "but the umpire at the striker's end never has to adjudicate on an LBW appeal". I, of course, agree but my reply is, "an umpire at the bowling wicket never has to adjudicate on appeals for stumped or hit wicket, which are just as important and at times more difficult than an LBW decision".

I remember Barrie Meyer being taken ill overnight when we umpired together at Bristol in May 1976 and the Gloucestershire secretary recruited a local Bristol League umpire until David Halfyard could get to the ground from his home, which was not until shortly after the tea interval. I felt that the "reserve" did a great job. He had many decisions to consider and received numerous appeals while standing at the striker's wicket for the best part of the day.

Law 3.2 now places the onus on the captains to agree on only one matter: should a replacement be allowed to take a full part in the match, umpiring at both the bowling end and striker's end? Should they not agree, the replacement may umpire only at the striker's wicket throughout the match. They do not have to agree on the individual, as they had to do in the past, only the position in which he is to officiate from: both ends or only one.

Law 3.9 caused the working party much deep thinking, with at least ten items of text to consider in this part of Law 3 alone. Key words in our progress here were "unsuitable" in Law 3.9 (b) and (c) and "unreasonable or dangerous" in Law 3.9 (d). In (b) and (c) the umpires are giving the captains the opportunity to leave the field of play or to appeal against the prevailing conditions. It is still only the one captain, the batting captain, who has an opportunity to make an appeal regarding the light and its fitness for play, or otherwise. In the past, when an appeal has been made by the batsmen in respect of the light conditions, the condition of the light must have become worse than when the position was reviewed previously. In the 2000 code an important change is to be found under Law 3.9 (c) (i) and (ii). It states that conditions only need to be "the same" or to have "deteriorated" since it was last reviewed for the umpires to take the players from the field of play.

I am sure that the following change will have a major effect on the game of cricket, but it had to come and it is found under Law 3.9 (d). Since the unfortunate injury to a young man in a rugby match some years ago, which left him paralysed and the referee with legal proceedings being taken against him, all officials in sport must now observe a "duty of care" in regard to all of the participants. Now, under this law, should the umpires find themselves in a situation where neither side wishes to leave the field of play and the umpires feel that conditions have deteriorated to such an extent that they are "unreasonable" and/or "dangerous", then acting together, the umpires shall suspend play. It is a decision and action for the umpires alone to make and there will obviously be many factors which have to be taken into consideration by them before arriving at such a decision. It will be for the good of the game that they come to such a decision and I sincerely hope that they will have that thought in mind, not that they may well be the first umpires to implement this part of Law 3.9, when the decision is taken.

It is when we get to Law 3.9 (f) that we see both of the words, "unsuitable" and "dangerous", used together. Whichever applies at the conclusion of an agreed interval will be adopted. If it is "unsuitable", we place the matter back into the hands of the captain or captains, as in Law 3.9 (b). If the umpires consider conditions "dangerous", then they implement Law 3.9 (d).

I would like to offer a little piece of advice in regard to the third and final paragraph of Law 3.11, which relates to who should be told about the change of position of an umpire. In addition to informing the three mentioned in the law, I consider it to be good field technique to inform the wicketkeeper. This has certainly been appreciated, as it saves him the embarrassment of appealing to the vacant side.

The second line of Law 3.12 explains that an innings which has been forfeited will count as a completed innings, even though it has never even been started. I know that in the past, when there has been one innings taken by a side and then there have been two innings forfeited, with the side batting last to win the match, umpires have not changed ends. This just explains such a situation and points out that, as there has been one innings completed by each side, the umpires will change ends.

Law 3.14 brings five new signals. First, new ball. This is not really a new signal at all for, as we all know, when a new ball is taken into play, it is always held up so the scorers are able to see that this action is being taken. Second, revoke last signal. Since I returned from umpiring in New Zealand on February 7, 1981 this is a signal which I have endeavoured to bring into the laws on a number of occasions. I had seen it used by the umpires in that country and felt it to be good for the game. It is a method by which the umpire revokes his last signal to the scorers, where he is saying "oops, sorry, I have made a mistake, that hit was not an allowance of six runs, it was only four runs", and he then gives the correct signal to the scorers. Third, commencement of last hour. A signal of various sorts has been in operation for years, whereby the umpire indicates to the scorers that the final hour of the match is due to start. They may have waved a coloured piece of paper, simply shouted, blown a whistle or, for all I know, may well have let off a firecracker. There is now an official signal. The umpire will point to his raised wrist with his other hand or, as I feel that it should say, point to his watch.

It is the other two signals, as yet untried, by which an umpire signals the award of penalty runs to one side or the other which is a major change in the game. To signal the award to the batting side, the umpire will "tap repeatedly one shoulder with the opposite hand". I suggest that the number of taps is five, the same as the number of runs to be awarded. Should the award of the penalty runs be to the fielding side, then the umpire simply "places a hand on his opposite shoulder". It is a pity that umpires had to be saddled with this sort of duty, but I am afraid that it had to come.

I took great exception to part of the wording of Law 3.14 in the 1980 code and I took it on behalf of all of my friends, the scorers. It read "that umpires shall be responsible for satisfying themselves on the correctness of the scores throughout and at the conclusion of the match". I am pleased to have been part of a working party that has been instrumental in having the word "throughout" deleted from what is now Law 3.15 in the 2000 code. Umpires are now instructed to agree with the scorers certain facts, only at intervals and at the conclusion of a match.

LAW 4
THE SCORERS

1. Appointment of scorers
Two scorers shall be appointed to record all runs scored, all wickets taken and, where appropriate, number of overs bowled.

2. Correctness of scores
The scorers shall frequently check to ensure that their records agree. They shall agree with the umpires, at least at every interval, other than a drinks interval, and at the conclusion of the match, the runs scored, the wickets that have fallen and, where appropriate, the number of overs bowled. See Law 3.15 (Correctness of scores).

3. Acknowledging signals
The scorers shall accept all instructions and signals given to them by the umpires. They shall immediately acknowledge each separate signal.

Some of this law has been covered under Law 3 and much more will be covered under Law 42 but I just make a few relevant points in an effort to help those who have no interest in the game, other than as a spectator. I know that in the future, many will be surprised why the score has moved forward at a faster pace than in the past. I will try to explain.

Law 4.1 states that "two scorers shall be appointed", to which I say, "if we are lucky". The wording of this part of Law 4 suggests that scorers are almost redundant and once again we show a great discourtesy to them. All we now say they are there for is, to record runs scored, wickets taken and, maybe, overs bowled. I know that the art of scoring, certainly at the top level of the game, is fast disappearing as computers become used more and more. I am pleased to say that, at club level, we can still find the most wonderful scorebooks, meticulously kept, with wonderful illustrations in colour for the various players taking part in the match. You can pick up many scorebooks, look through them, even years after the event, and by the facts and figures contained in them, still see the game being played out in front of you.

Those who know my reverence for scorers will understand that I am delighted that the word "throughout" has been erased from Law 4.2. There is nothing more degrading for a scorer nor unsightly for the game of cricket, than to see an umpire run across to the scoring position and acquaint the scorer that his score is not correct. I have seen it and I have even umpired with a colleague when he has taken such action. As for him getting a flea in his ear, when I had finished with him he did not have an ear left into which a flea could have been deposited.

It still makes the point that scorers should check with each other to ensure that their respective books tally and that they shall agree with the umpires at various intervals on certain matters. While there is a cross-reference to Law 21.8, "that umpires are responsible for the correctness of the scores", I do hope that we have seen the last of the umpire who has a scorebook strapped to his forearm and a top pocket full of coloured pencils. If the scorers agree on the scores, then I will agree with them, at the conclusion of the match.

Law 4.3 states that scorers must "acknowledge each *separate* signal". When I questioned this, I was told that it was the correct manner in which an umpire should pass on information to the scorers. The following example illustrates how complicated this could become. For example, a no ball makes no contact with the bat and the ball then carries on to cross the boundary line. The umpire obviously makes a no-ball signal to the scorers. I was told that the umpire must wait for an acknowledgement from the scorers, then he must again signal no ball to the scorers and again await an acknowledgement from them. Then he must indicate to the scorers with a signal that the striker did not hit the ball – arm raised above the head – and again wait for an acknowledgement from the scorers. He must then signal to the scorers a boundary allowance of four, and again wait for an acknowledgement from the scorers before he allows the game to continue. By this time the bowler will be asking you for at least one sweater, as he is getting cold waiting to deliver the next ball, and the batsmen will be considering an appeal against the light.

I shall retain the procedure I have always adopted of signalling no ball with my right arm outstretched to the side, accompanied by the left arm raised above the head, denoting that the ball was not hit by the bat, immediately followed by the boundary allowance signal of four runs. I am simply saying to the scorers, "it is a no ball, he did not hit it and it is four of them". I, of course, shall await one acknowledgement from the scorers. I know that I may receive only a few marks in an ACU&S exam for this action, but what I am really talking about here is the art and technique of umpiring a cricket match.

To move to more serious matters in regard to this law, I feel that this is the correct place to inform scorers of how to credit what will now be known as penalty runs and when to take this action. The whole aspect is covered in Law 42.17 (b) and (c). In part (c) (i) of that law, scorers should note that penalty runs are in addition to any other runs which are scored or penalties awarded from that delivery. When penalty runs are awarded to the batting side under Law 2.6, Law 41.2 or 3 or Law 42.3, 4, 5, 9 or 13, instruction is given as to how to separate the penalties from the runs which are scored by the batsmen.

I acquaint scorers more fully in my writing on Law 42 but here is an example. A bowler delivers a no ball, so there is one n.b. extra to credit immediately. The striker hits the ball and both batsmen embark on a run, during which, and in the opinion of both umpires, an act of deliberate obstruction takes place by a member of the fielding side against one of the batsmen. In the meantime, the ball has reached and crossed the boundary line. So, four runs to credit to the striker, five to debit against the bowler and now, under Law 42.5, "Obstruction of a batsman", there will be an award of five penalty runs to be awarded to the batting side's total in a new column in the scorebook. That is a total of ten runs. I think players will soon get the message.

In Law 42.17 (d) it will be seen that when penalty runs are awarded to the fielding side under Laws 18.5 (b) or Law 42.10, 14, or 16, these runs shall be "added as penalty extras to that side's total in its most recently completed innings". If penalty runs are awarded to the fielding side in a one-innings match, while they are fielding first, when they begin their innings they start with plus five runs. I have covered in greater detail all matters in regard to penalty runs under the relevant parts of Law 42. It will be seen that in a one-innings match, if the side fielding first receives two awards of penalty runs – 10 in all – and they dismiss their opponents for a total of 9, they will have won the match without even going in to bat.

With the advent of penalty runs, new-style scorebooks will have to be designed but I am sure that scorers will have no difficulty with it. To my friends in the scoring position, professional or amateur, I do apologise for making their great work even more difficult. But, as I have stated, it unfortunately had to come.

LAW 5
THE BALL

1. Weight and size
The ball, when new, shall weigh not less than 5½ ounces/155.9g, nor more than 5¾ ounces/163g, and shall measure not less than 8 $^{13}/_{16}$ in/22.4cm, nor more than 9 in/22.9cm in circumference.

2. Approval and control of balls
(a) All balls to be used in the match, having been approved by the umpires and captains, shall be in the possession of the umpires before the toss and shall remain under their control throughout the match.
(b) The umpire shall take possession of the ball in use at the fall of each wicket, at the start of any interval and at any interruption of play.

3. New ball
Unless an agreement to the contrary has been made before the match, either captain may demand a new ball at the start of each innings.

4. New ball in match of more than one day's duration
In a match of more than one day's duration, the captain of the fielding side may demand a new ball after the prescribed number of overs has been bowled with the old one. The Governing Body for cricket in the country concerned shall decide the number of overs applicable in that country, which shall not be less than 75 overs.
The umpires shall indicate to the batsmen and the scorers whenever a new ball is taken into play.

5. Ball lost or becoming unfit for play
If, during play, the ball cannot be found or recovered or the umpires agree that it has become unfit for play through normal use, the umpires shall replace it with a ball which has had wear comparable with that

which the previous ball had received before the need for its replacement. When the ball is replaced the umpires shall inform the batsmen and the fielding captain.

6. Specifications

The specifications as described in 1 above shall apply to men's cricket only. The following specifications will apply to

Women's cricket
Weight: from 4 $^{15}/_{16}$ ounces/140g to 5 $^{5}/_{16}$ ounces /151g
Circumference: from 8π in/21.0cm to 8 $^{7}/_{8}$ in/22.5cm

Junior cricket – under 13
Weight: from 4 $^{11}/_{16}$ ounces/133g to 5 $^{1}/_{16}$ ounces/144g
Circumference: from 8 $^{1}/_{16}$ in/20.5cm to 8 $^{11}/_{16}$ in/22.0cm

While the ball is the implement of the game that has given the greatest problems over the past decade, the changes to Law 5 are few. It is only when we arrive at Law 42.3 that we find a major change which appertains to this law, and again that is in regard to the award of penalty runs.

Since 1744, the law governing the weight and size of the ball, now Law 5.1, has seen few changes, only three in fact, all of which have been specific and clear. In this early code the ball could weigh between 5oz and 6oz and the umpires were instructed to mark it, so it was unable to be changed. What a laugh! Over the past decade it has been the players who have altered the condition of the surface of the ball and many of these changes have not taken place by legal means.

The first change to this law took place in 1774 when the tolerance to its weight was given as 5 $^{1}/_{2}$oz to 5 $^{3}/_{4}$oz, just as it is today. This part of Law 5 has stood the passage of time well as it is now more than 225 years since the last change.

In 1836 the size of the ball was specified for the first time. Its circumference was to be between 9 inches and 9 $^{1}/_{4}$ inches. It was some 90 years later, on May 4, 1927, that this measurement was altered to be between 8 and 8 $^{3}/_{16}$ inches in circumference and that still applies today, some 73 years later. When I am holding seminars with umpires and I am stating certain measurements, I always think of this as the most silly measurement that has ever been applied to any sport. I tell all those who attend that they should never forget it, simply because it is so strange.

John Jameson received information from one of his friends overseas that the metric conversions given in the 1980 code of the laws in relation to the ball were wrong. That information proved correct but the inaccuracies were so minute as to be of no consequence. Being someone with a fine attention to detail, John has altered them. I wonder if anyone can spot which they are?

Law 5.2 has consisted of fewer than 20 words in previous codes but under the 2000 code it is made up of a number of statements about the balls that are used in a match. As before, the balls have to be approved by the umpires but now they must be in their possession before the toss for innings and remain under their control until the match has finished. This applies not only to the one being used for play but all spare balls as well, an eminently sensible action.

Law 5.2 (b) instructs umpires to take into their possession the match ball, at the fall of a wicket, at the start of any agreed interval and at any interruption in play. This, again, makes good sense as it is during such a pause in play that illegal interference to the ball usually takes place. I feel Law 5.2 is well thought out and well set down. There now should be no doubts as to what is happening to a ball while play is not taking place.

Law 5.4 has changed in as much as the number of days for a match have now been decreased, from three or more to more than one, when a fielding captain can demand a new ball after the prescribed number of overs have been bowled. Please note that there is now no mention of eight-ball overs, as there was in the 1980 code. Also note that the umpire must indicate to batsmen and scorers when a new ball is being taken.

In Law 5.5, which covers a ball being lost or becoming unfit for play, the three words, "through normal use", have been inserted. I feel these words to be of great significance and if they had been there before, we may well have been spared the ramifications of the ball-tampering trials of 1993 and 1996. We know, of course, that in those two cases, the damage to the ball was not through normal use. This law now instructs that the fielding captain as well as the batsmen should be informed of the change of ball.

LAW 6
The Bat

1. Width and length
The bat overall shall not be more than 38 inches/96.5cm in length. The blade of the bat shall be made solely of wood and shall not exceed 4? inches/10.8cm at the widest part.

2. Covering the blade
The blade may be covered with material for protection, strengthening or repair. Such material shall not exceed $^{1}/_{16}$ inches/1.56mm in thickness, and shall not be likely to cause unacceptable damage to the ball.

3. Hand or glove to count as part of bat
In these Laws
(a) reference to the bat shall imply that the bat is held by the batsman.
(b) contact between the ball and
either (i)   the striker's bat itself
or   (ii)   the striker's hand holding the bat
or   (iii) any part of a glove worn on the striker's hand holding the bat shall be regarded as the ball striking or touching ~~the bat, or being struck~~ by the bat.

This is another law with few fundamental changes from the 1980 code, although great efforts are being made by the manufacturers of cricket bats, both in this country and overseas, to bend and in some cases not to comply with this law. It is the construction of the blade of the bat that has caused MCC most concern during the shaping of the 2000 code. In the main, the problem hinges on just one word in Law 6.1, which states that the blade of the bat shall be made "solely" of wood. First, I will deal with changes to this law and then discuss some of the problems in regard to the manufacture of bats.

The width and length of the bat, as in Law 6.1, are as in past codes and have been the same since at least 1771 in regard to the width. It was after a match in that season that the gentlemen of the Hambledon club ruled upon this dimension. There are a number of bats in use at the present time that exceed the stipulated width, "4.25 inches at the widest part", and they are mostly made by one overseas manufacturer.

Law 6.2 is, to all intents and purposes, the note to Law 6 in the 1980 code with the addition of a statement, that the protective material used "shall not be likely to cause unacceptable damage to the ball". In the late 1980s I had to report a number of times that a ball had been damaged by the covering on a bat. It was not a deliberate act by the batsman but simply that the material which had been used had come away from the face of the bat, close to the point at which the splice joined the blade. This material was very strong and the edge of it actually cut a slice off the surface of the ball. I think it was Graham Cowdrey who told me that the material being used at the time was a covering which was used on helicopter blades. Whatever it was, and whatever it was used for, it most certainly was strong and in my report I stated that "it looked as if the ball had been through a bacon slicer".

Law 6.3 now builds up a picture of the striker, with bat in hand, and carries on to describe the parts of the striker or his equipment that are to be defined as the ball coming into contact with the bat. I have already mentioned the problems with the manufacturers and the construction of a bat that fully complies with Law 6. I have seen correspondence from South Africa which gives the information that a company is manufacturing a bat from glass fibre and accordingly cannot be used in first-class cricket. It then carries on to say, "there is no reason bats cannot be utilised in non-representative cricket matches". The South African Cricket Board then states that "they would most favourably recommend the utilisation of this bat in non-representative cricket". These statements astound me, coming from what I am sure is a most reputable manufacturer of cricket equipment and from one of the major cricket boards in the world. The laws of cricket are designed for the game as a whole, no matter at what level, nor in which part of the world the game is played. They have stood the test of time well.

One of the advantages given for the use of such a bat is that "the bat can be manufactured to customers' specifications". If they wish to break the part of Law 6 in regard to the material used in the construction of the blade of the bat, then they would probably allow a customer to request one which has a blade measuring 12.75 inches wide. Have we to say that the work of those worthy gentlemen at Hambledon many years ago counts for nothing? If we look at another so-called "advantage" in allowing the manufacture of such bats, we find the most relevant point. It says that "the manufacturing process lends itself readily to colour processing". Where next will sporting bodies look for the magic dollar? Perhaps in time they will desire the players to wear funny hats and to don a false nose, or maybe to dress in a clown's outfit.

There is another bat manufacturer, in this country, who has used a type of filler within the blade of the bat and I do have great difficulty in saying that it abuses Law 6. The company makes a bat, of which the blade is 95 per cent willow. Encapsulated within the blade are inserts that are, as stated by the company, made from "wood pulp". If this is so, I see nothing wrong. It is in respect of the composition of the resin that abuse of this law may take place.

Neither company need tell me how scarce good willow is. I have visited my great friend John Cook's farm down in Hampshire over the last 18 years and have watched the wonderful willow trees that he has nurtured year after year come to fruition. His efforts are now reaping a dividend and some of the trees are being taken for the purpose of making cricket bats. Now when I visit, it is as if good friends have departed.

I am not against modifications to bats as long as they comply with Law 6. Neither am I against changes to this law, but let us not go back to the days of D.K. Lillee and his aluminium bat, which abused the law in many ways. Probably not under Law 6.1, in regard to the dimensions, but definitely the material used. Under Law 6.2, there would most certainly have been damage to the ball from the blade itself, let alone any covering which may have been applied to the surface of it.

LAW 7
The Pitch

1. Area of pitch
The pitch is a rectangular area of the ground 22 yards/20.12m in length and 10ft/3.05m in width. It is bounded at either end by the bowling creases and on either side by imaginary lines, one each side of the imaginary line joining the centres of the two middle stumps, each parallel to it and 5ft/1.52m from it. See Laws 8.1 (Width and pitching) and 9.2 (The bowling crease).

2. Fitness of the pitch for play
The umpires shall be the final judges of the fitness of the pitch for play. See Laws 3.8 (Fitness of ground, weather and light) and 3.9 (Suspension of play for adverse conditions of ground, weather or light).

3. Selection and preparation
Before the match, the Ground Authority shall be responsible for the selection and preparation of the pitch. During the match, the umpires shall control its use and maintenance.

4. Changing the pitch
The pitch shall not be changed during the match unless the umpires decide that it is unreasonable or dangerous for play to continue on it and then only with the consent of both captains.

5. Non-turf pitches
In the event of a non-turf pitch being used, the artificial surface shall conform to the following measurements:
  Length - a minimum of 58ft/17.68m
  Width - a minimum of 6ft/1.83m
See Law 10.8 (Non-turf pitches).

Except for two small but informative alterations, parts 2, 3, and 4 of Law 7 are the same as in the 1980 code but now are numbered parts 3, 4, and 5.

Law 7.1 has changed little but as it is now set down I feel it gives a better explanation. We stipulate a length of 22 yards, which is the old chain measurement and the one part of law which has never changed and can be found in the 1755 code of The Laws of Cricket. We then give a width either side of the imaginary centre line of the two middle stumps. The wickets are to be pitched opposite and parallel as in Law 8. Armed with this information, nobody needs a degree in geometry to realise that the area is now a rectangle.

The members of the working party did spend much time talking about wickets which appeared not to be opposite and parallel, therefore throwing everything else out of line. When I have felt uncomfortable in regard to this point, I take up a position of looking straight down the length of the return crease at my end and see how it corresponds with the one at the opposite end. One of the things that can give a wrong impression is the cut of the pitch if it has been mown at a slight angle. All groundsmen are meticulous when they square off the area of ground upon which pitches are to be selected before a season gets under way. They take a great deal of pride in their pitches being exact and the manner in which they present them.

Law 7.2 simply makes the statement that umpires shall be "the final judges of the fitness of the pitch for play", not players, ground authorities or captains. In first-class regulations umpires were instructed to take into consideration the views of the captains in regard to such matters. Almost without exception we knew the respective views before we asked for them. The side which at that time had, or appeared to have, the upper hand desired to start at least two hours previously, while their opponents felt that we should already have abandoned play for the day. In any such situation the umpires cannot win.

Law 7.4 brings in a few very important words, "unreasonable and dangerous for play to continue on it". This is when umpires are giving consideration for the changing of the pitch upon which the match is already being played because of the reasons mentioned. This is a decision for the umpires alone to make, but we are only able to effect such a change with the consent of both captains, as in the 1980 code.

Law 7.5 deals with non-turf pitches, which are now seeing a great deal of cricket, especially in the emerging European countries. Everyone, not just umpires, must not forget that such surfaces may receive the same attention as a natural turf pitch, before and during a match. Such attention is set down in Laws 10 and 11. I would not expect any groundsman to try to implement Law 10.3 (a), which is about mowing, but I have heard strange stories of some who have tried, so you never know.

LAW 8
The Wickets

1. Width and pitching
Two sets of wickets shall be pitched opposite and parallel to each other at a distance of 22 yards/20.12m between the centres of the two middle stumps. Each set shall be 9 in/22.86cm wide and shall consist of three wooden stumps with two wooden bails on top. See Appendix A.

2. Size of stumps
The tops of the stumps shall be 28 inches/71.1cm above the playing surface and shall be dome shaped except for the bail grooves. The portion of a stump above the playing surface shall be cylindrical, apart from the domed top, with circular section of diameter not less than $1^{3}/_{8}$ in/3.49cm nor more than 1π in/3.81cm See Appendix A.

3. The bails
(a) The bails, when in position on the top of the stumps,
    (i)   shall not project more than π in/1.27cm above them.
    (ii)   shall fit between the stumps without forcing them out of the vertical.

(b) Each bail shall conform to the following specifications. See Appendix A.

Overall length:	- $4^{5}/_{16}$ in/10.95cm
Length of barrel:	- $2^{1}/_{8}$ in/5.40cm
Longer spigot:	- $1^{3}/_{8}$ in/3.49cm
Shorter spigot:	- $1^{3}/_{16}$ in/2.06cm

4. Junior cricket
In junior cricket, the same definitions of the wickets shall apply subject to following measurements being used.
    Width: - 8 in/20.32cm

Pitched for under 13:	– 21 yards/19.20m
Pitched for under 11:	– 20 yards/18.29m
Pitched for under 9:	– 18 yards/16.46m
Height above playing surface:	– 27 in/68.58cm

Each stump

Diameter:	– not less than 1¼ in/3.18cm nor more than 1³⁄₈ in/3.49cm

Each bail

Overall:	– 3 ¹³⁄₁₆ in/9.68cm
Barrel:	– 1 ¹³⁄₁₆ in/4.60cm
Longer Spigot:	– 1 ¼ in/3.18cm
Shorter Spigot:	– ¾ in/1.91cm

5. Dispensing with bails

The umpires may agree to dispense with the use of bails, if necessary. If they so agree then no bails shall be used at either end. The use of bails shall be resumed as soon as conditions permit. See Law 28.4 (Dispensing with bails).

In the first code of The Laws of Cricket in 1744, a wicket consisted of two stumps, both 22 inches high and between them we had a gap of 6 inches. There was only one bail, which was 6 inches in length and was laid across the top of the stumps. Between and at the base of the stumps was a small hole, into which the batsman had to pop the toe of his bat before a member of the fielding side could place the ball there. If the batsman failed to do so, he was run out. Thus, to obtain a run, 22 yards had to be completed, not as now, 19yd 1ft.

Because of happenings during a match played at Hambledon in 1775, the three-stump wicket was introduced but it was 1785 before any reference to this type of wicket was found in any of the laws. It was still only six inches wide with one bail. The following year there is a reference to the use of two bails but this evidence is not considered reliable. In 1798 the size of the wicket was increased to 24 inches high and seven inches wide, but still with only one bail, 7 inches in length. Between 1803 and early 1809 there is a reliable reference to the use of bails, in the plural. The height of the wicket was increased again in 1821, to 26 inches, and between 1823 and 1825 there was yet another change to the size of the wicket: 27 inches in height and 8 inches in width.

In May 1931 two sizes of wickets were accommodated. They were to be not less than 27 inches in height and not more than 28 inches. In the latter case the width would be of 9 inches instead of 8 inches, with two bails that were allowed to project no more than half an inch above the top of the stumps. It was not until the 1947 code that we see the measurements of the wicket as they are today: 28 inches high, 9 inches wide, and with two bails 4 3/8 inches long. In the same code there was a statement that stumps with metal fittings were considered dangerous and their use was discouraged.

Nowadays this is an area of the laws which sees little change and Law 8.1 of the 2000 code is word for word the same as the 1980 code. Parts 2, 3 and 4 of Law 8, with the measurements set down in full, in imperial and metric, may appear verbose in places but this is, I think, unavoidable.

The first two lines of Law 8.2 are written in a similar manner to the 1980 code. Then the 2000 code deviates to describe the shape of a stump as "cylindrical". I hear you ask, "what other shape would you expect them to be?" Well, the manner in which the 1980 code is written, a wicket could be constructed of three wooden stumps, square in shape. They could have been the correct length with the correct height of 28 inches above the ground but measuring 2 7/8 inches square. The new Law 8.2, as written, therefore makes great sense.

Law 8.3 (a) (ii) simply states that the bails "shall fit between the stumps without forcing them out of the vertical". I hope umpires have observed this in the past and will continue to do so, no matter what measurements are laid down in Law 8.3 (b). In my position as an umpire, I have and use hundreds of sets of bails. All are of the same length because I always ensure that the law is complied with. If they are more than the stipulated length when they come into my possession, I sand them down. If they are shorter, I give them to clubs that run junior sides. At the lower club levels, we may struggle to find two sets of bails, let alone two sets of the correct dimensions. If umpires do not have their own bails, I suggest they take out with them a piece of sandpaper and simply do their best.

If umpires did not have their own bails, I hope they took out with them a piece of sandpaper and simply did their best. I trust that with the new dimensions laid down for stumps and bails, this will alleviate all such problems. The eagle-eyed will note that the overall length of a bail has changed from $4^{3}/_{8}$ inches to $4^{5}/_{16}$. Whatever the measurements, the most important thing to remember with bails is that they sit well in the grooves on top of the stumps.

Law 8.5 aims to clarify when bails should be dispensed with. The statement in this law is in answer to the often-raised question: "What do we do if, in a strong wind, the bails keep blowing off from the wicket at one end only?" Now it is clear what action umpires should take and no one can say that this clarification is either verbose or cosmetic. The umpires shall remove them from both wickets, replacing them when it is possible to do so, on both wickets.

LAW 9

THE BOWLING, POPPING AND RETURN CREASES

1. The creases
A bowling crease, a popping crease and two return creases shall be marked in white, as set out in 2, 3 and 4 below, at each end of the pitch. See Appendix B.

2. The bowling crease
The bowling crease, which is the back edge of the crease marking, shall be the line through the centres of the three stumps at that end. It shall be 8ft 8 in/2.64m in length, with the stumps in the centre.

3. The popping crease
The popping crease, which is the back edge of the crease marking, shall be in front of and parallel to the bowling crease and shall be 4ft/1.22m from it. The popping crease shall be marked to a minimum of 6ft/1.83m on either side of the imaginary line joining the centres of the middle stumps and shall be considered to be unlimited in length.

4. The return creases
The return creases, which are the inside edges of the crease markings, shall be at right angles to the popping crease at a distance of 4ft 4 in/1.32m either side of the imaginary line joining the centres of the two middle stumps. Each return crease shall be marked from the popping crease to a minimum of 8ft/2.44m behind it and shall be considered to be unlimited in length.

Law 9 has had only slight changes made to it. Law 9.1 is new and the old Law 9.1, 2 and 3 have been moved down to become 9.2, 3 and 4.

Law 9.1 now states that all of the creases "shall be marked in white" and that is certainly cosmetic in more senses than one. The sponsors of the game have missed this one, or perhaps they will take note with this wording of the new law. Sponsorship, in all of its weird and wonderful designs, now adorns most matters sacred to the game. It always reminds me of that lovely, informative book, written by G.D. Martineau and first published in 1950, "Bat, Ball, Wicket and All". These now all carry advertising material. Now that we are being prevailed upon by manufacturers of cricket bats for them to be made of many colours, we may soon have a paint manufacturer seeking to paint the creases and boundary line in the colours of a rainbow. It may not be that far into the future, for I can think of some in the hierarchy of the game who would sell that idea for a few pieces of silver.

Law 9.2, on the bowling crease, now makes the point, as does Law 9.3, on the popping crease, that it is the back edge of the crease marking from which distances are measured. However, we have still left in this part of the law words that have given confusion for years. In the 2000 code we state that this line shall run "through the centres of the three stumps at that end", which is far better than in the previous code. The words which caused confusion and still remain are in relation to the stipulated length of this crease, "8ft 8inches/2.64m in length, with the stumps in the centre". In my early days of umpiring and at all levels of the game, I found many wickets pitched with the stumps in the centre of the "width" of the bowling crease rather than on its back edge. Law 9, I feel, is worded much better now, but I still wish that we had done something about the words "with the stumps in the centre".

Law 9.4 deals with the return creases. The 1980 code mentioned "a forward extension" of the return crease and stated that "the return crease shall be marked to a minimum of 4ft/1.22m behind the wicket". The "forward extension" also measured 4ft/1.22m in a forward direction to join with the popping crease. Now, in the 2000 code, it is taken from and to the rear of the popping crease and will be marked to a minimum of 8ft/2.44m in length. The measurements are all as they were but I feel that the manner in which this law has been worded is an improvement.

Some may think that these changes, although only small, are revolutionary but as long ago as 1865, Alfred Shaw, one of the great old-time cricketers, was instrumental in having adopted "the whitewash crease". In the very early days of the game, 1744, the popping crease was cut into the turf and was at a distance of 3ft 10in in front of the wicket. This distance was what is known as an ell. An ell is 3ft 9in, with an inch added for the width of the cut crease. Reference was made that, for a batsman to be within his ground, "he has to be within his ell".

I have found one piece of information which is of great interest in relation to the return crease. It explains that strange local variations could still be found as recently as 1950, such as the "return creases going off at a 45-degree angle from the end of the bowling crease", instead of at a right angle. I can find nothing in the laws to support this statement and indeed as early as the 1823 code, it mentions a "return crease at each end and at right angles to the bowling crease". I am not sure if this was a reference to the forward extension", as it is only in the 1845 code that I find reference to the "return creases at each end of the bowling crease and at right angles 'behind' the wicket". I was only 18 when the 1947 code came into being and my only interest in the game was to hit the ball as hard and as far as I possibly could and to chase, stop, throw and catch the ball. I certainly was not interested in a close study of the laws but I do remember seeing the creases marked out as a rectangular box, with no extension of the popping crease and no return crease marked behind the line of the wicket. An interesting point for those who are old enough.

In the 1809 code, under a law that relates to the bowler, it states that "the bowler shall deliver the ball with one foot behind the bowling crease and within the return crease". While it is not conclusive, it points to the fact that the return crease may not, in those early days, have been marked to the rear of the wicket.

LAW 10

Preparation and Maintenance of the Playing Area

1. Rolling

The pitch shall not be rolled during the match except as permitted in (a) and (b) below.

(a) Frequency and duration of rolling

During the match the pitch may be rolled at the request of the captain of the batting side, for a period of not more than 7 minutes, before the start of each innings, other than the first innings of the match, and before the start of each subsequent day's play. See (d) below.

(b) Rolling after a delayed start

In addition to the rolling permitted above, if, after the toss and before the first innings of the match, the start is delayed, the captain of the batting side may request to have the pitch rolled for not more than 7 minutes. However, if the umpires together agree that the delay has had no significant effect on the state of the pitch, they shall refuse the request for the rolling of the pitch.

(c) Choice of rollers

If there is more than one roller available the captain of the batting side shall have the choice.

(d) Timing of permitted rolling

The rolling permitted (maximum 7 minutes) before play begins on any day shall be started not more than 30 minutes before the time scheduled or rescheduled for play to begin. The captain of the batting side may, however, delay the start of such rolling until not less than 10 minutes before the time scheduled or rescheduled for play to begin, should he so desire.

(e) Insufficient time to complete rolling

If a captain declares an innings closed, or forfeits an innings, or enforces the follow-on, and the other captain is prevented thereby from exercising his option of the rolling permitted (maximum 7 minutes), or if he is so prevented for any other reason, the extra time required to complete the rolling shall be taken out of the normal playing time.

2. Sweeping

(a) If rolling is to take place the pitch shall first be swept to avoid any possible damage by rolling in debris. This sweeping shall be done so that the 7 minutes allowed for rolling is not affected.

(b) The pitch shall be cleared of any debris at all intervals for meals, between innings and at the beginning of each day, not earlier than 30 minutes nor later than 10 minutes before the time scheduled or rescheduled for play to begin. See Law 15.1 (An interval).

(c) Notwithstanding the provisions of (a) and (b) above, the umpires shall not allow sweeping to take place where they consider it may be detrimental to the surface of the pitch.

3. Mowing

The pitch

The pitch shall be mown on each day of the match on which play is expected to take place, if ground and weather conditions allow.

The outfield

In order to ensure that conditions are as similar as possible for both sides, the outfield shall be mown on each day of the match on which play is expected to take place, if ground and weather conditions allow.

If, for reasons other than ground and weather conditions, complete mowing of the outfield is not possible, the Ground Authority shall notify the captains and umpires of the procedure to be adopted for such mowing during the match.

Responsibility for mowing

All mowings which are carried out before the match shall be the responsibility of the Ground Authority.

All subsequent mowings shall be carried out under the supervision of the umpires.

Timing of mowing

  (i) Mowing of the pitch on any day of the match shall be completed not later than 30 minutes before the time

           scheduled or rescheduled for play to begin on that day.
- (ii) Mowing of the outfield on any day of the match shall be completed not later than 15 minutes before the time scheduled or rescheduled for play to begin on that day.

4. Watering
The pitch shall not be watered during the match.

5. Re-marking creases
The creases shall be re-marked whenever either umpire considers it necessary.

6. Maintenance of footholes
The umpires shall ensure that the holes made by the bowlers and batsmen are cleaned out and dried whenever necessary to facilitate play. In matches of more than one day's duration, the umpires shall allow, if necessary, the re-turfing of footholes made by the bowler in his delivery stride, or the use of quick-setting fillings for the same purpose.

7. Securing of footholds and maintenance of pitch
During play, the umpires shall allow the players to secure their footholds by the use of sawdust provided that no damage to the pitch is caused and that Law 42 (Fair and unfair play) is not contravened.

8. Non-turf pitches
Wherever appropriate, the provisions set out in 1 to 7 above shall apply.

In the earliest code of the Laws of Cricket, the 1744 code, there were no provisions for the rolling, cutting or covering of the pitch during a match, subjects which are now included in Law 10. The first time that such matters were brought into the laws was in 1788 and in addition to those three provisions above, the "beating of the pitch during a match" was also allowed. I take this to mean by the batsmen with their bats. All of this could happen only by "mutual consent".

    Shortly before the 1831 season the provision whereby a bowler was permitted to water his run-up to the wicket was deleted. I have always been amazed that any bowler should have considered it an advantage to use this concession. In this day and age the last thing a bowler wishes to see are wet or damp areas of ground over which he has to accelerate prior to the delivery of the ball. Now, with the covering arrangements under Law 11, although the law fails to put it into words, the covers can be placed to the rear of the wickets as far back as the boundary line. This ensures that the approach area over which a bowler passes is nearly always dry and firm.

I think it fair to say that the greatest cause of lost time in a match is when these areas have been affected by the elements. Umpires are most careful before declaring that a ground is fit for play. Should these areas not be 100 per cent, there could well be an unacceptable risk of injury to the bowlers.

In 1986, before a Benson & Hedges Cup match in Glasgow, my colleague Barry Dudleston and I approached the captains of the two sides, Scotland and Worcestershire, and suggested to them that the only way we were going to be able to play the match was if we could use some sort of matting on which the bowlers could run up to deliver the ball. The run-up area at one end was a quagmire and both captains readily agreed. The groundsman hunted around and came up with two 20-yard lengths of carpet-type material, which I believe came from a local school hall. It was heavy enough not to move about and neither was the weave so open that a bowler's studs might get caught in it. Without taking this extreme action, the match, which turned out to be a thrilling encounter, would never have been played.

In 1849 "a pitch could be swept and rolled between innings", as long as the request to do so was made "by either side within one minute of an innings ending". This time limit, I feel, could well be used now, but only the side which is next to bat should have this prerogative, not "either side". It was in 1860 that a law was used for the first time giving "the side next to bat" the right to request that rolling be undertaken.

In May 1883 a law was passed, although it did not come into force until the next season, whereby "a duration of 10 minutes" was allowed for a pitch to be rolled "before the start of play". In 1931 this length of time was reduced to "7 minutes for sweeping and rolling of the pitch before the start of each day's play and between the innings". This law is just as it is today, some 70 years later.

Law 10.1 (b) contains the other change that I managed to have adopted after my visit to New Zealand in the 1980-81 season. It concerns the whole of this part of the law in relation to a delayed start of a match after the initial rolling has taken place. I felt it crazy that, if the start of play was delayed for five minutes after the toss, the batting captain could legally have the pitch rolled. Hence we now have what I consider a good law and one which was already in use in New Zealand when I umpired there.

There is a change of some significance under Law 10.1 (d), on the timing of permitted rolling, which emphasises again why an umpire must report to the ground 45 minutes before play starts on any day. It states that the rolling of the pitch shall "be started not more than 30 minutes before the scheduled start of play". Obviously, an umpire who is in charge of such matters must be on the ground in time to ascertain if the batting captain desires the pitch to be rolled? And, if so, with which roller? With the maximum allowed duration of such rolling only seven minutes, it must also be ascertained at what time the batting captain desires the rolling to take place: 30 minutes before the start or rescheduled start of play, or not later than 10 minutes after the start of the day's play; or at any time during this time-span. Remember, these are only his duties in respect of the rolling of the pitch. There are many others.

Law 10.1 (e) deals with the situation where there is insufficient time to complete rolling when "a captain declares an innings closed, or forfeits an innings or enforces the follow-on". The captain of the side next to bat must be allowed enough time for the rolling of the pitch to take place, a maximum of seven minutes. If information is conveyed to him so late that it will not allow him his option, then the time required for any rolling, should it be necessary, will be taken out of the playing time.

A few years ago, Allan Border, the Australia captain, created an unusual situation for David Shepherd, the English umpire, who was a member of the Independent Panel of Umpires, during an overseas Test match. This matter was brought to the attention of the working party and, after much thought, changes have been made. During an interval for a meal, Border approached the umpires and told them that he did not wish the groundsman to clear the pitch of debris, bits of earth and grass kicked up by the players, bowlers in the main. Law 10.2 of the 1980 code referred only to the sweeping of a pitch before rolling takes place.

From time immemorial groundsmen have presented their pitches in an immaculate manner and they endeavour to retain this impression throughout a match. At all intervals, they re-mark the creases and clear away all dust and debris from the bowlers footholds and also any pieces from the surface of the pitch. They do not sweep them off; all they do is flick them away with the brush. Anyway, David saw no reason to alter what has taken place for some 250 years. His decision is the sort that helps maintain the continuity of the game and I am certain that he was correct.

Law 10.2 (a) of the 2000 code states that, if the pitch is to be rolled, it will first be swept so as no damage is caused to its surface by the rolling into it of any debris. Part (b) adds that a pitch can be cleared of any debris by the groundsman before a day's play, between innings and at all intervals for meals, as in the situation which confronted David. Finally, part (c) allows the umpires the power not to allow any sweeping, should they consider it detrimental to the surface of the pitch. These changes now make this law very clear and should not pose problems for any umpire, let alone one of the best in the world.

Law 10.3 (d) again illustrates why the reporting time by umpires at the ground is much more wisely set at 45 minutes. The mowing of the pitch "shall be completed not later than 30 minutes before the time scheduled or rescheduled for play to begin". As mowing takes at least ten minutes, I wonder if the reporting time should not have been laid down as 60 minutes before the time for the start of play, because all mowings by the ground staff have to be "under the supervision of the umpires", except on the first day of the match.

I wonder if we may have missed something here? We all know that the responsibility for the pitch preparation lies in the hands of the ground authority before a match starts. Other than on the first day of a match, a pitch must have been mown 30 minutes before the time for play to start. On the first day, how would you view this situation? Twelve minutes before the start of the match, the groundsman, who is usually the ground authority, comes to the umpires and informs them that he is about to mow the pitch. The toss will have already taken place at least three minutes before, under Law 12.3.

Law 10.3 (a) states that "the pitch shall be mown on each day of the match on which play is expected to take place" while Law 10.3 (c) states that "all mowings which are carried out before the match shall be the responsibility of the Ground Authority". This one is not being carried out before the toss but after it and therefore it comes under the supervision of the umpires. While such action is an abuse of Law 10.3 (d) (i), the groundsman may be late on parade. Of course, it would never happen in cricket played at a professional level, nor at good club level, but do remember that cricket also takes place for the enjoyment of many small village clubs. The local farmer probably owns the field upon which the team plays and it is only he, by turning out a flock of sheep to graze, that keeps the grass to a reasonable length from the start of the season until its close. As for the players seeing a pitch cut, that is rarer than a total eclipse. One thing is certain, it could lead to a hell of a row. Commonsense says that the umpires should discuss their problem with the captains. If they wish for it to be mown, then a further toss must take place.

Law 10.4, which is about watering, refers only to "the pitch". Perhaps we have always allowed a bowler to water his approach to the wicket. As I said earlier, if any bowler took such action, it would probably be to his own, his wicketkeeper's and other members of his side's detriment. Anyway, umpires do not wish to stand on wet ground when they can stand on a dry surface.

Law 10.5 deals with the re-marking of creases and this is now worded slightly differently. It now gives umpires the licence to stop the game and to ask the groundsman to undertake this duty, should the need arise. It would, of course, have to be an extreme case and certainly something which umpires should try to avoid.

Law 10.6, on the maintenance of footholds, indicates the area where the bowler can land as he delivers the ball. This law mentions "the bowler in his delivery stride". I feel that this law should allow the maintenance to take place on any of a bowler's stride marks, on any part of his approach to deliver the ball and indeed as far as 5ft in front of the popping crease. Groundsmen at the top level have certainly taken such action for years.

Law 10.7 covers the securing of footholds with sawdust and maintenance of the pitch. I would allow and have allowed the use of sawdust, but only to a distance of 4ft in front of the popping crease. Now this distance has been extended to 5ft, I would allow both bowlers and batsmen to secure their footholds by the use of sawdust up to this point, but certainly no further forward.

LAW 11

Covering the Pitch

1. Before the match
The use of covers before the match is the responsibility of the Ground Authority and may include full covering if required. However, the Ground Authority shall grant suitable facility to the captains to inspect the pitch before the nomination of their players and to the umpires to discharge their duties as laid down in Laws 3 (The umpires), 7 (The pitch), 8 (The wickets), 9 (The bowling, popping and return creases) and 10 (Preparation and maintenance of the playing area).

2. During the match
The pitch shall not be completely covered during the match unless provided otherwise by regulations or by agreement before the toss.

3. Covering bowlers' run ups
Whenever possible, the bowlers' run ups shall be covered in inclement weather, in order to keep them dry. Unless there is agreement for full covering under 2 above the covers so used shall not extend further than 5ft/1.52m in front of each popping crease.

4. Removal of covers
(a) If after the toss the pitch is covered overnight, the covers shall be removed in the morning at the earliest possible moment on each day that play is expected to take place.
(b) If covers are used during the day as protection from inclement weather, or if inclement weather delays the removal of overnight covers, they shall be removed promptly as soon as conditions allow.

While the working party agreed to neither add to, nor delete from, the 42 Laws of Cricket in their recommendations, this is one which they may well have erased. The reason is that professional and league cricket, at all except the lower levels, allow for full covering of the pitch at all times during a match. The working party, being mindful of the fact that there are still some clubs of limited means, naturally decided that it had to stay. Law 11 and Law 42.11 (b) hinge to a great extent upon each other and I will set down the reasons we felt a change in the latter had to be made.

Law 11 has only two changes and while both are small, one of them is of great significance. Information contained in previous codes of the Laws of Cricket, which came to light in my research into this law, was of considerable interest. Parts 1, 2 and 4 are as set down in the 1980 code, although part 4 was actually note (a) in that code. It is only when we come to Law 11.3, which deals with covering bowlers' run-ups, that we see the changes. The first is the addition of the words "in inclement weather", which refers to the situation when the bowler's approach to the stumps shall be covered. The other change is the replacement of "4ft/1.22m" with "5ft/1.52m" in reference to the distance that covers can extend in front of the popping crease.

There are times when umpires and groundsmen have to take extreme action in their efforts to make play possible. I have known a situation and have instructed groundsmen, or perhaps it would be better to state that I have acted upon their advice, not to cover the bowler's run-ups overnight. This has happened when these areas have been so wet and soggy that to have covered them would have restricted their drying by the elements for some 16 hours. By taking this action, some of the moisture already in the ground was allowed to evaporate and, if blessed with an overnight breeze, the overnight drying process was hastened still further.

Some may contest these actions but I believe that, in these extreme situations, even if it had rained on the unprotected area, it would have been in no worse condition than if it had been covered. If it had rained, we would not have been able to play; if it had not rained but we had covered these areas, we still would not have been able to play. We took a gamble and I am delighted to say that it paid off.

It is the other change to this law, the extending of the distance that can be covered in front of the popping crease, that may have a dramatic effect on the manner in which the game is played. When this law was introduced it was stated that this was a recommended danger area "which should be protected from damage by a bowler".

This wording in itself has led to possibly the greatest inconsistency in umpiring since 1980 but I will say more in regard to this point under Law 42.12. This part of the 2000 code, Law 11.3, will work in unison with Law 42.11 (b) and in effect Law 42.12, since there was no point in changing one if we did not change the other. We could not let a bowler run on the pitch 4ft 9in in front of the "popping crease", if we did not then take steps to protect that area from the elements.

It was on May 30, 1788, that a law was first laid down in regard to the covering of the pitch but it failed to stipulate the area that could be covered. It is only when we get to 1916 that a recommendation was given to the counties which contained the distance of 3ft 6in by which covering could extend in front of each popping crease. That distance stayed the same until the 1980 code, when it was increased to 4ft. As early as 1970 the counties came forward with a recommendation to protect what was to become known as a "danger area", when the attention of umpires "was drawn to" and "purely as a guide" an area of ground "contained by an imaginary line 4ft from the popping crease and parallel to it, and within two imaginary and parallel lines drawn down the pitch from points 1ft either side of the middle stump and 4ft from the popping crease". This distance applied until the working party saw fit to recommend a change to 5ft, a much more realistic distance, in the 2000 code.

LAW 12

Innings

1. Number of innings
(a) A match shall be one or two innings of each side according to agreement reached before the match.
(b) It may be agreed to limit any innings to a number of overs or by a period of time. If such an agreement is made then
    (i) in a one innings match it shall apply to both innings.
    (ii) in a two innings match it shall apply to
        either the first innings of each side
        or the second innings of each side
        or both innings of each side.

2. Alternate innings
In a two innings match each side shall take their innings alternately except in the cases provided for in Law 13 (The follow-on) or Law 14.2 (Forfeiture of an innings).

3. Completed innings
A side's innings is to be considered as completed if
    (a) the side is all out
or (b) at the fall of a wicket, further balls remain to be bowled, but no further batsman is available to come in
or (c) the captain declares the innings closed
or (d) the captain forfeits the innings
or (e) in the case of an agreement under 1(b) above,
    either (i) the prescribed number of overs has been bowled
    or (ii) the prescribed time has expired.

4. The toss
The captains shall toss for the choice of innings on the field of play not

earlier than 30 minutes, nor later than 15 minutes, before the scheduled or any rescheduled time for the match to start. Note, however, the provisions of Law 1.3 (Captain).

5. Decision to be notified

The captain of the side winning the toss shall notify the opposing captain of his decision to bat or to field, not later than 10 minutes before the scheduled or any rescheduled time for the match to start. Once notified the decision may not be altered.

This law has two main changes and they are both of some significance. One is in Law 12.3, the other in Law 12.4.

Law 12.1 (a) is as in the 1980 code while part (b) has simply incorporated notes (a) and (b) of that code. I feel that it is a throwback to the old first-class regulation, when the first innings of each side was a maximum of 100 overs.

Law 12.2 deals with the matter of alternate innings. In a two-innings match, innings are taken alternately, except in the cases provided for in Law 13 (the follow-on) and Law 14 (declaration and forfeiture). Please remember that, should a captain take up any of these options, that innings will be counted as a completed innings. During England's 1999-2000 tour of South Africa, there was great joy when England were adjudged to have won the fifth and final Test match. Those of us who knew the laws were not at all sure of the validity of this result, but more in regard to this later, under Law 21, "The result".

Law 12.3 covers the subject of completed innings and in the past it has been asked many times what constitutes a completed innings? Few believed that a forfeiture by the captain of his side's second innings would count as a completed innings. Some thought that if a captain declared his side's innings closed, this did not constitute a completed innings. Also, in the case of a batsman or batsmen being injured and unable to resume in that innings, was that then a completed innings? Yes it was. All are now regarded as completed innings. These situations have now been dealt with in Law 12.3 and none of the above questions need arise again.

Law 12.4 brings to our attention the point that the toss for choice of innings shall take place "not earlier than 30 minutes, nor later than 15 minutes, before the scheduled or any rescheduled time for the match to start". With a cross-reference to what I have written in Law 1.3 and Law 3.1, you will see some of the reasons for this time-span. The 1980 code recommended that umpires should report to the ground at least 30 minutes before the start of play. As I said earlier, that would be too late under the 2000 code and, to my mind, always has been.

Law 12.5, entitled "Decision to be notified", was Law 12.4 and called "Choice of Innings" in the 1980 code. The wording has been changed in places but the essence is the same.

In the 1980 code Law 12.5 dealt with the "Continuation After One Innings of Each Side". There is now no law in respect of this in the 2000 code as the working party felt it to be pointless. Should a side win a one-innings match in a very short time, all that needs to happen to benefit from that lovely summer's day is to play another game, hopefully of cricket.

LAW 13

The Follow-on

1. Lead on first innings
(a) In a two innings match of 5 days or more, the side which bats first and leads by at least 200 runs shall have the option of requiring the other side to follow their innings.
(b) The same option shall be available in two innings matches of shorter duration with the minimum required leads as follows:
- (i) 150 runs in a match of 3 or 4 days;
- (ii) 100 runs in a 2-day match;
- (iii) 75 runs in a 1-day match.

2. Notification
A captain shall notify the opposing captain and the umpires of his intention to take up this option. Law 10.1(e) (Insufficient time to complete rolling) shall apply.

3. First day's play lost
If no play takes place on the first day of a match of more than one day's duration, 1 above shall apply in accordance with the number of days remaining from the actual start of the match. The day on which play first commences shall count as a whole day for this purpose, irrespective of the time at which play starts.

Play will have taken place as soon as, after the call of Play, the first over has started. See Law 22.2 (Start of an over).

The first law pertaining to the follow-on appears in the MCC revision of the laws in 1835, "obliging a side to bat again if 100 runs behind on the first innings".

With the dawning of the 2000 code of The Laws of Cricket exactly 100 years have elapsed since an option was provided for in regard to a follow-on. Before that, if the side batting second failed to get to a certain number of runs fewer than their opponents, it was mandatory for them to bat again. Over the years before 1900, the follow-on figure changed a lot. For example, in 1887, if a side scored 80 runs or more fewer than their opponents, they had to bat again. If it was a one-day match, the figure was 60 runs. In 1895 a score of 120 or more fewer than their opponents was required. In 1900 the follow-on figures were increased again to 150 for a three-day match, 100 for a two-day match and 75 for a one-day match. These figures have stood for a century and are now under Law 13.1 (b).

It was not until 1927 that any reference was made to a match of more than three days but, when it was, the follow-on figure was still 150 runs in "matches of three days or more". In 1963 we saw the first experimental law, which only applied in Test matches, where a lead of 200 was required before a side could ask their opponents to bat again. In those years there were a number of lovely expressions used and in this situation it states "that the opponents were invited to follow-on". This experimental law must have worked well because the follow-on in county championship matches had been abolished in 1961 but was reintroduced in 1964. There was no further change to this law until the 1972 season, when the words "5 days or more" were brought in.

And so to the minutiae of the follow-on law in the 2000 code. Law 13.1 has been phrased slightly differently but, as I said, is the same as it has been for many years in regard to the lead required. Law 13.2 deals with notification of the follow-on. While notification should be given by the captain wishing to take advantage of a follow-on situation almost immediately, sometimes there is a slight delay in doing so. He must notify the other captain and the umpires, as the latter are in charge of the rolling requirements. The duration of such rolling (maximum seven minutes) and the type of roller he requires are instructions that the umpires have to pass on to the groundsman. There will also be other matters such as sweeping the pitch, re-marking of the creases and perhaps maintaining of the footholds. Ten minutes is not really enough time between innings to complete these duties. Provision is given in Law 13.2, with reference to Law 10.1 (e), that if such duties are not completed when the time arrives to restart the match, then any time for the rolling of the pitch that exceeds the ten-minute interval will come out of the playing time. This, of course, applies equally for a declaration or a forfeiture of an innings.

Law 13.3 states that, in matches of a certain number of days, when play may not take place at all on one or a number of them, the follow-on figure will reflect the number of days upon which play actually takes place, with a proviso. The days which will count are those from the start of the match, even if there is no play on a subsequent day. So, if play only takes place for a short time on the first day of a five-day match, it is still regarded as a five-day match, even if no play takes place on day two and day three. However, if a five-day match is unable to start until the third day, it will be classed as a three-day match for the purposes of this law. Similarly, if there is no play on the first day of a three-day match, it becomes a match of two days, as long as some play takes place on the second day. Should no play take place on the second day, then it will become a one-day match.

See page 104 below for my comments on Law 13.3.

LAW 14

Declaration and Forfeiture

1. Time of declaration
The captain of the batting side may declare an innings closed, when the ball is dead, at any time during a match.

2. Forfeiture of an innings
A captain may forfeit either of his side's innings. A forfeited innings shall be considered as a completed innings.

3. Notification
A captain shall notify the opposing captain and the umpires of his decision to declare or to forfeit an innings. Law 10.1(e) (Insufficient time to complete rolling) shall apply.

This is now the shortest law of all but it nonetheless contains two important answers and clarifications regarding certain incidents that arise in matches.

Before 1889 there was no such thing in the laws as declaring an innings closed but in that year a law was introduced stating that "the batting side could declare its innings closed at any time on the last day of the match".

Between 1889 and 1927 there were alterations to what was then Law 15. These were in respect of allowing such action to take place either on certain days or when a certain amount of time remained for play on that day. It also allowed this action if a certain number of runs had been scored or a certain amount of time had expired in the match. By 1968 the law had become so complicated that it was changed to read "the captain of the batting side may declare an innings closed at any time during a match, irrespective of its duration". With a slight proviso this regulation had applied in first-class cricket since 1952, the proviso being in regard to the amount of time lost in the match.

Since that time the age-old question of what happens in the following situation has been asked. The captain of the batting side has scored 99 when he hits the ball high into the air. The batsmen complete one run when the striker shouts "innings declared", after which a catch is taken. What should be the umpires' decision? As the law read, the decision should have been "not out", which I, along with all the other members of the working party and many others who follow the game, would have thought ludicrous. The new code gives clarification, should such an incident arise.

Law 14.1 now states that the captain of the batting side may declare an innings closed, when the ball is dead, at any time during a match. As regards the above example, the key phrase, which was not in the 1980 code, is obviously "when the ball is dead".

Law 14.2 also gives important clarification to matters that have bothered umpires over a number of years and states a major decision of law. A captain may forfeit either of his side's innings and a forfeited innings shall be considered a "completed innings". An innings that has been declared will also be considered completed, no matter at what score or even if no wickets have fallen.

Because of collusion, the word "forfeit" was brought into the game at first-class level in 1967. In the first-class regulations before 1967, emphasis was put on the fact that, should the umpires feel that collusion had taken place in regard to declarations, the matter must be reported and the sides would not receive any points.

In the laws previous to the 2000 code, only the second innings could be forfeited and this was not introduced until the 1969 code. In fact there has been provision for both innings to be forfeited in English county championship cricket for a number of years but now it applies to all cricket.

I began to wonder why captains wished to complete an innings in this manner. I thought back to my early years as a member of the First Class Panel of Umpires and how many times I had seen a side declare at 0 runs for 0 wickets. To comply with the law, a side had to start a first innings before it could declare it closed. This regulation allowed for one side to bat and make a certain score, and the second side to declare at 0 runs for 0 wickets. The side which had made the score in its first innings would then forfeit its second innings, which was within the law. The side which had declared its first innings closed on 0 for 0 would bat for a second time to try to score one more run than had been scored by their opponents in the one innings in which they had batted. These actions by captains only took place, in the main, as a time-saving measure when rain had restricted play by a number of hours. At least I would like to think so. It certainly did save time under the 1980 code and now it will save even more time, if only the ten minutes between innings.

Law 14.3 gives instruction that a captain taking either action of declaration or forfeiture must notify his opposite number and the umpires. This is in case matters arise in regard to Law 10.1, which deals with rolling the pitch. In my research into this law I turned up an interesting point which really pertains to Law 13. In one of the early codes it stated that "a captain had to notify his opposite number within one minute of the end of an innings if he required his opponents to follow on". It might be useful if we returned to the wording of that law.

LAW 15

Intervals

1. An interval

The following shall be classed as intervals.

The period between close of play on one day and the start of the next day's play.

Intervals between innings.

Intervals for meals.

Intervals for drinks.

Any other agreed interval.

All these intervals shall be considered as scheduled breaks for the purposes of Law 2.5 (Fielder absent or leaving the field).

2. Agreement of intervals

(a) Before the toss:
- (i) the hours of play shall be established;
- (ii) except as in (b) below, the timing and duration of intervals for meals shall be agreed;
- (iii) the timing and duration of any other interval under 1(v) above shall be agreed.

(b) In a one-day match no specific time need be agreed for the tea interval. It may be agreed instead to take this interval between the innings.

(c) Intervals for drinks may not be taken during the last hour of the match, as defined in Law 16.6 (Last hour of match – number of overs). Subject to this limitation the captains and umpires shall agree the times for such intervals, if any, before the toss and on each subsequent day not later than 10 minutes before play is scheduled to start. See also Law 3.3 (Agreement with captains).

3. Duration of intervals

(a) An interval for lunch or for tea shall be of the duration agreed under

2(a) above, taken from the call of Time before the interval until the call of Play on resumption after the interval.

(b) An interval between innings shall be 10 minutes from the close of an innings to the call of Play for the start of the next innings, except as in 4, 6 and 7 below.

4. No allowance for interval between innings

In addition to the provisions of 6 and 7 below,

(a) if an innings ends when 10 minutes or less remain before the time agreed for close of play on any day, there will be no further play on that day. No change will be made to the time for the start of play on the following day on account of the 10 minutes between innings.

(b) if a captain declares an innings closed during an interruption in play of more than 10 minutes duration, no adjustment shall be made to the time for resumption of play on account of the 10 minutes between innings, which shall be considered as included in the interruption. Law 10.1(e) (Insufficient time to complete rolling) shall apply.

(c) if a captain declares an innings closed during any interval other than an interval for drinks, the interval shall be of the agreed duration and shall be considered to include the 10 minutes between innings. Law 10.1(e) (Insufficient time to complete rolling) shall apply.

5. Changing agreed times for intervals

If for adverse conditions of ground, weather or light, or for any other reason, playing time is lost, the umpires and captains together may alter the time of the lunch interval or of the tea interval. See also 6, 7 and 9(c) below.

6. Changing agreed time for lunch interval

(a) If an innings ends when 10 minutes or less remain before the agreed time for lunch, the interval shall be taken immediately. It shall be of the agreed length and shall be considered to include the 10 minutes between innings.

(b) If, because of adverse conditions of ground, weather or light, or in exceptional circumstances, a stoppage occurs when 10 minutes or less remain before the agreed time for lunch then, notwithstanding 5 above, the interval shall be taken immediately. It shall be of the agreed length.

Play shall resume at the end of this interval or as soon after as conditions permit.

(c) If the players have occasion to leave the field for any reason when more than 10 minutes remain before the agreed time for lunch then, unless the umpires and captains together agree to alter it, lunch will be taken at the agreed time.

7. Changing agreed time for tea interval

(a) (i) If an innings ends when 30 minutes or less remain before the agreed time for tea, then the interval shall be taken immediately. It shall be of the agreed length and shall be considered to include the 10 minutes between innings.

(ii) If, when 30 minutes remain before the agreed time for tea, an interval between innings is already in progress, play will resume at the end of the 10 minute interval.

(b) (i) If, because of adverse conditions of ground, weather or light, or in exceptional circumstances, a stoppage occurs when 30 minutes or less remain before the agreed time for tea, then unless

either there is an agreement to change the time for tea, as permitted in 5 above

or the captains agree to forgo the tea interval, as permitted in 10 below

the interval shall be taken immediately. The interval shall be of the agreed length. Play shall resume at the end of this interval or as soon after as conditions permit.

(ii) If a stoppage is already in progress when 30 minutes remain before the time agreed for tea, 5 above will apply.

8. Tea interval – 9 wickets down

If 9 wickets are down at the end of the over in progress when the agreed time for the tea interval has been reached, then play shall continue for a period not exceeding 30 minutes, unless the players have cause to leave the field of play, or the innings is concluded earlier.

9. Intervals for drinks

(a) If on any day the captains agree that there shall be intervals for drinks, the option to take such intervals shall be available to either side. Each interval shall be kept as short as possible and in any case shall not exceed 5 minutes.

(b) (i) Unless both captains agree to forgo any drinks interval, it shall be taken at the end of the over in progress when the agreed time is reached. If, however, a wicket falls within 5 minutes of the agreed time then drinks shall be taken immediately. No other variation in the timing of drinks intervals shall be permitted except as provided for in (c) below.

(ii) For the purpose of (i) above and Law 3.9(a)(ii) (Suspension of play for adverse conditions of ground, weather or light) only, the batsmen at the wicket may deputise for their captain.

(c) If an innings ends or the players have to leave the field of play for any other reason within 30 minutes of the agreed time for a drinks interval, the umpires and captains together may rearrange the timing of drinks intervals in that session.

10. Agreement to forgo intervals

At any time during the match, the captains may agree to forgo the tea interval or any of the drinks intervals. The umpires shall be informed of the decision.

11. Scorers to be informed

The umpires shall ensure that the scorers are informed of all agreements about hours of play and intervals, and of any changes made thereto as permitted under this Law.

This is one of two laws which has had a change of law number from the 1980 code. This one, "Intervals", was Law 16 in the 1980 code. Law 15, "Start of play", and Law 17, "Cessation of play", from the 1980 code have been brought together under the combined title in the 2000 code as the new Law 16. Law 17, "Practice on the field", is virtually a new law in the 2000 code.

While there has seldom been a problem with this law, Nigel Plews and I were both adamant that we desired clarification to be set down in law upon two points. He for what was written under Law 16.6 in the 1980 code and myself over what I can only refer to as hours of play. Both of these matters were in relation to Law 2.8 of the 1980 code.

In some of the countries Nigel visited, they showed a great reluctance to agree with him that a drinks interval was indeed an interval in respect of implementing Law 2.8 of the 1980 code, which refers to substitutes. That it is a proper interval is beyond question because in Law 15, "Start of play", umpires are instructed to call "play" after any interval. Likewise, Law 17, "Cessation of play", instructs umpires to call time before the start of any interval. The correct application of these two laws appears to have escaped the dissenters. Should the cricketing bodies of other countries wish not to observe this law, they must write a special regulation to that effect in their competitions.

Similarly, I met with opposition when I stated that the time between the end of a day's play and the start of play on the day that the match resumes is also an interval. It always was and still is, for the reasons that I have given in the preceding paragraph. In Law 15.1 of the 2000 code these two situations have been classified as intervals and there is no room for any ambiguity.

Law 15.2 deals with the agreement of intervals. The hours of play are usually laid down before a competition or a match starts, and they generally include the times of the intervals for meals. If they do not, the captains must agree on them before the toss. If it is felt that drinks intervals will be required during a match, this matter must be agreed on by the captains, along with the timing of such intervals. Please note that the timing of drinks intervals may be reviewed at the start of each day's play. Sometimes, indeed, we not only wish to change the timing and the frequency of them, but also the beverage to be consumed. Or perhaps we do not wish to take them at all. On the first day of a match in this country it may be so cold that drinks never cross anybody's mind, except for a large Scotch after close of play. By the start of play on the third day the temperature may well have soared to 80 degrees, circumstances in which drinks are not just a pleasure but a necessity.

Law 15.3, "Duration of intervals", contains a change that is most welcome. It makes the point that intervals for meals shall be of such duration as have been agreed. Many a time I have been in a situation where a wicket has fallen with just over two minutes remaining for play before the lunch interval, this being from the first delivery of an over. By the time the new batsman has taken his place at the wicket and taken his guard, and the captain has set his field for the new batsman, the clock is ticking past the allotted hour. Then, if the captain has perhaps not set the field to good effect, his fielders may have to retrieve a number of those last five deliveries from the boundary. When, eventually, the umpire is able to call "over" and "time", the hands on the clock are reading five or six minutes past the agreed time of the lunch interval. Forty minutes, to my mind, never has been a long enough time for the lunch interval but something considerably under 35 minutes is ridiculous. Law 15.3, as now written, means that players and umpires are always able to have 40 minutes for a lunch interval, or indeed whatever time has actually been agreed.

Law 15.4, "No allowance for interval between innings", is mostly self-explanatory but I would like to point out that in parts (b) and (c), if the declaration or forfeit is within ten minutes of the end of any interval, the ten minutes will be taken from the moment the information is dispensed to the umpires. In regard to part (a) I do not think that anyone would ever dream of starting five minutes late when a match is resumed on a succeeding day, should an innings have closed or a declaration have been made five minutes before the time for the close of play on the previous day.

Law 15.5 makes the sensible statement that, in situations when time has been lost to the elements, captains and umpires together may alter the time of the meal intervals. This is, of course, to enable us to play as much cricket as possible. Law 16.2 of the 1980 code has not operated as written for many years and I never found myself in a position when it could have done so. In the various editions of the 1980 code, the wording allowed for a lunch interval of a greater length of time than that originally agreed. For example, should an innings have closed nine minutes before the time agreed for the start of that interval, nine minutes was added to the interval, giving an interval of 49 minutes, with play still starting at the originally agreed time for the end of the lunch interval. This law is now worded in a manner which will ensure that, while the lunch interval will begin on the fall of that last wicket at nine minutes to the agreed time for the lunch interval, the interval itself will be only of "the agreed duration" and play will restart nine minutes earlier than the previously agreed time.

This alteration is to be found in Law 15.6 (a) of the 2000 code while Law 15.6 (b) confirms that, should a suspension of play take place within ten minutes of the lunch interval, the interval will be taken immediately. Law 15.6 (c) covers the situation when a suspension of play occurs with more than ten minutes remaining to a lunch interval. Unless there is agreement between captains and umpires, lunch will still be taken at the time agreed before the start of the match.

I have not always agreed with matters pertaining to the playing regulations of the first-class game being included in the Laws of Cricket but, with those which are good for the game, I certainly have. Law 15.8, headed "Tea interval – 9 wickets down", is one of them. I have implemented it many times in county championship matches during my career and again it is in an effort to play more cricket. No one need fear it. It is an easy law to follow and easy to apply during a match. I am certain that many will agree with me that, if at the appointed time for the tea interval, nine wickets have fallen and the umpires call "time" and depart the field of play, that is not really sensible. Certainly it would not be if, upon the resumption of play 20 minutes later, the final wicket of the innings falls from the first ball delivered. We then depart the scene for a further ten minutes, the time between innings. That would be a complete waste of time and this law endeavours to eliminate such a situation, except in the following very rare case. Umpires should be aware of this situation. A batsman has been injured and leaves the field of play and, as far as you are aware, is still at the ground. A wicket falls and you know that there is only the last man to come to the wicket. Do not call "time", thinking that nine wickets have fallen. They have not; it is only eight down, because the injured man's wicket has not yet fallen.

Law 15.10 brings to the fore the point that, should the captains have agreed to drinks intervals during a match, the option to take those drinks remains available to both sides, even if one declines. More than once I have seen a fielding captain wave away the drinks waiters as they assemble at the boundary edge. I, in turn, have asked the non-striker if he desired to take advantage of the right to take a drink. One batsman to whom I posed this question said: "I am gasping." I simply pointed out to the fielding captain that, while he and his team may not desire to take drinks, they were still available to both sides. He was none too pleased but he got the message and the batsmen got their drinks.

During an England v Australia Test match at Lord's, I observed one of the Australian batsmen signal to the dressing room for a drink, just after the final hour of the match had been signalled to the scorers. I could not believe this but out they came, at least as far as the boundary line, when I signalled in a direct manner for them to be taken away. This caused some slight consternation for the batsmen but I just said, "sorry, not in the final hour". At the conclusion of the match everyone was invited into the Australian dressing room for a tin or two and I was approached by the Australian manager, Fred Bennett. He apologised to me for trying to send on the drinks and explained to me that, under the playing regulations in his country, should drinks be required during the final session of play on the last day of a match, they can only be taken *after* the final hour has started. As will be seen, this is somewhat different to Law 16.6 of the 1980 code, now Law 15.2 of the 2000 code.

LAW 16

Start of Play; Cessation of Play

1. Call of Play
The umpire at the bowler's end shall call Play at the start of the match and on the resumption of play after any interval or interruption.

2. Call of Time
The umpire at the bowler's end shall call Time on the cessation of play before any interval or interruption of play and at the conclusion of the match. See Law 27 (Appeals).

3. Removal of bails
After the call of Time, the bails shall be removed from both wickets.

4. Starting a new over
Another over shall always be started at any time during the match, unless an interval is to be taken in the circumstances set out in 5 below, if the umpire, after walking at his normal pace, has arrived at his position behind the stumps at the bowler's end before the time agreed for the next interval, or for the close of play, has been reached.

5. Completion of an over
Other than at the end of the match,
- (a) if the agreed time for an interval is reached during an over, the over shall be completed before the interval is taken except as provided for in (b) below.
- (b) when less than 2 minutes remain before the time agreed for the next interval, the interval will be taken immediately if
  either (i) a batsman is out or retires
  or (ii) the players have occasion to leave the field

whether this occurs during an over or at the end of an over. Except at the end of an innings, if an over is thus interrupted it shall be completed on resumption of play.

6. Last hour of match – number of overs

When one hour of playing time of the match remains, according to the agreed hours of play, the over in progress shall be completed. The next over shall be the first of a minimum of 20 overs which must be bowled, provided that a result is not reached earlier and provided that there is no interval or interruption in play.

The umpire at the bowler's end shall indicate the commencement of this 20 overs to the players and the scorers. The period of play thereafter shall be referred to as the last hour, whatever its actual duration.

7. Last hour of match – interruptions of play

If there is an interruption in play during the last hour of the match, the minimum number of overs to be bowled shall be reduced from 20 as follows.

(a) The time lost for an interruption is counted from the call of Time until the time for resumption of play as decided by the umpires.

One over shall be deducted for every complete 3 minutes of time lost.

(c) In the case of more than one such interruption, the minutes lost shall not be aggregated; the calculation shall be made for each interruption separately.

(d) If, when one hour of playing time remains, an interruption is already in progress,

- (i) only the time lost after this moment shall be counted in the calculation;
- (ii) the over in progress at the start of the interruption shall be completed on resumption of play and shall not count as one of the minimum number of overs to be bowled.

(e) If, after the start of the last hour, an interruption occurs during an over, the over shall be completed on resumption of play. The two part-overs shall between them count as one over of the minimum number to be bowled.

8. Last hour of match – intervals between innings

If an innings ends so that a new innings is to be started during the last hour of the match, the interval starts with the end of the innings and is to end 10 minutes later.

(a) If this interval is already in progress at the start of the last hour, then to determine the number of overs to be bowled in the new innings, calculations are to be made as set out in 7 above.

(b) If the innings ends after the last hour has started, two calculations are to be made, as set out in (c) and (d) below. The greater of the numbers yielded by these two calculations is to be the minimum number of overs to be bowled in the new innings.

(c) Calculation based on overs remaining.
- (i) At the conclusion of the innings, the number of overs that remain to be bowled, of the minimum in the last hour, to be noted.
- (ii) If this is not a whole number it is to be rounded up to the next whole number.
- (iii) Three overs to be deducted from the result for the interval.

(d) Calculation based on time remaining.
- (i) At the conclusion of the innings, the time remaining until the agreed time for close of play to be noted.
- (ii) Ten minutes to be deducted from this time, for the interval, to determine the playing time remaining.
- (iii) A calculation to be made of one over for every complete 3 minutes of the playing time remaining, plus one more over for any further part of 3 minutes remaining.

9. Conclusion of match

The match is concluded

(a) as soon as a result, as defined in sections 1,2,3 or 4 of Law 21 (The result), is reached.

(b) as soon as both
- (i) the minimum number of overs for the last hour are completed

and (ii) the agreed time for close of play is reached

unless a result has been reached earlier.

(c) if, without the match being concluded either as in (a) or in (b) above, the players leave the field, either for adverse conditions of ground, weather or light, or in exceptional circumstances, and no further play is possible thereafter.

10. Completion of last over of match

The over in progress at the close of play on the final day shall be completed unless:

either (i) a result has been reached

or (ii) the players have occasion to leave the field. In this case there shall be no resumption of play except in the circumstances of Law 21.9 (Mistakes in scoring), and the match shall be at an end.

11. Bowler unable to complete an over during last hour of match

If, for any reason, a bowler is unable to complete an over during the last hour, Law 22.8 (Bowler incapacitated or suspended during an over) shall apply.

This is the second of the two laws that have had a change of numbering from the 1980 code. The new Law 16 in the 2000 code is made up of Laws 15 and 17 from the 1980 code. I think this is a sensible move as it draws together many matters relating to the progress of a match.

While two laws have been incorporated in the new Law 16, it actually contains only one small paragraph from the old Law 15, "Start of play". It was the first paragraph of the old law and is now Law 16.1, "Call of play". Umpires are often asked the question, "when has a match actually started?" Because other codes were not completely clear, the answer to this question has altered from time to time. At one time it was the call of "play" that started the match. At other times it was when the bowler began his forward progress to deliver the first ball. More recently a clarification from the ACU&S was to the effect that the match started as soon as an incident took place whereby an entry should be made in the scorebook. Under the 2000 code, the start of the match is the moment that the umpire at the bowling wicket calls "play".

The remainder of the new Law 16 is taken from the old Law 17, with a little renumbering of parts.

Law 16.5 is entitled "Completion of an over" and has an important first line "Other than at the end of the match". That line will, I am sure, satisfy my old friend and colleague in Australia, Tom Brooks. Tom was the exceptionally good Sheffield Shield and Test match umpire who came over to England in what were supposed to be the early days of the exchange of umpires scheme. Tom has been in conflict with many people on this one point of law and he quite rightly posed the question, "why should it be different at the end of a match, in regard to the starting of another over, than it is prior to all other intervals?" He always said: "If it is within two minutes for all other intervals, why not if a wicket falls prior to the end of the match?" I always told Tom that I could see his point but that was not how the law was applied. Now that one-line rider makes it crystal clear.

Law 16.6 clears up a point that barrack-room lawyers have often raised. They believe that the last hour can only be of 60 minutes. If the time for close of play on the last day of a match is 6pm, they say that the last hour should be signalled when the big hand is exactly on 12 and the little hand is on 5, even if it is during an over. The clarification is in the final sentence. It has been well stated and should lay to rest this particular point of conflict.

Law 16.7 deals with the "Last hour of match – interruptions of play". There is nothing new in the calculations in this part of the law but I do wish to point out part 8 (c). During one of our meetings discussions centred round this point and someone stated that stoppages had never been aggregated. Fortunately I had with me many books of reference and I soon dispelled such thoughts from the individual's mind. They, of course, knew that many years ago this was the manner by which the calculations were made. However, I simply want to make the point that now each stoppage is calculated as a single entity.

In Law 16.8, "Last hour of match – interval between innings", there is an important change in part (c) (ii). Under Law 17.7 (c) (iv) of the 1980 code, if a match was in the final hour and an innings came to a close, say, after four overs and four balls had been bowled of the 20, the first calculation that should have gone through an umpire's mind was four overs bowled, forget the four balls. Those four balls would not enter calculations at all. We would then finalise our calculations on the basis by which we have done in the past and will do so in the future, with one exception.

Under the 2000 code and taking the same example, four overs and four balls bowled of the minimum 20 to be bowled in the final hour, our first thought is, how many more to be bowled? This is obviously 15 overs and two balls. The new law states "if this is not a whole number, it is to be rounded up to the next whole number". This would be 16 and then we deduct three for the 10 minutes between innings, leaving us with a minimum of 13 to bowl to complete the minimum of 20 overs in that final hour. The thing that must not be forgotten is the other calculation based on time remaining. This is exactly as in the 1980 code. Whichever calculation gives the most overs, that is the one to be adopted.

With the overs calculation under the 1980 code we would still end up with the same amount of overs. Taking the same example of four overs and four balls bowled, our first thought would have been to forget the four balls, leaving four overs bowled. Then we add the three overs for the ten minutes between innings, making seven bowled, which again would leave us with 13 to bowl to reach the minimum of 20 in the final hour.

LAW 17

Practice on the Field

1. Practice on the field

(a) There shall be no bowling or batting practice on the pitch, or on the area parallel and immediately adjacent to the pitch, at any time on any day of the match.

(b) There shall be no bowling or batting practice on any other part of the square on any day of the match, except before the start of play or after the close of play on that day. Practice before the start of play

- (i) must not continue later than 30 minutes before the scheduled time or any rescheduled time for play to start on that day.
- (ii) shall not be allowed if the umpires consider that, in the prevailing conditions of ground and weather, it will be detrimental to the surface of the square.

(c) There shall be no practice on the field of play between the call of Play and the call of Time, if the umpire considers that it could result in a waste of time. See Law 42.9 (Time wasting by the fielding side).

(d) If a player contravenes (a) or (b) above he shall not be allowed to bowl until at least 5 complete overs have been bowled by his side after the contravention. If an over is in progress at the contravention he shall not be allowed to complete that over nor shall the remaining part-over count towards the 5 overs above.

2. Trial run up

No bowler shall have a trial run up between the call of Play and the call of Time unless the umpire is satisfied that it will not cause any waste of time.

Despite the working party having stated from time to time that there would be no new laws in the 2000 code and that there would there be no deletions from the 1980 code, Law 17 is completely new. I must add that it is one which was certainly required. This is because of what takes place, in the main, when a captain changes his bowling attack.

I have often seen players who are about to begin a spell of bowling deliver the ball three or four times to another member of his side standing 20 or so yards away in the outfield. This has taken place many times and I have often been tempted to ask them whether they would like us to move the wickets over to accommodate their actions. Other colleagues have told me that they have seen players deliver six balls in this manner. I asked them if the player had then taken his sweater from the umpire but, of course, such actions take place before the player discards his sweater. The bowler then decides to mark out his approach to deliver the first real ball. All very tedious.

It is not only bowlers who waste a great deal of time as many fielders adopt a slovenly approach to taking up their position between overs and some captains take an eternity in the setting of the field. Nor is it just the bowling side who are guilty of time-wasting. All such incidents are now covered under Laws 42.9 and 42.10 and interesting reading they make.

The new Law 17 is, in the main, the old Law 15, except that Law 15.1 has now been incorporated into Law 16, as mentioned earlier. Law 17, "Practice on the field", is the old Law 15.2 from the 1980 code with several additions and clarifications.

Law 17.1 (a) allows no batting or bowling practice on the pitch, and in addition does not allow similar practices "parallel and immediately adjacent to it". I am assured that, at the higher levels of the game, it is now common practice for coaches to take out the opening bowlers and let them bowl right on the edge of the match pitch, with the purpose of getting them to bowl the required length. This must now cease.

Law 17.1 (b) ensures that no bowling or batting practice will take place on the remainder of the square during the hours of play. It will permit practice up to 30 minutes prior to play commencing, and also after the end of a day's play. A player can still comply with this part of the law and bowl the ball, before a day's play or after it, some 15ft 3in wide of the wickets on the pitch on which the match is being played.

Law 17.1 (c) is to my mind what this new law is all about – wasting time during the day's play. I have mentioned earlier some of the actions that constitute wasting time and, as other laws have been formulated to allow for as much cricket as possible to be played, it was felt that the players should play their part.

Law 17.1 (d) sets down the penalty should any member of the fielding side, not just a bowler, contravene this law. Some may think that there is a flaw in this law in that it allows a non-bowler to waste whatever time he so desires. He will not mind being suspended from bowling for "5 complete overs", as the law states. However, there is still serious redress in Law 42.9 (b) and this is why I am sure that Law 42 will have a great bearing on how the game of cricket is played in the future, a bearing certainly for the better. Although it may seem a hollow penalty to suspend a non-bowler from bowling, he will also incur five penalty runs each time he offends and I am sure that would not endear him to the rest of his team. Also, as he and his captain will be reported for such actions under Law 42.9 (b) (iii), I do feel that Law 42 is going to be a great deterrent.

Law 17.2, on trial run-ups, is more or less Law 15.3 from the 1980 code.

LAW 18

Scoring Runs

1. A run
The score shall be reckoned by runs. A run is scored
so often as the batsmen, at any time while the ball is in play, have crossed and made good their ground from end to end.
when a boundary is scored. See Law 19 (Boundaries).
when penalty runs are awarded. See 6 below.
(d) when Lost ball is called. See Law 20 (Lost ball).

2. Runs disallowed
Notwithstanding 1 above, or any other provisions elsewhere in the Laws, the scoring of runs or awarding of penalties will be subject to any disallowance of runs provided for within the Laws that may be applicable.

3. Short runs
(a) A run is short if a batsman fails to make good his ground on turning for a further run.
(b) Although a short run shortens the succeeding one, the latter if completed shall not be regarded as short. A striker taking stance in front of his popping crease may run from that point also without penalty.

4. Unintentional short runs
Except in the circumstances of 5 below,
if either batsman runs a short run, unless a boundary is scored the umpire concerned shall call and signal Short run as soon as the ball becomes dead and that run shall not be scored.
if, after either or both batsmen runs short, a boundary is scored, the umpire concerned shall disregard the short running and shall not call or signal Short run.

if both batsmen run short in one and the same run, this shall be regarded as only one short run.

(d) if more than one run is short then, subject to (b) and (c) above, all runs so called shall not be scored.

If there has been more than one short run the umpire shall inform the scorers as to the number of runs scored.

5. Deliberate short runs

(a) Notwithstanding 4 above, if either umpire considers that either or both batsmen deliberately run short at his end, the following procedure shall be adopted.

- (i) The umpire concerned shall, when the ball is dead, warn the batsman or batsmen that the practice is unfair, indicate that this is a first and final warning and inform the other umpire of what has occurred.
- (ii) The batsmen shall return to their original ends.
- (iii) Whether a batsman is dismissed or not, the umpire at the bowler's end shall disallow all runs to the batting side from that delivery other than the penalty for a No ball or Wide, or penalties under Laws 42.5 (Deliberate distraction or obstruction of batsman) and 42.13 (Fielders damaging the pitch), if applicable.
- (iv) The umpire at the bowler's end shall inform the scorers as to the number of runs scored.

(b) If there is any further instance of deliberate short running by either of the same batsmen in that innings, when the ball is dead, the umpire concerned shall inform the other umpire of what has occurred and the procedure set out in (a)(ii) and (iii) above shall be repeated. Additionally, the umpire at the bowler's end shall

- (i) award 5 penalty runs to the fielding side. See Law 42.17 (Penalty runs).
- (ii) inform the scorers as to the number of runs scored.
- (iii) inform the batsmen, the captain of the fielding side and, as soon as practicable, the captain of the batting side of the reason for this action.
- (iv) report the occurrence, with the other umpire, to the Executive of the batting side and any Governing Body

responsible for the match, who shall take such action as is considered appropriate against the captain and player or players concerned.

6. Runs scored for penalties

Runs shall be scored for penalties under 5 above and Laws 2.6 (Player returning without permission), 24 (No ball), 25 (Wide ball), 41.2 (Fielding the ball), 41.3 (Protective helmets belonging to the fielding side) and 42 (Fair and unfair play).

7. Runs scored for boundaries

Runs shall be scored for boundary allowances under Law 19 (Boundaries).

8. Runs scored for Lost ball

Runs shall be scored when Lost ball is called under Law 20 (Lost ball).

9. Batsman dismissed

When either batsman is dismissed

(a) any penalties to either side that may be applicable shall stand but no other runs shall be scored, except as stated in 10 below. Note, however, Law 42.17(b) (Penalty runs).

(b) 12(a) below will apply if the method of dismissal is Caught, Handled the ball or Obstructing the field. 12(a) will also apply if a batsman is Run out, except in the circumstances of Law 2.8 (Transgression of the Laws by a batsman who has a runner) where 12(b) below will apply.

(c) the not out batsman shall return to his original end except as stated in (b) above.

10. Runs scored when a batsman is dismissed

In addition to any penalties to either side that may be applicable, if a batsman is

(a) dismissed Handled the ball, the batting side shall score the runs completed before the offence.

(b) dismissed Obstructing the field, the batting side shall score the runs completed before the offence.

If, however, the obstruction prevents a catch from being made, no runs other than penalties shall be scored.

(c) dismissed Run out, the batting side shall score the runs completed before the dismissal.

If, however, a striker with a runner is himself dismissed Run out, no runs other than penalties shall be scored. See Law 2.8 (Transgression of the Laws by a batsman who has a runner).

11. Runs scored when ball becomes dead

(a) When the ball becomes dead on the fall of a wicket, runs shall be scored as laid down in 9 and 10 above.

(b) When the ball becomes dead for any reason other than the fall of a wicket, or is called dead by an umpire, unless there is specific provision otherwise in the Laws, the batting side shall be credited with

      (i) all runs completed by the batsmen before the incident or call

and   (ii) the run in progress if the batsmen have crossed at the instant of the incident or call. Note specifically, however, the provisions of Laws 34.4(c) (Runs from ball lawfully struck more than once) and 42.5(b)(iii) (Deliberate distraction or obstruction of batsman).

and   (iii) any penalties that are applicable.

12. Batsman returning to wicket he has left

If, while the ball is in play, the batsmen have crossed in running, neither shall return to the wicket he has left, except as in (b) below.

The batsmen shall return to the wickets they originally left in the cases of, and only in the cases of

    (i) a boundary;

    (ii) disallowance of runs for any reason;

    (iii) the dismissal of a batsman, except as in 9(b) above.

The changes to this law, which affect the way that runs are accrued, are among many that will have a dramatic influence on the playing of the game of cricket. Under the 2000 code, all penalty runs will be in addition to the runs which are scored from the bat or as byes or leg byes. In the 1980 code, if the striker hit a no ball for four, that would be the sum total of the runs scored. Under the new code the no-ball penalty will be scored in addition to all other runs or extras credited. In similar vein, should a wide ball be bowled and extras are obtained, the sum total will be one wide penalty added to any other extras. In this instance, all will be entered in the scorebook as wides. Furthermore, should the fielding or batting side infringe Law 42 and have penalty runs awarded against them, these will be awarded, in the case of the batting side, in addition to all other runs or penalties which have been scored.

Law 18.1 describes all circumstances when runs shall be credited to the batting side. The wording of part (c), "when penalty runs are awarded", is the same as the 1980 code but, as mentioned above, there are far more situations in which this will occur and this part of Law 18.1 ends with a cross-reference to Law 18.6, "Runs scored for penalties". A study of Law 18.6 of the 1980 code throws up a couple of anomalies, which have obviously now been corrected. For example, Law 19, "Boundaries", is referred to under that section. Of course, they never were and never have been penalties. They have always been credited to the striker as it was his skill, or in some cases good fortune, that placed the ball beyond that part of the playing area of the field. Similarly, Law 20, "Lost ball", should not have been classed as a penalty as it is simply an award of runs to the batting side. As I have stated, both of these matters have been addressed and corrected in the new code.

Parts 3, 4 and 5 of Law 18 are the old Law 18.2, which has been divided up and enlarged. In the new Law 18.4, "Unintentional short runs", the action taken by the umpires is exactly as before. In Law 18.5, "Deliberate short runs", it is somewhat different, or should I say extended. I am one of only a few umpires to have disallowed runs for this offence and probably the only one at first-class level who has applied this part of the laws. The incident that prompted my action occurred in a county championship match between Kent and Leicestershire at Tunbridge Wells in 1975. When I saw it I knew just what to do as I had learnt it by heart when I first embarked on my study of the Laws of Cricket. After the incident, when colleagues asked me where they could look for confirmation of the action I had taken, I just said: "Read Law 19, note 3, part (iii)." By the way, that was in the 1947 code. It was that long ago.

During our deliberations on this part of the new laws, the working party went into lengthy discussion as to when and if the umpires should call "dead ball". In the end we decided to delete this call from the law and will now only take action after the ball has been made "dead" automatically. Parts (i) to (v) of Law 18.5 (a) detail the actions that an umpire must take when the ball is "dead". They warn the batsmen that the "practice is unfair" and the batsmen, as in the incident at Tunbridge Wells, are returned to their original ends. All runs taken by the batsmen will be disallowed, legal or otherwise. The law now informs us that penalties shall be credited to the batting side for the delivery of a no ball or a wide ball and now also under Law 42.5, "Deliberate distraction or obstruction of batsman", and Law 42.13, "Fielders damaging the pitch", if applicable. We have failed to turn the coin over, though, for we could in an incident of this nature also penalise the batting side, thereby awarding "penalty runs" to the fielding side under Law 42.14, "Batsman damaging the pitch".

Law 18.5 (b) contains the extension of this law that I mentioned earlier. After warnings have been issued and the deletion of runs in an incident of this nature, should a similar situation by either or both batsmen arise, the umpires will adopt the procedures as set down in Law 18.5 (a) (ii) to (v) and in addition shall award five penalty runs to the fielding side. At the opportune moment the umpires will inform both batsmen and both captains what has taken place and will report the matter to the appropriate authorities.

In my research into Law 18 I came across an interesting proposal that was considered during the revision of the Laws of Cricket in 1835. It was suggested that two runs be deducted when a batsman runs short "because such striker, not having run home in the first instance, cannot have started the second from the proper goal". There is no record of this ever being more than a proposal but it may have been the reason for the clarification in later codes "that for a run to be short, the batsman must have failed to make good his ground in turning for a further run; although a short run shortens the succeeding one, the latter if completed shall not be regarded as short".

Parts 6, 7 and 8 of Law 18 describe how runs are credited to the batting side. Part 6 lists the five types of penalties: wide ball, no ball, illegal fielding, the ball striking a protective helmet placed on the ground by the fielding side, and finally penalty runs awarded under Law 42, "Fair and unfair play". Part 7 covers runs scored for a boundary allowance, remembering that at some grounds this is not always four or six runs. Part 8 is simply "Runs scored for lost ball". In the 1980 code the last two methods of scoring runs were described as penalties. That was incorrect and it will be seen that the mistakes have been rectified.

When either batsman is dismissed, as in part 9 (a) of Law 18, no runs shall be credited, except the penalties as described, if applicable, not forgetting the penalty runs. It must also be remembered that, even if a batsman is dismissed, penalty runs can be awarded to the fielding side. There is provision for other runs to be scored by the batting side under Law 18.10.

Part 9 (b) of Law 18 lists the four types of dismissals (caught, handled the ball, obstructing the field and run out) when batsmen shall not be returned to their original wicket. There is one exception to this and that is when we have an injured striker using a runner and the injured striker himself is run out. The new batsman will then take up a position at the wicket where the injured striker himself was dismissed, and not as the law states, "where 12 (b) below will apply", the reason being that one of those batsmen will not be there "to return to the wicket".

In addition to the above, runs are also scored, as under Law 18.10, which are completed before the offences of "Handled the ball" and "Obstructing the field". Should there be obstruction of a fielder trying to take a catch, no runs will be credited. If either batsman is run out, all runs completed before the dismissal will be scored. However, in the case of an injured striker who has a runner operating for him, should the injured party be run out, no runs will be scored even if the two parties responsible for making those runs, the runner and the non-injured batsman, have completed runs in the correct manner.

Law 18.11, "Runs scored when the ball becomes dead", conjures up the following situation for an umpire and the signals that he would have to convey to the scorers. A no-ball delivery hits the striker on the body, with the striker playing a shot at the ball. The ball then crosses the boundary. During the action of running by the batsmen, one of them is charged to the ground by the bowler. When the ball is dead, the umpire will repeat the no-ball signal, accompanied by the bye signal, denoting that the ball was not hit by the striker. There will then be a boundary signal for an allowance of four runs. The umpire will then tap one shoulder with the opposite hand five times to denote that there are five penalty runs to be awarded to the batting side. And we are supposed to be making life easier for the scorers! If, of course, the umpires intervene with a call of dead ball prior to the ball crossing the boundary line, then only the runs completed and crossed upon by the batsmen will be credited, not the boundary allowance. These, of course, will be added to the no-ball penalty along with the allowance of five penalty runs for the obstruction.

The following recent incident was brought to the attention of Nigel Plews and he then on to myself, as in most matters on the Laws of Cricket we are in total agreement. The striker plays no stroke at a delivery from the bowler and from a deflection off his person the batsmen endeavour to take a run. The striker is then run out at the bowling wicket before a run is completed. All of this was quite clear but the question which was posed to us was, at which wicket will the incoming batsman take up his position? In both of our minds this was an easy answer; he will take his position at the wicket where the dismissal occurred. It is only in Law 18.11 (b) (ii) that a batsman will return to the wicket he has left, if there is a "disallowance of runs for any reason". The umpires would not have been able to disallow a run in this case, as no run had been completed. The striker was run out.

LAW 19

BOUNDARIES

1. The boundary of the field of play
(a) Before the toss, the umpires shall agree the boundary of the field of play with both captains. The boundary shall if possible be marked along its whole length.
(b) The boundary shall be agreed so that no part of any sight-screen is within the field of play.
(c) An obstacle or person within the field of play shall not be regarded as a boundary unless so decided by the umpires before the toss. See Law 3.4(ii) (To inform captains and scorers).

2. Defining the boundary – boundary marking
(a) Wherever practicable the boundary shall be marked by means of a white line or a rope laid along the ground.
(b) If the boundary is marked by a white line,
  (i) the inside edge of the line shall be the boundary edge.
  (ii) a flag, post or board used merely to highlight the position of a line marked on the ground must be placed outside the boundary edge and is not itself to be regarded as defining or marking the boundary. Note, however, the provisions of (c) below.
(c) If a solid object is used to mark the boundary, it must have an edge or a line to constitute the boundary edge.
  (i) For a rope, which includes any similar object of curved cross section lying on the ground, the boundary edge will be the line formed by the innermost points of the rope along its length.
  (ii) For a fence, which includes any similar object in contact with the ground, but with a flat surface projecting above the ground, the boundary edge will be the base line of the fence.
(d) If the boundary edge is not defined as in (b) or (c) above, the umpires

and captains must agree, before the toss, what line will be the boundary edge. Where there is no physical marker for a section of boundary, the boundary edge shall be the imaginary straight line joining the two nearest marked points of the boundary edge.

(e) If a solid object used to mark the boundary is disturbed for any reason during play, then if possible it shall be restored to its original position as soon as the ball is dead. If this is not possible, then

(i) if some part of the fence or other marker has come within the field of play, that portion is to be removed from the field of play as soon as the ball is dead.

(ii) the line where the base of the fence or marker originally stood shall define the boundary edge.

3. Scoring a boundary

(a) A boundary shall be scored and signalled by the umpire at the bowler's end whenever, while the ball is in play, in his opinion

(i) the ball touches the boundary, or is grounded beyond the boundary.

(ii) a fielder, with some part of his person in contact with the ball, touches the boundary and has some part of his person grounded beyond the boundary.

(b) The phrases 'touches the boundary' and 'touching the boundary' shall mean contact with

either (i) the boundary edge as defined in 2 above

or (ii) any person or obstacle within the field of play which has been designated a boundary by the umpires before the toss.

(c) The phrase 'grounded beyond the boundary' shall mean contact with

either (i) any part of a line or a solid object marking the boundary, except its boundary edge

or (ii) the ground outside the boundary edge

or (iii) any object in contact with the ground outside the boundary edge.

4. Runs allowed for boundaries

(a) Before the toss, the umpires shall agree with both captains the runs to be allowed for boundaries. In deciding the allowances, the umpires and captains shall be guided by the prevailing custom of the ground.

(b) Unless agreed differently under (a) above, the allowances for boundaries shall be 6 runs if the ball having been struck by the bat pitches beyond the boundary, but otherwise 4 runs. These allowances shall still apply even though the ball has previously touched a fielder. See also (c) below.

(c) The ball shall be regarded as pitching beyond the boundary and 6 runs shall be scored if a fielder

    (i)   has any part of his person touching the boundary or grounded beyond the boundary when he catches the ball.

    (ii)   catches the ball and subsequently touches the boundary or grounds some part of his person beyond the boundary while carrying the ball but before completing the catch. See Law 32 (Caught).

5. Runs scored

When a boundary is scored,

(a) the penalty for a No ball or a Wide, if applicable, shall stand together with any penalties under any of Laws 2.6 (Player returning without permission), 18.5(b) (Deliberate short runs) or 42 (Fair and unfair play) that apply before the boundary is scored.

(b) the batting side, except in the circumstances of 6 below, shall additionally be awarded whichever is the greater of

    (i)   the allowance for the boundary.

    (ii)   the runs completed by the batsmen, together with the run in progress if they have crossed at the instant the boundary is scored.

           When these runs exceed the boundary allowance, they shall replace the boundary for the purposes of Law 18.12 (Batsman returning to wicket he has left).

6. Overthrow or wilful act of fielder

If the boundary results either from an overthrow or from the wilful act of a fielder the runs scored shall be

    (i)   the penalty for a No ball or a Wide, if applicable, and penalties under any of Laws 2.6 (Player returning without permission), 18.5(b) (Deliberate short runs) or 42 (Fair and unfair play) that are applicable before the boundary is scored

and (ii) the allowance for the boundary
and (iii) the runs completed by the batsmen, together with the run in progress if they have crossed at the instant of the throw or act.

Law 18.12(a) (Batsman returning to the wicket he has left) shall apply as from the instant of the throw or act.

This law has changed dramatically from the 1980 code and so I have set down in detail comparisons between that code and the 2000 code.

In the early codes there was no mention of a boundary line or of any allowance; all hits were run out to their limit. It was not until 1884 that there is any reference in law to a boundary line, although it is known that they were in use many years earlier. That code stated: "The umpires shall arrange boundaries where necessary and allowances to be made for them." With the words "where necessary" being used, it would appear that it was only when there were large gatherings of spectators present at a match that boundaries were brought into use, more probably to save injuries than to ease the burden of running upon the batsmen.

In those early days of cricket, when the game started to become popular, marquees and tents were erected for the benefit of the dignitaries in attendance at the big matches of the day. Should a ball be hit and it enter one of the marquees, it would be declared a dead ball. Such hits became known as "booth balls" and a certain allowance of runs was allotted. Should the hit not enter these tents, it was chased by the fielder into the crowd, scattering all and sundry. Spectators and fielders were often knocked over, with both parties sustaining injuries. Sometimes deliberate obstruction of the fielder by an interested party of the batting side would take place. I imagine it was spectators who had made a large wager on the result who were often the culprits. Some individuals were even known to have pocketed the ball. At the Oval, which is a large ground and in the early days was an even larger expanse of grass, a number of sevens were recorded, without overthrows.

While the boundary allowance, generally four runs, came into being in 1884, it was not until 1910 that a greater allowance, usually one of six runs, was given for hits pitching over the boundary line. MCC did, however, allow six runs for such a hit in their matches when Australia toured England five years earlier. Before 1910, the custom was only to allow six runs for hits that sent the ball "right out of the ground". This may not have been too difficult a feat to accomplish on some of the smaller village grounds but on many of the larger grounds, it must have been almost impossible. If such a law were in operation in county cricket today, there would only be a very small percentage of the boundaries which are recorded that would count as the maximum.

Having said that, I have seen Tony Cordle, of Glamorgan, hit a ball over the stand and over the River Rea at Edgbaston, Graham Barlow hit a ball over the old

Tavern at Lord's and onto the road, and Clive Lloyd make a prodigious hit of 146 yards 8 inches out of the Oval and over Harleyford Road. I recall Jim Love clearing the rugby stand at Headingley and, while I do not remember the individuals making the hit, I have seen a number of balls despatched out of Trent Bridge in the direction of Sherwood Forest. As for Old Trafford, although I cannot remember seeing any hits out of the ground, I do know the story of a wonderful cricketer by the name of Ben Ehrenfried, a tremendous smiter of a cricket ball. While playing for Lincolnshire against Lancashire in a Minor Counties match there, he struck the ball onto the station platform, which is well outside the ground. While Ben would never boast of that hit, many of the players of both sides have described it to me as the biggest hit they have seen.

I have seen many other big hits sail out of county grounds. Pat Pocock, of Surrey, was bowling from my end to Ian Botham at Taunton one day and the ball was struck very hard and high towards the river end of the ground. Pat turned to me and said: "Listen for the splash." There never was one, the reason being that the ball cleared the ground, cleared the river and finished in the wood-yard on the far side. I am sure that most grounds have at some time witnessed a ball being hit right out of the ground but there is one which would surprise me if it figured among them. It is the ground at Derby. Depending on which side of the square the pitch is, the shortest hit to clear the confines of the ground is something approaching 400 yards. This hit would be towards mid-wicket on the shorter side. On the other, you would have to hit the ball past the seven-furlong pole for, as many will know, the ground used to be the racecourse at Derby.

It should be noted that there never has been a set-down or stated allowance of runs when the ball reaches or crosses the boundary line. The umpires and captains should always have agreed these allowances before the toss. In the 1980 code the wording was, "the allowance for a boundary shall normally be 4 runs and 6 runs for hits pitching over and clear of the boundary line". Now, in Law 19.4 (b) of the 2000 code, "Runs allowed for boundaries", we get as close to a definite laid-down allowance as we have ever been. It reads "unless agreed differently under (a) above, the allowance for boundaries shall be 6 runs if the ball having been struck by the bat pitches beyond the boundary, but otherwise 4 runs". What is in (a) above? "Before the toss, the umpires shall agree with both captains the runs to be allowed for boundaries".

While it is common practice to think of boundaries as four runs and six runs, nobody must assume that this is so. For example, on many small club grounds, the club will have a good reason for trying to discourage big hitting. It could be that public pathways or roads run through the playing area. Or it could be that nearby private dwellings have children playing in the garden. Perhaps the reason is that a river runs close to the boundary line. Indeed, I know a ground where the riverbank is normally the boundary line and, when it floods, the boundary is the edge of the grass meeting the water. Clubs with such difficulties have to make regulations and they will always take precedence over the Laws of Cricket.

There is a ground close to where I live which has a regulation that the ball has to be hit over the hedge to be awarded six runs. At one end of the ground, though, it is impossible to score six as there is a house there and hitting it over the hedge, or even over the house, will yield only four runs, just as it would for hitting the ball all along the ground into the base of the hedge.

On my favourite ground in Spain, that of Javea CC, they have a 3ft wall running round the ground on three sides with a 5ft wire-mesh fence on top of the wall. For a hit to be awarded six runs, the ball must clear the fence. Any contact with the wall or fence, and it is only four runs, as in the case of a boundary fence in Law 18. To complicate matters, on one side of the ground there is a row of trees inside the wall but very close to it. In front of the trees is a rope to mark the boundary and also to help make the fielders aware of the trees. This rope denotes an allowance of four runs if the ball hits it or crosses it on the ground but in the air the ball still has to clear the fence behind the trees for the hit to be awarded six runs. It will be seen therefore that the ball can pass well above the boundary rope and hit the top of the fence and yet still earn only four runs. The reasons for these unusual allowances are that the ground is very small and there is a big river running behind the wall on one side.

It must be remembered that a club can set boundary allowances as it sees fit and it could even stipulate no runs for hitting the ball over a particular boundary. I do not know of a club where that is the case but there are grounds where the allowances are different to the normal four and six.

Law 19, "Boundaries", and Law 32, "Caught" have in the past and will still in the future hinge on one another. The deliberations on these laws were intense and did not have universal approval in the first instance. In the main, the objections came from Australia and the West Indies. These objections were in regard to matters connected with "boundary boards" and how it was felt the law should apply. The objection from the West Indies could be well understood, as most of their grounds only cover a small playing area. It was not so easy to understand the Australian objection, as their grounds, in the main, are the opposite. They have some of the largest playing areas in the world. They felt that one of the old traditions of the game was being erased and I for one have sympathy with that view. In the end, there was a consensus of sorts.

Law 19.1 (a) states that "the boundary, if possible, shall be marked along its whole length". There is not usually any problem with this but I have seen boundaries marked out with flags and stones, and this is where confusion could reign.

Part (b) of Law 19.1 contains a very important change. Now, no part of a sightscreen is to be regarded as inside the field of play, no matter in what position we may find it. It may only have its wheels on the line or it may be some 20 yards inside the field of play but should a ball which is crossing over the ground make contact with the screen, as before, this will be a boundary allowance of four runs. Unlike the 1980 code, should a ball be hit by the striker and it make contact with any part of a sightscreen full pitch, no matter where it may be placed, then the boundary allowance will be of six runs. It will be seen that this is a complete change from the previous code. I well remember when I was umpiring in a local league match, that at one end the sightscreen had its wheels inside the boundary line as well as about 18 inches of the axle but the perpendicular was about three feet behind the line. A big hit down the ground hit the screen about a couple of feet from its top and, because of the flimsy structure, broke through it. Players and spectators were amazed when I gave the signal, an allowance of only four runs. Now, under the 2000 code, even if that screen had been positioned some 25 yards nearer to the bowling wicket and the ball had struck and passed through it, the allowance would be six runs.

The question will then be asked: "What about the area behind the sightscreen, should a ball pass over it?" Under the 1980 code umpires knew that this area was "beyond the boundary line" and a ball had to pass over the sightscreen for it to be an allowance of six runs; if the ball hit the sightscreen, it was only four runs. While Law 19.2 makes no reference in any of its parts to a sightscreen, I do feel that the last sentence of part (d) of this law directs us towards clarification.

Law 19.2 (a) says that the boundary "shall be marked by a white line or rope laid along the ground". Many years ago the Panel of First-class Umpires pressed the TCCB for a rope to be used to mark the boundary. I am pleased to say that we were successful in this quest, for a rope is far better than a white line on grass. A rope can always be seen, unlike a white line, and it allows an umpire to see when the ball has reached the rope as, upon contact, the ball skips into the air. It is also an advantage to a fielder, when fielding or catching a ball. He can feel if he is in contact with a rope, whereas with a line he is rarely able to know if he is in contact with it.

Part (b) of Law 19.2 deals with circumstances where the boundary is marked by a white line and has clarified the anomaly that existed in regard to the ball having completely to clear a boundary line, which can be as much as 12 inches wide, for an allowance of six to be made. The law was four runs if the ball pitched on the line and six for a ball pitching clear and beyond it. That was the ruling, but not now. If a ball lands on any part of a boundary line or rope, no matter how wide, it is now an allowance of six runs. The dividing line is the edge of the white line or rope nearer to the pitch.

Part (c) of the same law covers the situation where "a solid object is used to mark the boundary", in other words a rope or fence. The boundary edge for a rope is "the line formed by the innermost points of the rope along its length". For a fence, or boards, "the boundary edge will be the base line of the fence", i.e. where the bottom of the face of the fence or board nearer to the pitch meets the grass. Should there be a gap between the bottom of the board and the grass, it will be taken as a straight line from the bottom of the board down to the grass. If, from a stroke of the bat, the ball hits a boundary fence full pitch, it will now be a boundary six, not four as in the previous code.

Difficulties always arise when there is no defined or marked boundary line and, as in the 1980 clarification, the boundary line in that situation becomes an imaginary straight line between the objects being used to define the boundary. It does not matter whether they are 5ft apart or 50ft apart, it is still the imaginary straight line that counts. Early markings took the form of sticks pushed into the ground. These gave way to stones and then flags. We have since progressed to white lines and now to ropes. Perhaps in time we will move to a laser beam that can detect when a ball passes over the line? If the boundary is marked by white stones, the assumed boundary line is a straight line between each stone. Should a ball roll up against a stone, it will be a boundary allowance of four runs but, if the ball from a stroke of the bat hits the stone full pitch, any part of it, it will be a boundary of six runs.

Law 19.3, "Scoring a boundary", has another important change from the 1980 code. Under that code, a ball hit along the ground to reach the edge of the boundary line closest to the pitch or to touch a rope or fence will be a boundary four. If a fielder in contact with the ball had at the same time any part of his person in contact with line or rope, that was a boundary four. This is still the case. Where the 2000 code has changed is in relation to a boundary board or fence. Under the 1980 code the ball had actually to touch such an object for it to be a boundary four while being fielded. Not now. If a fielder is in contact with the ball and at the same time is in contact with any boundary board, it is as if he were in contact with line or rope, and it is now a boundary four.

Yet another change concerns taking a catch on the boundary, which is covered under Law 19.4 (c). Should a fielder be catching the ball or has caught it and he treads on a line or rope or touches it with any part of his person while in contact with the ball, a boundary allowance of six is scored. Before the 2000 code a fielder could catch a ball and crash into a boundary board and a boundary would not be scored. Under the new code, if a fielder is in contact with the ball in endeavouring to catch it and at the same time makes contact with a boundary board or any similar object marking the boundary, the boundary allowance will be six runs.

Law 19.5 (a) of the new code emphasises that the penalty for bowling a wide ball or no ball will be added to the score of the boundary allowance. Should the fielding side incur penalty runs before the ball reaches the boundary, these shall be added to the batting side's score. However, in the case of the penalty runs being awarded against the batting side, such runs will be added to the fielding side's most recently completed innings. Should they not have batted, then the fielding side's innings will start at plus five runs. If, of course, two batsmen are so speedy that they have crossed on their fifth run before the ball reaches the boundary, they are allowed to count the five instead of the four.

Law 19.6 covers the situation where a boundary results from an overthrow or the wilful act of a fielder. As above, this will yield a boundary allowance of four runs, plus any no-ball or wide-ball penalty, and any penalty runs should a misdemeanour have been committed. However, in addition, the batsmen will score any runs completed and crossed before the throw that led to the boundary.

While looking at boundaries, I would ask readers to take special note of Law 32.3, "A fair catch", and how it has altered from the situation which existed previously. That law and Law 19 obviously have a strong bearing on one another.

LAW 20

Lost Ball

1. Fielder to call Lost ball
If a ball in play cannot be found or recovered, any fielder may call Lost ball. The ball shall then become dead. See Law 23.1 (Ball is dead). Law 18.12(a) (Batsman returning to wicket he has left) shall apply as from the instant of the call.

2. Ball to be replaced
The umpires shall replace the ball with one which has had wear comparable with that which the previous ball had received before it was lost or became irrecoverable. See Law 5.5 (Ball lost or becoming unfit for play).

3. Runs scored
(a) The penalty for a No ball or a Wide, if applicable, shall stand, together with any penalties under any of Laws 2.6 (Player returning without permission), 18.5(b) (Deliberate short runs) or 42 (Fair and unfair play) that are applicable before the call of Lost ball.
(b) The batting side shall additionally be awarded
either   (i)   the runs completed by the batsmen, together with the run in progress if they have crossed at the instant of the call,
or   (ii)   6 runs,
whichever is the greater.

4. How scored
If there is a one run penalty for a No ball or for a Wide, it shall be scored as a No ball extra or as a Wide as appropriate. See Laws 24.13 (Runs resulting from a No ball – how scored) and 25.6 (Runs resulting from a Wide – how scored). If any other penalties have been awarded to either side, they shall be scored as penalty extras. See Law 42.17 (Penalty runs).

Runs to the batting side in 3(b) above shall be credited to the striker if the ball has been struck by the bat, but otherwise to the total of Byes, Leg byes, No balls or Wides as the case may be.

This law, after much discussion by the working party, was almost erased from the 2000 code. However, when it was realised that there could still be situations when a call of "lost ball" by members of a fielding side might be made, we examined other avenues. We tinkered with efforts to frame a law under which it was the duty of an umpire to decide if a ball was lost or not and for either of them to make such a call. The working party felt, though, that any such actions taken by an umpire could lead to suggestions of favouritism, so it was decided to leave well alone.

It was thought by many that this was a law that is not used nowadays. It originated from the early days of cricket, when grass was long and played on fields of a huge size. It must be said, though, that two members of the working party, of which I was one, had umpired in a match when this call might have been made. So, having said that this law came close to extinction, it is interesting to note that the old Law 20 consisted of 106 words and that the new Law 20 has 285 words.

The "lost ball" law was introduced in 1804 when the striker was allowed to score all the runs which he made from a hit, with a minimum allowance of four. In 1823 the minimum was increased to six and again the striker was allowed all he could muster if no call was made. To this day the law is of a similar wording and the same minimum allowance of six runs still applies some 177 years later.

Law 20.1, "Fielder to call lost ball", has similar wording to the 1980 code but includes new words that are of benefit to umpires. It states, upon the call of "lost ball", that "the ball shall then become dead". This phrase will settle many arguments that might have arisen in the past.

As in all other laws regarding the ball being changed, except of course when a new ball is taken into use by the fielding side, the replacement ball shall be replaced with one of comparable wear. It failed to state this in Law 20 of the 1980 code but it is now Law 20.2.

Law 20.3 makes the point again that, if a delivery is adjudged a no ball or wide ball, the penalty for bowling it will be credited to the batting side in addition to those runs that are awarded under Law 20 for a ball being declared lost. Also, should there have been an award of penalty runs to the batting side under Law 42 before "lost ball" is called, these shall also be added to the total.

The next part of this law gives direction on how and to whom all of these runs are to be credited and reminds me of an incident that was brought to my attention by my umpiring friend and colleague in Canada, Ron Whitewood. During the interval in our match, Ron told me that he and his colleague had arrived at a ground for an early-season match and had noticed that at one end of the ground there was an area of grass about 18 inches high. There was a distinct boundary marked but the long grass extended some 25 yards into the field of play. The umpires spoke with the captains before the toss and informed them that, should a ball be hit into this area, they would accept a call of "lost ball". Sure enough, during the match, the ball was hit hard and high down the ground and it bounced into this area of long grass. A fielder went in after it and, as the batsmen were taking their third run, a ball was found and returned to the bowler. The bowler did not break the wicket as he saw that the batsman had made good his ground. Halfway back to his mark, the bowler observed to the umpire that it was not the same ball that he had previously bowled with and, when the umpires inspected it, he was found to be correct. The umpires therefore decreed the ball to be "dead". The match ball was found a short distance from where the other ball had been retrieved and the match resumed.

Ron then asked me what the correct decision would have been if the first ball found had been thrown back to the bowler in time to effect a run-out? At first I felt that, as the fielder and bowler both assumed that they had the original ball at that stage and that the umpire certainly would not know that it was not the ball which had whistled past his ears some moments earlier, it would have been correct for a run-out decision to have been given. However, I then thought about Law 5.2, "Approval and control of balls", which states that all balls must have been approved by the umpires. The one which would have been used by the bowler to run out the batsman would certainly not have been. Would the umpires therefore have been correct in recalling the batsman, once it was discovered that the ball was not the original one? Perhaps they would have been, perhaps not. Interesting.

LAW 21

The Result

1. A Win – two innings match
The side which has scored a total of runs in excess of that scored in the two completed innings of the opposing side shall win the match. Note also 6 below.

A forfeited innings is to count as a completed innings. See Law 14 (Declaration and forfeiture).

2. A Win – one innings match
The side which has scored in its one innings a total of runs in excess of that scored
by the opposing side in its one completed innings shall win the match. Note also 6 below.

3. Umpires awarding a match
(a) A match shall be lost by a side which
either (i) concedes defeat
or (ii) in the opinion of the umpires refuses to play
and the umpires shall award the match to the other side.
(b) If an umpire considers that an action by any player or players might constitute a refusal by either side to play then the umpires together shall ascertain the cause of the action. If they then decide together that this action does constitute a refusal to play by one side, they shall so inform the captain of that side. If the captain persists in the action the umpires shall award the match in accordance with (a)(ii) above.
(c) If action as in (b) above takes place after play has started and does not constitute a refusal to play
    (i) playing time lost shall be counted from the start of the action until play recommences, subject to Law 15.5 (Changing agreed times for intervals).

(ii) the time for close of play on that day shall be extended by this length of time, subject to Law 3.9 (Suspension of play for adverse conditions of ground, weather or light).

(iii) if applicable, no overs shall be deducted during the last hour of the match solely on account of this time.

4. A Tie
The result of a match shall be a Tie when the scores are equal at the conclusion of play, but only if the side batting last has completed its innings.

5. A Draw
A match which is concluded, as defined in Law 16.9 (Conclusion of a match), without being determined in any of the ways stated in 1,2,3 or 4 above, shall count as a Draw.

6. Winning hit or extras
(a) As soon as a result is reached, as defined in 1,2,3 or 4 above, the match is at an end. Nothing that happens thereafter shall be regarded as part of the match. Note also 9 below.

(b) The side batting last will have scored enough runs to win only if its total of runs is sufficient without including any runs completed before the dismissal of the striker by the completion of a catch or by the obstruction of a catch.

(c) If a boundary is scored before the batsmen have completed sufficient runs to win the match, then the whole of the boundary allowance shall be credited to the side's total and, in the case of a hit by the bat, to the striker's score.

7. Statement of result
If the side batting last wins the match, the result shall be stated as a win by the number of wickets still then to fall.

If the other side wins the match, the result shall be stated as a win by runs.

If the match is decided by one side conceding defeat or refusing to play, the result shall be stated as Match Conceded or Match Awarded as the case may be.

8. Correctness of result
Any decision as to the correctness of the scores shall be the responsibility of the umpires. See Law 3.15 (Correctness of scores).

9. Mistakes in scoring
If, after the umpires and players have left the field in the belief that the match has been concluded, the umpires discover that a mistake in scoring has occurred which affects the result, then, subject to 10 below, they shall adopt the following procedure.

If, when the players leave the field, the side batting last has not completed its innings, and

either (i) the number of overs to be bowled in the last hour has not been completed,

or (ii) the agreed finishing time has not been reached,

then unless one side concedes defeat the umpires shall order play to resume.

If conditions permit, play will then continue until the prescribed number of overs has been completed and the time remaining has elapsed, unless a result is reached earlier. The number of overs and/or the time remaining shall be taken as they were when the players left the field; no account shall be taken of the time between that moment and the resumption of play.

(b) If, when the players leave the field, the overs have been completed and time has been reached, or if the side batting last has completed its innings, the umpires shall immediately inform both captains of the necessary corrections to the scores and to the result.

10. Result not to be changed
Once the umpires have agreed with the scorers the correctness of the scores at the conclusion of the match – see Laws 3.15 (Correctness of scores) and 4.2 (Correctness of scores) – the result cannot thereafter be changed.

Parts 1 and 2 of Law 21 deal with "A Win", which I feel should be the final accolade to the finish of a match. In spite of the huge amounts of money being played for at the top levels of the game of cricket, I do hope that the players never lose sight of this fact. I am not sure what 1,000 guineas would be worth in today's terms but this was the amount staked as win money more than 250 years ago on matches between the top sides.

Part 1, covering two-innings matches, has one significant change in the statement that "a forfeited innings is to count as a completed innings". Part 2, which deals with one-innings matches, says unremarkably that the side gaining the higher number of runs is the winner. There are still some leagues who cater for such a thing as a winning draw but the apportioning of points for such a result is laid down in the regulations pertaining to those leagues.

Law 21.3, which is headed "Umpires awarding a match", has a plethora of subsections. Part (a) gives two instances of when a match is lost other than in the above. The first is when a side concedes defeat. There are a number of circumstances when this might occur and I once played in a match where it happened. The second is where a side refuses to play, and I would hope these occasions are so rare as to be thought of as extinct. Part 3 (b) sets down the procedure to be adopted by umpires when they feel that a player or players may be refusing to play. This procedure would appear reasonably straightforward if it is a member or members of the fielding side taking the action but the umpires must be very careful should it be a member or members of the batting side. In that situation, I feel that Law 31.1 (a), "Out timed out", should take precedence. Law 31.1 (b) mentions a "protracted delay". To my mind any protracted delay may result in a batsman being given out under Law 31.1 (b) but the delay will have to be of greater duration than three minutes before we adopt Law 21.3 (b). We do not wish to spoil a lovely day's cricket because of the selfish attitude of one player.

Law 21.3 (c) explains how any time is to be added to a day's play, should umpires consider that any delay by players did not "constitute a refusal to play". Section (i) directs us to count any time lost from the start of the action, but when did the action start? Was it when the batsman did not set foot on the field of play, or was it when there was no batsman ready to receive the next delivery within three minutes from the fall of the previous wicket? Perhaps it should be from when the umpires leave the field to investigate the delay?

Bringing together Laws 21 and 31 means that if no batsman appears for five minutes, the umpires can leave the field of play to ascertain why nobody has appeared. Let us suppose that, after enquiries, it is found that the delay did not constitute a refusal to play. The umpires return to their positions on the field, accompanied by another batsman two minutes later. There will then be four minutes to add at the end of the day's play. An appeal is then made under Law 21.1 (a) and the umpires' first action is to give the incoming batsman out.

Law 21.3 (c) (iii) directs us not to deduct any overs in the final hour. If the time to be added is on the last day, the final hour will start later by the number of minutes to be added. If the delay itself takes place in that final hour, the close of play will be later by the number of minutes to be added.

All of this takes me back to the injury to Eddie Hemmings, of Nottinghamshire, in a match against Middlesex at Trent Bridge in 1981. While it was for an injury, and not for a delay as mentioned in Law 21.3 (c) (iii), we took exactly the action now advocated.

There are two vital points to note about Law 21.6, the first of which I fought hard and long for. It is that, once a side has scored the run in excess of their opponents' score, the match is over. That was, in my opinion, implicit in the 1980 code but since then a number of individuals have stated that, if the striker hits the ball to the boundary, he should be credited with those runs. This is not so in all cases and now, under this law and Law 24 "No ball" and Law 35 "Wide ball", about which I shall enlarge later, it is clarified.

It follows from the above that if one run is required to win the match and the batsman hits the ball and one is completed before the ball crosses the boundary, only the one run will be credited. Batsmen who desire those extra three runs must now use their heads. Run by all means but do not complete if you feel that the shot is well struck and the ball will reach the boundary. Should a brilliant feat of fielding stop the ball from crossing the boundary line, all the batsmen have to do is put their bat or person over the popping crease at the opposite wicket. The game is then finished.

The exception to the above is covered under Law 32.2, "Caught to take precedence", and the reason will be seen when we arrive at that law.

Law 21.8, headed "Correctness of result", says that the correctness of the scores shall be the responsibility of the umpires and refers the reader back to Law 3.15, "Correctness of scores". Please do not forget that the significant word "throughout" has been deleted from this last-mentioned law in the 2000 code.

Law 21.9 deals with mistakes in scoring. I can recall such a mistake being discovered after the sides had left the field with the batting side certain that the match has been won by them. When the captains were informed, the fielding captain decided to concede the match as there were ten overs left, seven wickets to fall and one run required to win the match. He and a number of his players were in the shower and he felt that it was far more beneficial for them to stay there than return to the field of play.

It is when the batting side win off the last ball, or at least think that they have, only to find that they require one more run when they arrive in the dressing-room, that all hell breaks loose. To avoid this, umpires are advised in a tight finish to stop the game before the final over and check the situation with the scorers. I have taken this action many a time.

And so to the result that never was, as hinted at in my words on Law 12.2, "Alternate innings". The day after the fifth Test between South Africa and England in January 2000, Nigel Plews rang me to ask my opinion on the validity of England's "victory". I said that I thought the outcome was "most strange" but added that, "having been out of things at that level since 1993, I was not fully conversant with the relevant regulations". As Nigel had only finished his first-class umpiring career the previous September, he verified to me that the Laws of Cricket still applied at this level.

That being the case, it was clear at that time that only a second innings could be forfeited in a Test match and that the 1980 code of the Laws of Cricket had been abused. Test matches are not the same, or at least were not the same, as the county championship, where it has been possible to forfeit the first innings of a two-innings match since a regulation was brought in to that effect in 1980. This was a good regulation at that level and was made to allow county captains to try to gain a positive result from what was often a hopeless position, made so by the great amount of time lost to the elements.

Before 1980 a side had to go out to bat for its first innings and declare immediately. Many a time I stood in matches where a score of 0 runs for 0 wickets declared was posted. However, it wasted at least ten minutes and it was unsightly to watch the fielding side walk out, the batsmen follow, a bowler walk back so many paces in pretence that he was going bowl, the umpire call "play" and then for the captain of the batting side to state "we are declaring". The 1980 county regulation stopped all this nonsense and often since then I have had the captains come to me and my colleague after a great deal of time has been lost through rain. One captain would say: "When you consider starting, umpires, I have forfeited my first innings." And the other captain would add: "And I have forfeited my second innings." It made good sense and often made for a great game of cricket.

Those regulations did not apply to Test cricket played under the 1980 code and, for the result of the fifth Test against South Africa to have been legal, England would have had to have gone out and declared at 0 for 0. Then Hansie Cronje, the South Africa captain, would have had to forfeit his second innings, a move which would have been legitimate, and England could then have batted again to try to win the match.

However, no legal declaration of England's first innings took place and no forfeiture of that innings was permitted under Law 14.2 of the 1980 code of the Laws of Cricket. As a consequence, the innings in progress at close of play on the final day was England's first innings. Therefore the real result of the match was not a "victory" for England but a draw.

LAW 22

The Over

1. Number of balls
The ball shall be bowled from each wicket alternately in overs of 6 balls.

2. Start of an over
An over has started when the bowler starts his run up or, if he has no run up, his delivery action for the first delivery of that over.

3. Call of Over
When 6 balls have been bowled other than those which are not to count in the over and as the ball becomes dead - see Law 23 (Dead ball) - the umpire shall call Over before leaving the wicket.

4. Balls not to count in the over
(a) A ball shall not count as one of the 6 balls of the over unless it is delivered, even though a batsman may be dismissed or some other incident occurs before the ball is delivered.
(b) A ball which is delivered by the bowler shall not count as one of the 6 balls of the over
    (i)   if it is called dead, or is to be considered dead, before the striker has had an opportunity to play it. See Law 23 (Dead ball).
    (ii)   if it is a No ball. See Law 24 (No ball).
    (iii) if it is a Wide. See Law 25 (Wide ball).
    (iv) if it is called dead in the circumstances of either of Laws 23.3 (vi) (Umpire calling and signalling Dead ball) or 42.4 (Deliberate attempt to distract striker).

5. Umpire miscounting
If an umpire miscounts the number of balls, the over as counted by the umpire shall stand.

6. Bowler changing ends

A bowler shall be allowed to change ends as often as desired, provided only that he does not bowl two overs, or parts thereof, consecutively in the same innings.

7. Finishing an over

(a) Other than at the end of an innings, a bowler shall finish an over in progress unless he is incapacitated, or he is suspended under any of Laws 17.1 (Practice on the field), 42.7 (Dangerous and unfair bowling – action by the umpire), 42.9 (Time wasting by the fielding side), or 42.12 (Bowler running on the protected area after delivering the ball).

(b) If for any reason, other than the end of an innings, an over is left uncompleted at the start of an interval or interruption of play, it shall be completed on resumption of play.

8. Bowler incapacitated or suspended during an over

If for any reason a bowler is incapacitated while running up to bowl the first ball of an over, or is incapacitated or suspended during an over, the umpire shall call and signal Dead ball. Another bowler shall complete the over from the same end, provided that he does not bowl two overs, or parts thereof, consecutively in one innings.

Law 22.1 now only allows for an over to consist of six balls legally delivered. It can no longer consist of eight deliveries, as it could under the 1980 code, unless, of course, "special regulations" so provide.

The first code of laws only allowed for an over to consist of four balls. That was in 1744 and it remained thus for 145 years until 1889, when the number was increased to five. The next change was much swifter, 11 years to be exact. On May 2, 1900 MCC decreed that the number of deliveries be increased to six per over. Then, in the 1947 code, latitude was given for an over to be of either six or eight deliveries, as prescribed by the league or competition in which matches were being played. This was simply to accommodate the desires of Australia and New Zealand. Eight-ball overs were also bowled in South Africa for their Currie Cup matches in the 1937-38 season and the MCC tour matches in that country in the 1938-39 season. In England in 1939 a trial was given to eight-ball overs in all first-class matches and this was extended to the England v West Indies Test series that season.

Law 22.2 is headed "Start of an over" and it is here that I would like to enlarge on a point I raised at the end of my words on Law 13.3. Law 22.2 makes it clear that the over starts when a bowler, at any time after the call of "play", begins his approach to the bowling wicket to deliver the first ball. It will not matter if that approach is over 30 yards or a couple of paces; once he begins a forward momentum to deliver the ball, the over has started.

This law, as written, goes against all the previous teaching given to umpires. There were three specific actions to start the proceedings of a cricket match: the call of "play" by the bowler's umpire started the match; the forward momentum of the bowler after that call decreed that the ball was in play and from that moment either batsman could be dismissed; finally, it was the first legal delivery bowled that started the over. Now, under Law 22.2, the call of "play" is as before and from that moment the match has started. The moment that the bowler starts his forward momentum will now mean that, not only is the ball in play but that the over has started. I do hope that this change in law will not cause any problems for umpires.

I wonder how the following situation would be interpreted? As a young man I played in the Lincolnshire League and in one of our fixtures in the Scunthorpe area, against Redbourne if I remember correctly, one of their bowlers began his momentum from about five paces behind the bowling wicket. He ran about 15 paces before he delivered the ball, the first five of which were toward the boundary line directly behind the bowling wicket. He would then bank sharply to port, come back towards the wicket and deliver the ball. It was unusual but highly effective as he took many wickets.

Part (a) of Law 22.4, Balls not to count in the over", may startle a few people and prompt the question "how can a batsman be dismissed if the ball is not delivered?" This is an obvious reference to a bowler dismissing the non-striker prior to the delivery of the ball. In part (b), sections (ii) and (iii) are as we have always known them, with neither a wide nor a no ball counting in the over. Section (i) is surely what all good umpires have known for many years but section (iv) needs some clarification and the points it raises will be explained under the relevant Law numbers 23.3 and 42.4.

Parts 5, 6 and 8 of Law 22 are more or less the same as under the 1980 code, as is much of part 7, "Finishing an over", except for slight changes of number reference to the other laws. There are, however, two new misdemeanours that may lead to a bowler being ejected from the fray before he can finish his over. They are also to be found under Law 17.1, "Practice on the field", and Law 42.9, "Time wasting by the fielding side". There are full explanations under those laws and, while some may think the measures draconian, something had to be done to stop players abusing the game of cricket.

LAW 23

Dead Ball

1. Ball is dead
(a) The ball becomes dead when
- (i) it is finally settled in the hands of the wicket-keeper or the bowler.
- (ii) a boundary is scored. See Law 19.3 (Scoring a boundary).
- (iii) a batsman is dismissed.
- (iv) whether played or not it becomes trapped between the bat and person of a batsman or between items of his clothing or equipment.
- (v) whether played or not it lodges in the clothing or equipment of a batsman or the clothing of an umpire.
- (vi) it lodges in a protective helmet worn by a member of the fielding side.
- (vii) there is a contravention of either of Laws 41.2 (Fielding the ball) or 41.3 (Protective helmets belonging to the fielding side).
- (viii) there is an award of penalty runs under Law 2.6 (Player returning without permission).
- (ix) Lost ball is called. See Law 20 (Lost ball).
- (x) the umpire calls Over or Time.

(b) The ball shall be considered to be dead when it is clear to the umpire at the bowler's end that the fielding side and both batsmen at the wicket have ceased to regard it as in play.

2. Ball finally settled
Whether the ball is finally settled or not is a matter for the umpire alone to decide.

3. Umpire calling and signalling Dead ball
(a) When the ball has become dead under 1 above, the bowler's end

umpire may call Dead ball, if it is necessary to inform the players.

(b) Either umpire shall call and signal Dead ball when

- (i) he intervenes in a case of unfair play.
- (ii) a serious injury to a player or umpire occurs.
- (iii) he leaves his normal position for consultation.
- (iv) one or both bails fall from the striker's wicket before he has the opportunity of playing the ball.
- (v) he is satisfied that for an adequate reason the striker is not ready for the delivery of the ball and, if the ball is delivered, makes no attempt to play it.
- (vi) the striker is distracted by any noise or movement or in any other way while he is preparing to receive or receiving a delivery. This shall apply whether the source of the distraction is within the game or outside it. Note, however, the provisions of Law 42.4 (Deliberate attempt to distract the striker).

    The ball shall not count as one of the over.
- (vii) the bowler drops the ball accidentally before delivery.
- (viii) the ball does not leave the bowler's hand for any reason other than an attempt to run out the non-striker before entering his delivery stride. See Law 42.15 (Bowler attempting to run out non-striker before delivery).
- (ix) he is required to do so under any of the Laws.

4. Ball ceases to be dead

The ball ceases to be dead – that is, it comes into play – when the bowler starts his run up or, if he has no run up, his bowling action.

5. Action on call of Dead ball

(a) A ball is not to count as one of the over if it becomes dead or is to be considered dead before the striker has had an opportunity to play it.

(b) If the ball becomes dead or is to be considered dead after the striker has had an opportunity to play the ball, except in the circumstances of 3(vi) above and Law 42.4 (Deliberate attempt to distract striker), no additional delivery shall be allowed unless No ball or Wide has been called.

From an umpire's viewpoint, I have always thought Law 23 to be the most important of the 42. If an umpire does not have a full command and knowledge of Law 23, he will put himself at a great disadvantage and may commit a number of errors. Few players know when a ball is "dead" and even fewer spectators, but this is a law which, since the 1947 code, I feel has been set down well. With only a small amount of time spent on its study, the reader will have a good understanding of it.

When I first began my umpiring career at the professional level in 1972, I feared that an appeal might be made by a member of the fielding side when a batsman had interfered with the ball before it was "dead". I was never sure if the players simply did not know that an appeal could be made in such situations and would be upheld, or whether it was because of the sporting nature of all of the participants in the game. In my 21 years of umpiring at that level, not once did I receive an appeal and neither did I hear one made. I certainly think it was sportsmanship rather than ignorance that governed their actions, for those who play are, in the main, very genuine people.

I am therefore delighted that this law has remained much the same as in the 1980 code. Unfortunately, there is an insertion that, to my mind, will cause umpires many problems. Some may think that it is good for the game; if so, it should have been inserted into another part of Law 23 and umpires should have been given directions on action to be taken. More of that shortly.

The words "dead ball" were first used in the laws in 1798 and they were in a law which was introduced in that season, under what we would now refer to as Law 41.2, "The fieldsman". It stated that a penalty of five runs would be awarded to the batting side "if the fieldsman stops a ball with his hat". Note that the word "cap" is not used. If we look at the old prints of matches being played in those years, many of the players were wearing stovepipe hats, which were very effective for stopping a ball. Before 1798 the words "dead ball" were not used but the meaning was implicit in some of the other laws of the day.

The main change to Law 23.1, "Ball is dead", is the addition of part (a) (iv). This is very similar to part (v), which was in the 1980 code as part (d). The crucial word in part (iv) is "trapped" and this has been brought in as the direct result of an incident in a New Zealand v England Test match a few years ago. Andrew Caddick was batting against a spin bowler, played forward and the ball became trapped, or lodged, or whatever word you wish to use, between his bat and his pad. The ball was stationary for probably less than two seconds and, as he took the bat away, the ball fell onto the top of his boot, from where it bounced about six inches into the air. In that time the fielder at silly mid-off dived forward and took a clean catch. An appeal was made but the decision of the umpire, Darrell Hair, was not out.

At the time I thought that it was a great decision and hoped that he had arrived at it for the right reasons. Through the good offices of Nigel Plews, I knew within 48 hours that he had. A lodgement of the ball had taken place, albeit for little more than a second. Critics of the decision said that the word "in" meant that the ball had to be enclosed by the "clothing or equipment of a batsman". Not so. They should have read the word as meaning "in between" for that is what happened in regard to the lodgement. The ball had lodged "in between" bat and pad, and both are items of "equipment of a batsman". What a great decision.

The other insertion is Law 23.1 (b). It is the one I do not like as I feel it will bring trouble for umpires, when the laws should be seeking to make things as easy as possible for them. It was felt prudent to bring it in because of the situation where the ball is passed around the fielders on its way back to the bowler, without ever having been with the wicketkeeper. The final throw of the ball to the bowler is missed by him and the batsmen take a run. Several thought this unfair and so Law 23.1 (b) was inserted. A great deal of discussion took place on this point, and the reason for the decision was that it was felt to be against the Spirit of the Game for either side to take what was considered an unfair advantage of such a situation. I have spoken with many umpires, and almost without exception they have been in agreement about this.

Part (vi) of Law 23.3 (b) contains a clarification that I feel is good and concerns distraction of the striker. It makes the point that it need not be a distraction by noise or movement within the game but could be by any outside agency from within or from outside the confines of the ground. For example, it could be a glint of sunlight off something in the crowd or a nearby building, or the age-old problem of spectators passing in front of the sightscreen. I can tell you that when you umpire at Chelmsford and a car backfires as it crosses the bridge over the river, it can be of a great distraction, not only to the striker but to the fielders and umpires as well. I remember seeing Ray East dive to the ground as he was about to deliver the ball from the river end of the ground and a noisy old banger passed by. He played "dead player", and the crowd loved it. Where do we find such great characters now?

LAW 24

No Ball

1. Mode of delivery

(a) The umpire shall ascertain whether the bowler intends to bowl right handed or left handed, over or round the wicket, and shall so inform the striker.

It is unfair if the bowler fails to notify the umpire of a change in his mode of delivery. In this case, the umpire shall call and signal No ball.

(b) Underarm bowling shall not be permitted except by special agreement before the match.

2. Fair delivery – the arm

For a delivery to be fair in respect of the arm the ball must not be thrown. See 3 below.

Although it is the primary responsibility of the striker's end umpire to ensure the fairness of a delivery in this respect, there is nothing in this Law to debar the bowler's end umpire from calling and signalling No ball if he considers that the ball has been thrown.

(a) If, in the opinion of either umpire, the ball has been thrown, he shall
  (i) call and signal No ball.
  (ii) caution the bowler, when the ball is dead. This caution shall apply throughout the innings.
  (iii) inform the other umpire, the batsmen at the wicket, the captain of the fielding side and, as soon as practicable, the captain of the batting side of what has occurred.

(b) If either umpire considers that after such caution a further delivery by the same bowler in that innings is thrown, the umpire concerned shall repeat the procedure set out in (a) above, indicating to the bowler that this is a final warning. This warning shall also apply throughout the innings.

(c) If either umpire considers that a further delivery by the same bowler in that innings is thrown,

- (i) the umpire concerned shall call and signal No ball. When the ball is dead he shall inform the other umpire, the batsmen at the wicket and, as soon as practicable, the captain of the batting side of what has occurred.
- (ii) the umpire at the bowler's end shall direct the captain of the fielding side to take the bowler off forthwith. The over shall be completed by another bowler, who shall neither have bowled the previous over nor be allowed to bowl the next over.

  The bowler thus taken off shall not bowl again in that innings.
- (iii) the umpires together shall report the occurrence as soon as possible to the Executive of the fielding side and any Governing Body responsible for the match, who shall take such action as is considered appropriate against the captain and bowler concerned.

3. Definition of fair delivery – the arm

A ball is fairly delivered in respect of the arm if, once the bowler's arm has reached the level of the shoulder in the delivery swing, the elbow joint is not straightened partially or completely from that point until the ball has left the hand. This definition shall not debar a bowler from flexing or rotating the wrist in the delivery swing.

4. Bowler throwing towards striker's end before delivery

If the bowler throws the ball towards the striker's end before entering his delivery stride, either umpire shall call and signal No ball. See Law 42.16 (Batsmen stealing a run). However, the procedure stated in 2 above of caution, informing, final warning, action against the bowler and reporting shall not apply.

5. Fair delivery – the feet

For a delivery to be fair in respect of the feet, in the delivery stride
- (i) the bowler's back foot must land within and not touching the return crease.
- (ii) the bowler's front foot must land with some part of the foot, whether grounded or raised, behind the popping crease.

If the umpire at the bowler's end is not satisfied that both these conditions have been met, he shall call and signal No ball.

6. Ball bouncing more than twice or rolling along the ground

The umpire at the bowler's end shall call and signal No ball if a ball which he considers to have been delivered, without having previously touched the bat or person of the striker,
either (i) bounces more than twice
or (ii) rolls along the ground
before it reaches the popping crease.

7. Ball coming to rest in front of striker's wicket

If a ball delivered by the bowler comes to rest in front of the line of the striker's wicket, without having touched the bat or person of the striker, the umpire shall call and signal No ball and immediately call and signal Dead ball.

8. Call of No ball for infringement of other Laws

In addition to the instances above, an umpire shall call and signal No ball as required by the following Laws.
Law 40.3 - Position of wicket-keeper
Law 41.5 - Limitation of on side fielders
Law 41.6 - Fielders not to encroach on the pitch
Law 42.6 - Dangerous and unfair bowling
Law 42.7 - Dangerous and unfair bowling – action by the umpire
Law 42.8 - Deliberate bowling of high full pitched balls.

9. Revoking a call of No ball

An umpire shall revoke the call of No ball if the ball does not leave the bowler's hand for any reason.

10. No ball to over-ride Wide

A call of No ball shall over-ride the call of Wide ball at any time. See Law 25.1 (Judging a Wide) and 25.3 (Call and signal of Wide ball).

11. Ball not dead

The ball does not become dead on the call of No ball.

12. Penalty for a No ball
A penalty of one run shall be awarded instantly on the call of No ball. Unless the call is revoked this penalty shall stand even if a batsman is dismissed. It shall be in addition to any other runs scored, any boundary allowance and any other penalties awarded.

13. Runs resulting from a No ball – how scored
The one run penalty for a No ball shall be scored as a No ball extra. If other penalty runs have been awarded to either side, these shall be scored as in Law 42.17 (Penalty runs). Any runs completed by the batsmen or a boundary allowance shall be credited to the striker if the ball has been struck by the bat; otherwise they also shall be scored as No ball extras. Apart from any award of a 5 run penalty, all runs resulting from a No ball, whether as No ball extras or credited to the striker, shall be debited against the bowler.

14. No ball not to count
A No ball shall not count as one of the over. See Law 22.4 (Balls not to count in the over).

15. Out from a No ball
When No ball has been called, neither batsman shall be out under any of the Laws except 33 (Handled the ball), 34 (Hit the ball twice), 37 (Obstructing the field) or 38 (Run out).

Since its inception in the 1744 code, this law has altered completely in respect of the propulsion of the ball, the position from which this action may take place and the scoring of any runs or penalties. In that code a no ball was only called when the "hinder foot", better known as the back foot, was in front of the bowling crease. Now it is the front foot and the popping crease that are the critical issues. Law 24.5 says that "in the delivery stride some part of the front foot, grounded or raised, must be behind the popping crease". There is also instruction as to where the back foot may land but, even in this part of the law, there is no mention of the bowling crease.

In that early code, if a no ball was delivered, the ball was to be regarded as "dead" and the striker could not score off it. Neither was there any penalty awarded for the delivery of that ball. In 1811 we saw the first change to the no-ball law. The striker was allowed to play it and to count any runs scored from the hit. The only way in which he could be dismissed was run out.

It was not until 1829 that a one-run penalty was introduced for a no ball that was not scored off. That same year a decision was made in regard to the delivery of the ball: it had to be delivered underhand and the hand had to be below the height of the elbow on delivery. Nowadays, of course, as Law 24.1 (b) states, "underarm bowling shall not be permitted except by special agreement before the match".

It was in 1864 that the arm was able to be raised to any height to deliver the ball and from that year we have been bedevilled by what is known as "throwing". In those days it was only the umpire at the bowling end who made such a call and it was not until the 1900 season that the law was changed so that either umpire could make the call. The question is often asked, if the bowler throws the ball, will the ball travel the 22 yards quicker than if he had bowled it quickly? I can tell you that it most certainly will and I have experienced it in a number of matches.

In 1912 a law was introduced that a striker was not able to be stumped off a no ball but could be run out. Then the 1947 code clarified that a striker had to be in the act of running to be dismissed under this law, not merely standing out of his ground. So it can be seen that, as I mentioned earlier, all three parts of the law have changed completely: the action of the bowler delivering the ball, the position from which the bowler is able to make that delivery and that initially no runs could ensue from a no-ball delivery.

In Law 24.1 it is interesting to note the words, "the umpire shall ascertain", with regard to whether the bowler is left-handed or right-handed and whether he is bowling over or around the wicket. This should have always taken place, with the information then being passed by the umpire to the striker as he takes guard. However, the 1980 code only talked about "failure by the bowler to indicate in advance a change in his mode of delivery". Indicate to whom? Now the law is very clear. It is the umpire who will initially ascertain from the bowler his mode of delivery and then it is up to the bowler to indicate any change to the umpire, so that he may in turn inform the striker.

There have been too many silly incidents in the past. For example, under the previous code, the first ball of a match might be called and signalled a no ball and, when asked why, the umpire could say: "You failed to inform me of your mode of delivery." That cannot happen now as the onus is on the umpire to ascertain the information and pass it on.

Let us take another example. A bowler changes his mode of delivery, say, from over the wicket to round the wicket without informing the umpire and he is correctly no-balled by the umpire. When the bowler finds out the reason for the no ball from the umpire, the bowler replies to the effect that he had informed the striker of his change. That now is not good enough and never has been. How will the umpire know that the bowler's mode has changed if he is not acquainted with the fact? There is now no cop-out for either the umpire or the bowler. The law is there and it is quite clear.

Law 24.2, "Fair delivery – the arm", has been greatly enlarged since the 1980 code and the credit for this lies both with the ICC throwing committee and MCC.

The ICC came up with two definitions and the laws working party had to decide which it felt was the better of the two. Bobby Simpson, the great Australian captain, slip catcher and batsman, came to one of the meetings and spoke at length on this matter in an effort to rid the game of one of its great ills, the propulsion of the ball in an illegal manner, in other words "throwing". It is not possible to explain all of the discussions that took place on this matter but when you arrive at Law 24.3 you will see the great amount of work put in by members of our committee, particularly Bobby, by which we arrived at the decision to alter this part of the law.

Previously, an umpire could not withdraw a bowler from an innings for delivering a ball illegally by unfair action and I pressed the point that he must be able to. In my career as a first-class umpire, I have seen four bowlers, all of different nationalities, deliver illegally and since 1993, while umpiring at other levels, I have seen a further four. Nigel Plews was also a member of the working party and a member of the ICC's throwing committee, for the want of a better name. He, along with myself and all of the other members of our working party, realised that stronger action was required and hence the law as it is now written. However, I still feel that two warnings is at least one too many.

In previous codes an umpire could no-ball a bowler if he was "not entirely satisfied with the absolute fairness of the delivery". Now, under the 2000 code, he should take this action "if he considers the ball has been thrown". Some may think that this is not much of a change but when you read on I think you will see that the changes are considerable.

Simpson felt that, in the past, we had been trying to describe what was not a fair delivery and he asked us to consider instead what he had set down, describing what constitutes a fair delivery. This had been mooted as long ago as 1958 in that illuminating book, "Straight from the Shoulder", by Ian Peebles. There were two propositions put forward, not that different from each other, and the one that was agreed on now forms part 3 of Law 24. When it is read and understood by umpires, I think that they will have a better chance of discharging their duties in a proficient manner. I hope that the wording of this law will help the game to eliminate those who seek success by abuse of its laws.

Law 24.4 concerns the bowler throwing towards the striker's end before delivery and there is just one small but pertinent point I would like to make here. If the throw is made before the delivery stride, it must obviously be an attempt to run out the striker. The action by the umpire of calling "no ball" will still be put into operation but not followed by the warning procedure.

Part 6 of Law 24 brings into the laws something that has existed for a number of years in county cricket. In respect of the delivery, it will be deemed unfair if the ball delivered by the bowler bounces more than twice or rolls along the ground before it reaches the popping crease. This came into being when underarm bowling was first banned, then reintroduced for a couple of years after the infamous Trevor Chappell incident in Australia. The law has been retained, even though that type of delivery is not now allowed. I think that it is a good thing, as it is not really fair, no matter what type of bowling is taking place.

Law 24.7, "Ball coming to rest in front of striker's wicket", was dealt with under Law 25, "Wide ball", in the 1980 code but now follows on quite naturally from Law 24.6 and is the natural cousin of the two situations in that law. If, and when, the ball came to rest in front of the striker's wicket, the striker was previously allowed "one free hit at the stationary ball", no matter how wide of the pitch it was when it became stationary. It was felt that the spectacle of the striker moving to where the ball had come to rest and trying to hit it was not good for the game. Also there was the risk of serious injury to a member of the fielding side if a ball became stationary close to any fielder. Now, under the 2000 code, the umpire must call and signal "no ball", Followed immediately by "dead ball". I wonder if we have gone far enough as, under Law 24.6, although "no ball" must be called, we can still get the unsightly practice of a striker chasing a ball to any position in front of his wicket and hitting the ball, as long as it is still moving. I believe this to be a rare occurrence.

Law 24.12, "Penalty for a no ball", now becomes a most important point of law. Again it is one of the clarifications that I fought to have included. It is all contained in the first sentence, "a penalty of one run shall be awarded instantly on the call of no ball". For too long we have given batsmen runs to which they are not entitled when, with the scores level, a no ball is bowled. Should the striker hit that delivery to the boundary, he would often have been credited with four runs. He is not, nor has he ever been, entitled to those runs. Indeed he is not even entitled to hit the ball, as the match was over before he received it. This law now makes this clear as the run to win the match was "awarded instantly" on the call of no ball.

Part 13 of Law 24 deals with "Runs resulting from a no ball – how scored". These are scored as explained in Law 4, "The scorers", but again it can be seen how and to whom they are credited and/or debited. The exception is contained in the last sentence, which says that penalty runs will not be debited against the bowler. It would hardly be fair to do so, for example, in the case of penalty runs awarded when a fielder obstructs the batsman. This law now changes the situation when a striker hits a no ball against a fielder's helmet in a position behind the wicketkeeper. Now only the one run for the delivery of the "no ball' will be debited against the bowler, not the five runs for the hitting of the helmet by the ball, as under the 1980 code. These five runs will be entered in the new penalty runs column in the scorebook and the striker will not be credited with them, as he would have been under the 1980 code.

Those who make a close study of the Laws of Cricket may have noted that Law 24.5 of the 1980 code, "Bowler attempting to run out non-striker before delivery", has been omitted from the new Law 24. This is now Law 42.15 and is explained fully under that law.

LAW 25
WIDE BALL

1. Judging a Wide
(a) If the bowler bowls a ball, not being a No ball, the umpire shall adjudge it a Wide if according to the definition in (b) below, in his opinion, the ball passes wide of the striker where he is standing and would also have passed wide of him standing in a normal guard position.
(b) The ball will be considered as passing wide of the striker unless it is sufficiently within his reach for him to be able to hit it with his bat by means of a normal cricket stroke.

2. Delivery not a Wide
The umpire shall not adjudge a delivery as being a Wide
(a) if the striker, by moving,
either (i) causes the ball to pass wide of him, as defined in 1(b) above
or (ii) brings the ball sufficiently within his reach to be able to hit it with his bat by means of a normal cricket stroke.
(b) if the ball touches the striker's bat or person.

3. Call and signal of Wide ball
(a) If the umpire adjudges a delivery to be a Wide he shall call and signal Wide ball as soon as the ball passes the striker's wicket. It shall, however, be considered to have been a Wide from the instant of delivery, even though it cannot be called Wide until it passes the striker's wicket.
(b) The umpire shall revoke the call of Wide ball if there is then any contact between the ball and the striker's bat or person.
(c) The umpire shall revoke the call of Wide ball if a delivery is called a No ball. See Law 24.10 (No ball to over-ride Wide).

4. Ball not dead
The ball does not become dead on the call of Wide ball.

5. Penalty for a Wide

A penalty of one run shall be awarded instantly on the call of Wide ball. Unless the call is revoked (see 3 above), this penalty shall stand even if a batsman is dismissed, and shall be in addition to any other runs scored, any boundary allowance and any other penalties awarded.

6. Runs resulting from a Wide – how scored

All runs completed by the batsmen or a boundary allowance, together with the penalty for the Wide, shall be scored as Wide balls. Apart from any award of a 5 run penalty, all runs resulting from a Wide ball shall be debited against the bowler.

7. Wide not to count

A Wide shall not count as one of the over. See Law 22.4 (Balls not to count in the over).

8. Out from a Wide

When Wide ball has been called, neither batsman shall be out under any of the Laws except 33 (Handled the ball), 35 (Hit wicket), 37 (Obstructing the field), 38 (Run out) or 39 (Stumped).

Before 1828 a wide ball was not registered in a scorebook, even though in 1811 a law appeared for the first time regarding such a delivery. There was a penalty for bowling it but it was entered as a bye. To my mind this would have been harsh on the wicketkeeper, because if he were agile enough to move across and arrest the passage of the ball, nobody could say that it had gone "bye". In 1828 the law was altered for such a delivery to be recorded as a "wide" and not as a "bye".

The 1835 code stated that "on the call of wide ball, the ball was considered 'dead' and no more than the one-run penalty for the bowling of it was recorded". On June 17, 1844, the law was changed again in such a way that, from the delivery of a wide ball, the batting side could reckon all runs resulting from that ball. Unusually, this law was brought into use from that date, even though it was not officially confirmed until the annual meeting of MCC the following year.

While the 1980 code describes a wide ball, some people think that the umpires are now adjudicating balls as wides that pass a batsman within a couple of inches of his legs and that this is harsh on the bowler. All I can say is that the authorities have impressed on the umpiring bodies over many years that this is what they desire. I feel that, at the top level of the game, the umpires have been most consistent in the calling of wides.

One radical change that was considered, but not adopted, was not allowing a batsman to be stumped off a wide ball. Because a wide ball, like a no ball, is an illegal delivery, it was felt by some that it was unfair for a batsman to be able to be stumped off it. However, after much discussion, the status quo was preserved. A batsman can therefore still be stumped off a wide ball, but not a no ball.

Law 25.1, "Judging a wide", no longer contains a reference to "so high over", in relation to a ball passing the striker, as the 1980 code did. It will be seen that this is now covered in Law 42.6 (a) (ii) and that the penalty is a no ball, not a wide ball. I am surprised that Law 25.1 (a) makes no mention of "wide of the wicket". Part (b) of this law suggests that a bowler must always bowl a ball within the striker's reach, standing in normal guard position and being able to play a normal cricket stroke. Remember, we do not call wide until the ball has passed the wicket.

When discussing part 3 of Law 25, "Call and signal of a wide ball", it is time to state that a mistake was made at one of the MCC laws clarification committee meetings. This mistake was conveyed in issue No 5, published in December 1992, of the "green sheets", the ACU&S publication sent out to all of its members. It was in regard to the scores being level with the last pair of batsmen at the wicket. A wide ball is delivered to one of the batsmen and in his efforts to hit the ball, he only succeeds in hitting down his own wicket. The clarification given was that there was no run to credit and that the decision of "out" would be the correct one. Obviously the ruling could not be the same as it is at other times during a match, nor indeed if such an incident happened at the end of the first innings. If it were so, the side batting last would have won the match and at the same time would have lost all ten wickets as one run would have been credited as a wide ball penalty and the striker would have been dismissed "hit wicket". Shortly after the meeting when this decision was made, it was realised that the clarification should have been one run to credit as the wide-ball penalty and a decision of not out because the match was over. This error has now been addressed in Law 25.3 (a) of the 2000 code.

This states that a wide-ball penalty is an instant award and that it is judged as wide when it passes the striker but is not called until it passes the line of the striker's wicket. In this part of the law we see that the ball will be considered to be wide from the instant of delivery. This is fine during almost any part of a match as, if a striker is given out from that delivery, the one penalty run will be scored and the striker is able to be dismissed. However, if it is from a ball delivered when the scores are level, only the wide will be credited, even if by some mischance the wicket is broken by the striker before the ball passes the wicket. As Law 25.3 (a) emphasises, "it shall be considered a wide from the instant of delivery".

Part (c) of this law makes the point that, if the bowling-end umpire calls "wide" and the square-leg umpire calls "no ball", it will be the latter call that takes precedence, thus eliminating the call of "wide ball".

Law 25.5, "Penalty for a wide", again makes the very important point that the one-run penalty for the bowling of a wide is an instant award and the match is over should the scores have been tied up to that point.

I explained in Law 24.13 how the bowler is debited with just one run if a no ball hits the helmet positioned on the ground behind the wicketkeeper. Similarly, under Law 25, if a wide ball is delivered and it is deflected by a member of the fielding side onto the helmet or hits it directly, only the one penalty run will be debited against the bowler. The five runs for the ball making contact with the helmet will be entered into the new column in the scorebook as penalty runs, giving a total of six to the batting side. Under Law 24 and Law 25, if the ball fails to encounter the helmet and carries on to cross the boundary line, all five will be debited against the bowler, one for the delivery of the no ball or wide and four for the boundary.

LAW 26

BYE AND LEG BYE

1. Byes
If the ball, not being a No ball or a Wide, passes the striker without touching his bat or person, any runs completed by the batsmen or a boundary allowance shall be credited as Byes to the batting side.

2. Leg byes
(a) If the ball, not having previously touched the striker's bat, strikes his person and the umpire is satisfied that the striker has
either (i) attempted to play the ball with his bat,
or (ii) tried to avoid being hit by the ball,
then any runs completed by the batsmen or a boundary allowance shall be credited to the batting side as Leg byes, unless No ball has been called.
(b) If No ball has been called, the runs in (a) above, together with the penalty for the No ball, shall be scored as No ball extras.

3. Leg byes not to be awarded
If in the circumstances of 2(a) above, the umpire considers that neither of the conditions (i) and (ii) has been met, then Leg byes will not be awarded. The batting side shall not be credited with any runs from that delivery apart from the one run penalty for a No ball if applicable. Moreover, no other penalties shall be awarded to the batting side when the ball is dead. See Law 42.17 (Penalty runs). The following procedure shall be adopted.
(a) If no run is attempted but the ball reaches the boundary, the umpire shall call and signal Dead ball, and disallow the boundary.
(b) If runs are attempted and if
(i) neither batsman is dismissed and the ball does not become dead for any other reason, the umpire shall call and signal

Dead ball as soon as one run is completed or the ball reaches the boundary. The batsmen shall return to their original ends. The run or boundary shall be disallowed.

(ii) before one run is completed or the ball reaches the boundary, a batsman is dismissed, or the ball becomes dead for any other reason, all the provisions of the Laws will apply, except that no runs and no penalties shall be credited to the batting side, other than the penalty for a No ball if applicable.

Law 26 in the 2000 code shows little change and so I should like to take the liberty here of quoting a couple of passages from my first *Wisden Book of Cricket Laws*, written in 1993. My comments in that first book are still relevant, particularly the sentence that read: "I feel the law-makers have done well for, in my opinion, the law is now as fair to both sides as it is possible to achieve."

While I still hold those beliefs with regard to Law 26 in the 2000 code, I wish that something had been done to explain the vexed question of a certain legitimate signal that not many people appear to understand. Spectators, players – mainly wicketkeepers – and indeed some umpires have approached me and asked: "Why do you signal no ball and bye as well?" I would like to explain this by quoting again from that first *Wisden Book of Laws*. "When a bye is scored (from a delivery which makes no contact with the striker's bat, person or equipment) it is a matter of disgust to all wicketkeepers who take pride in ensuring that nothing is debited against them. This leads me to a point which many first-class wicketkeepers feel that I do not get right because of their lack of knowledge of the laws. Early in my career I am pretty sure that I was 'marked down' in captains' reports – certainly by one wicket-keeper captain – because my action in this connection was perfectly correct. I refer to the delivery of a no ball which makes contact with the striker's person and, say, a couple of runs result. These are legitimate. In this case the law states: 'When the ball is dead the umpire shall repeat the no-ball signal to the scorers accompanied by the bye signal.' I have known wicketkeepers go blue in the face and tell me that it should be leg byes and at times question my decision – even my sanity. I am sure that I have not been given the marks which my attention to the law have merited. Once a no ball, always a no ball; and in the instance I have cited, they will always be credited as such. They will never be credited as byes causing the wicketkeeper to feel I am doing him a disservice. The reason for the bye signal is to inform the scorers that no contact was made with the striker's bat, or hands holding the bat, by the ball. The signal also ensures that I do not do the bowler a disservice by having the runs debited against him. To all wicketkeepers I say: 'Trust me; I may get an occasional out or not out decision wrong but I certainly don't get that part of the game wrong!'"

It is the usual practice that the umpire shall signal bye to the scorers when the ball is "dead". However, I still feel that the following course of action is the best one to take. As soon as the batsmen start to run, I signal a bye. By doing this immediately, I am not affecting any other action I should be taking, e.g. moving to the correct position to adjudicate on a run-out attempt. The immediate signal and the continuance of it is a help to the scorers. When the ball is dead, and with my arm still upraised, I turn to the scoring position to observe the acknowledgement of my decision.

Moving on to leg byes, if the umpire is certain that the striker played a genuine stroke at the ball or made an attempt to avoid being hit by the ball, and it makes contact with the striker's person other than the hand or hands holding the bat, any runs obtained shall be credited as leg byes under Law 26.2. As stated in Law 18, "Scoring runs", any penalties awarded from that delivery, either with regard to the bowler in his delivery of the ball and/or any penalty runs incurred by the fielding side, will be scored in addition to any ensuing leg byes.

Law 26.3, "Leg byes not to be awarded", emphasises that from such a deflection, nothing after the deflection will count. What may have taken place prior to it, however, will count, e.g. the one-run penalty for the delivery of a no ball. No penalty runs under the new Law 42 can be awarded, so the old adage holds true: "No shot played, no runs to count."

In conclusion I would like to reiterate the final paragraph of my thoughts on Law 26 in the first *Wisden Book of Laws*. "If all the 42 laws were framed as well as this one, equating fairness and justice to both sides in equal proportions, maybe the game would be even better than it is."

LAW 27

APPEALS

1. Umpire not to give batsman out without an appeal
Neither umpire shall give a batsman out, even though he may be out under the Laws, unless appealed to by the fielding side. This shall not debar a batsman who is out under any of the Laws from leaving his wicket without an appeal having been made. Note, however, the provisions of 7 below.

2. Batsman dismissed
A batsman is dismissed if
either (a) he is given out by an umpire, on appeal
or (b) he is out under any of the Laws and leaves his wicket as in 1 above.

3. Timing of appeals
For an appeal to be valid it must be made before the bowler begins his run up or, if he has no run up, his bowling action to deliver the next ball, and before Time has been called.

The call of Over does not invalidate an appeal made prior to the start of the following over provided Time has not been called. See Laws 16.2 (Call of Time) and 22.2 (Start of an over).

4. Appeal "How's That?"
An appeal "How's That?" covers all ways of being out.

5. Answering appeals
The umpire at the bowler's end shall answer all appeals except those arising out of any of Laws 35 (Hit wicket), 39 (Stumped) or 38 (Run out) when this occurs at the striker's wicket. A decision Not out by one umpire shall not prevent the other umpire from giving a decision,

provided that each is considering only matters within his jurisdiction. When a batsman has been given Not out, either umpire may, within his jurisdiction, answer a further appeal provided that it is made in accordance with 3 above.

6. Consultation by umpires
Each umpire shall answer appeals on matters within his own jurisdiction. If an umpire is doubtful about any point that the other umpire may have been in a better position to see, he shall consult the latter on this point of fact and shall then give his decision. If, after consultation, there is still doubt remaining the decision shall be Not out.

7. Batsman leaving his wicket under a misapprehension
An umpire shall intervene if satisfied that a batsman, not having been given out, has left his wicket under a misapprehension that he is out. The umpire intervening shall call and signal Dead ball to prevent any further action by the fielding side and shall recall the batsman.

8. Withdrawal of an appeal
The captain of the fielding side may withdraw an appeal only with the consent of the umpire within whose jurisdiction the appeal falls and before the outgoing batsman has left the field of play. If such consent is given the umpire concerned shall, if applicable, revoke his decision and recall the batsman.

9. Umpire's decision
An umpire may alter his decision provided that such alteration is made promptly. This apart, an umpire's decision, once made, is final.

There is little in the early codes relating to appeals from the fielding side but I did find a lovely turn of phrase in the 1755 laws. In the section Laws for the Umpires, it states that "they are not to order any man out unless appealed to by one of the players". This wording was slightly altered between 1755 and 1809 so that it read, "they are not to order a player out, unless appealed to by the adversaries".

Law 27 in the 2000 code is much the same as in the 1980 code, although all of the sections have been given a different number. Some parts have been clarified and expanded. Also, an obscure legal point that was put to the working party has led to Law 27.2, "Batsman dismissed", being set out in the manner which it is. There are a few additions and I shall deal with them under the relevant sections.

The second paragraph of Law 27.1, "Umpire not to give batsman out without an appeal", gives either batsman the opportunity to leave his wicket should he feel that he is out, without any appeal being made. This was always the case for those who elected to play the game in the best sense of the word and now it is written into this law. I can think of just two instances in my professional career when a striker has inexplicably left his wicket without any semblance of an appeal and both are connected with Derbyshire players. One incident involved Peter Kirsten at Northampton in 1981. Peter received a ball from Neil Mallender which, from my viewpoint as the umpire at the bowler's end, struck him high on the pad and carried to Bob Carter at short leg. Bob took the ball and immediately tossed it back to the bowler. The next thing we all observed was Peter turning and walking from the field of play. Nobody appealed and, even if they had done, I certainly would not have given him out. Everyone looked at each other and, as Neil walked back past me to his bowling mark, he said: "He didn't hit that, did he?" My reply was: "Not in my opinion."

The other incident took place at Derby in a match against Sussex. The ball was hit to the square-leg position and the fielder dropped forward to take a very low catch. To the surprise of many, myself included, the fielder turned down the catch. The striker still elected to leave the field and I walked over to my colleague, Ray Julian, and said: "I am sure that the catch was good." Ray gave me good advice, as he has done many times in my career, when he said: "Yes, but leave it." So we did.

Law 27.2 sets out the two situations when a batsman is dismissed: (a) he is given out by either umpire on appeal; or (b) he elects to leave his wicket under his own volition as in Law 27.1, knowing that he is out under any of the laws.

Of course, from time to time, a sporting batsman will leave his wicket in the belief that he is out, when in fact he is not. This situation is covered under Law 27.7 and I hope umpires have always taken and will continue to take the following action. As quickly as possible, the umpire should call and signal "dead ball", thus stopping any action by the fielding side that may lead to resentment at a later stage of the match. He should then recall the batsman who is leaving the field of play. While all of this is implied in the 1980 code, it is now set down in a much broader and clearer manner in the new code.

I would like to conclude my thoughts on Law 27 by saying how much I like the very last line, "the umpire's decision, once made, is final".

LAW 28

THE WICKET IS DOWN

1. Wicket put down
(a) The wicket is put down if a bail is completely removed from the top of the stumps, or a stump is struck out of the ground by
- (i) the ball.
- (ii) the striker's bat, whether he is holding it or has let go of it.
- (iii) the striker's person or by any part of his clothing or equipment becoming detached from his person.
- (iii) a fielder, with his hand or arm, providing that the ball is held in the hand or hands so used, or in the hand of the arm so used.

  The wicket is also put down if a fielder pulls a stump out of the ground in the same manner.

(b) The disturbance of a bail, whether temporary or not, shall not constitute its complete removal from the top of the stumps, but if a bail in falling lodges between two of the stumps this shall be regarded as complete removal.

2. One bail off
If one bail is off, it shall be sufficient for the purpose of putting the wicket down to remove the remaining bail, or to strike or pull any of the three stumps out of the ground, in any of the ways stated in 1 above.

3. Remaking the wicket
If the wicket is broken or put down while the ball is in play, the umpire shall not remake the wicket until the ball is dead. See Law 23 (Dead ball). Any fielder, however, may
- (i) replace a bail or bails on top of the stumps.
- (ii) put back one or more stumps into the ground where the wicket originally stood.

4. Dispensing with bails

If the umpires have agreed to dispense with bails, in accordance with Law 8.5 (Dispensing with bails), the decision as to whether the wicket has been put down is one for the umpire concerned to decide.

(a) After a decision to play without bails, the wicket has been put down if the umpire concerned is satisfied that the wicket has been struck by the ball, by the striker's bat, person, or items of his clothing or equipment separated from his person as described in 1(a)(ii) or 1(a)(iii) above, or by a fielder with the hand holding the ball or with the arm of the hand holding the ball.

(b) If the wicket has already been broken or put down, (a) above shall apply to any stump or stumps still in the ground. Any fielder may replace a stump or stumps, in accordance with 3 above, in order to have an opportunity of putting the wicket down.

In the early days of this law it must have been much more difficult to put the wicket down than it is under the present-day laws. Under the earliest code, the wicket consisted of only two stumps with one bail laid across the top, and the dimensions were much smaller. The wicket was only six inches wide, which is two-thirds of the present measurement, and the height was only 22 inches, which is six inches lower than the present stipulation. The greatest disadvantage, though, must have been that if the ball passed between the two stumps without removing the bail, the wicket would not have been judged to have been put down. With the ball measuring less than 2 1/4 inches in diameter it was not unusual for it to pass through the gap between the two stumps and there are many recorded instances of it having done so.

As there was only one bail in the early days, of six inches in length, I expect the home side used stumps as thin as possible when they batted. I do hope that the dimensions were not increased when they were in the field. It was implicit in the laws that "the bail had definitely to fall from the top of the stumps for the wicket to be down". Then, as now, if the bail was off, a stump had to be struck out of the ground with ball in hand.

In 1775 a three-stump wicket, with one six-inch bail, was introduced, although it did not appear in the laws until 1786. The first MCC code of laws in 1788 made no mention of a three-stump wicket as by then it appeared that there was a common acceptance of this type of wicket. It was not until 1838 that it was specified in the laws that a wicket should consist of three stumps. In 1775 bowlers' eyes must have taken on a new twinkle for, with the gap between the two stumps having been filled by a third one, it was much easier to put the wicket down. The ball could not now pass between the stumps and under the one bail. In 1798 the bowlers' task was made a great deal easier again with the wicket size being increased to 24 inches in height and seven inches in width. However, there was still only one bail.

Some time shortly after 1803 there is a reliable edition of the laws that mentions bails, plural, and 1821 saw a further increase in the height of the wicket to 26 inches. Two years later the bowlers must have been rubbing their hands in glee again as the wicket height was increased to 27 inches and, perhaps more importantly, the width was increased by an inch to eight inches.

For more than a century there were no further changes until, in May 1931, the laws stated that two sizes of wicket could be used, the one as mentioned above or a wicket of 28 inches in height and nine inches in width. These dimensions were not entirely new, however, as they were experimented with in a match involving an MCC XI at Lord's in 1872. It should be made clear that a mix of these two sets of measurements, such as 27 inches in height and nine inches in width, was not allowed; they had to be one dimension or the other. I wonder if, during that transition period, a match was ever played with a wicket of one dimension at one end of the pitch and one of lesser proportions at the other. The size of the bails was also stipulated for the two dimensions of the wicket. They had to be not less than four inches and not more than 4 $^{1}/_{2}$ inches in length, depending upon which width dimension of the wicket was being used. As yet it appeared that nobody had thought about having a slight gap between the bails when they were in position.

In the 1947 code the dimension of the wicket was standardised and it remains to this day as 28 inches in height and nine inches in width. The two bails shall be of no more than 4 $^{3}/_{8}$ inches in length and when in position shall not project more than half an inch above the top of the stumps. The wicket can therefore be of an overall height of 28 $^{1}/_{2}$ inches, which clearly gives bowlers and fielders a much better chance of putting the wicket down than they had in those early days.

As will be seen from Law 28.1 of the 2000 code, to put down a wicket a bail must be completely removed from the top of the stumps, plural, not just one stump. What is new in this part of the law is, in section (ii) regarding the bat, the words "or has let go of it" and in section (iii) the words "becoming detached from his person". Right until the eleventh hour that piece of text was due to read "or being thrown from his person" but I was always against that phrase and it led me to ask: "What do we think the game is coming to, a coconut shy?" Anyway, late in the day it was changed to the more sensible wording that we now have.

Law 28.1 (b) says that "the disturbance of a bail shall not constitute its complete removal". In my playing days I often fielded close to the wicket and one day, while I was crouching at silly mid-on, a delivery whistled past the wicket. The wicketkeeper and I both observed the leg-side bail jump six inches or so into the air and drop back into the grooves on the top of the stumps. The only thing that either of us could do for about ten seconds was to point open-mouthed at the wicket. Our mouths may have been down but the wicket most certainly was not.

It is not unusual to see a wicket broken, i.e. the bails off, and the batsman to be not out. This frequently happens in a run-out attempt with the batsman having made his ground before the bails become detached. If, however, only one bail is off then, should there be efforts to take another run, the fielding side only has to remove the one remaining bail to put the wicket down in a legal manner.

During 1999 Nigel Plews and I visited many countries, he to hold seminars on the Duckworth/Lewis method of the recalculation of target scores in one-day matches and I to hold seminars on the Laws of Cricket. I made 19 trips to 12 countries while he made ten visits to seven countries. One of his trips was to the West Indies and, while he was there, he was asked a question that has prompted an addition to Law 28.3 and gave us one of the lighter moments during our many long days of deliberation. Law 28.3 of the 1980 code states that "if all of the stumps are out of the ground, the fielding side shall be allowed to put back one or more stumps in order to have an opportunity of putting the wicket down". Members of the West Indies Cricket Umpires' Association asked Nigel if that meant that a stump could be thrust back into the ground where it lay. We considered this a most sensible question, as the law read under that code. This was obviously not the meaning of the law and the answer to this question is now covered in the new clarification found in Law 28.3 (ii).

Also under this part of Law 28 I came across a situation while umpiring a match in Gibraltar that made me press for a clarification under the new code. It was, however, felt wise to allow it to be left to the local league or association to write its own regulation. Most cricket within Europe and in many other parts of the world is now played on artificial turf pitches, with a set of spring-loaded stumps at each end of the pitch. With both bails off, how can the wicket then be put down with this type of wicket? As many will know, this type of structure has a heavy metal base with the three stumps attached to it by a spring on each, all of which have a spindle running through them. This makes it impossible for a stump to be taken up in the correct manner. The lot has to be raised from the ground, with bail in hand – not an easy task – or the whole structure has to be forcibly knocked over, perhaps risking injury.

The situation I came across in Gibraltar was this. The bails were off when the captain of the national side, Chris Rocca, took the ball from a return from the outfield and with a hand hit the structure quite hard, spinning the base around and appealing for a run-out with the batsman well out of his ground. My reply was "not out", not because he had failed to raise the structure from the ground but because he had spun it round with his left arm while holding the ball in his right. As I moved in to remake the wicket, the captain said: "Don, we only have to make a discernible movement of the structure to dismiss the batsman." I have remembered those words and I shall press for this expression to be used in future clarifications of this law for games where spring-loaded stumps are being used.

It is not often that a situation arises under Law 28.4 (a), "Dispensing with bails", but when it happens, at least for any great length of time, it is unreal. I umpired for the week of August 11-17 at Portsmouth in 1979, the time when many yachts were lost in the Fastnet Race. Not only did we have to dispense with the bails but neither would the "heavies" stay on. Indeed the stumps were moving about in a wind that made the playing of the match almost impossible. Fortunately, every time the ball hit the stumps over those few days it made a hard, direct contact.

LAW 29
BATSMAN OUT OF HIS GROUND

1. When out of his ground
A batsman shall be considered to be out of his ground unless his bat or some part of his person is grounded behind the popping crease at that end.

2. Which is a batsman's ground
(a) If only one batsman is within a ground
    (i) it is his ground.
    (ii) it remains his ground even if he is later joined there by the other batsman.
(b) If both batsmen are in the same ground and one of them subsequently leaves it, (a)(i) above applies.
(c) If there is no batsman in either ground, then each ground belongs to whichever of the batsmen is nearer to it, or, if the batsmen are level, to whichever was nearer to it immediately prior to their drawing level.
(d) If a ground belongs to one batsman, then, unless there is a striker with a runner, the other ground belongs to the other batsman irrespective of his position.
(e) When a batsman with a runner is striker, his ground is always that at the wicket-keeper's end. However, (a), (b), (c) and (d) above will still apply, but only to the runner and the non-striker, so that that ground will also belong to either the non-striker or the runner, as the case may be.

3. Position of non-striker
The batsman at the bowler's end should be positioned on the opposite side of the wicket to that from which the ball is being delivered, unless a request to do otherwise is granted by the umpire.

This law consisted of 33 words in the 1980 code and quite why it now needs to be 244 words baffles me as it shows little significant change. However, it endeavours to give a number of clarifications, upon which I shall now try to enlarge. Although a batsman's ground has been specified and marked with bowling and popping creases for a great many years, certainly since 1755 and probably before, the fact that a batsman had to pop his bat into the hole between the two stumps that made up the wicket to complete a run makes me wonder whether, at an early date, for a batsman to be "within his ground" he had to take the action of placing the bat into this hole. The marking of return creases did not come into being until a much later date and they are nothing to do with a batsman being "within his ground".

In the early codes of the laws and after 1755, when creases were marked by them being cut into the turf, this area of ground was 3ft 9in in front of the wicket at each end of the pitch. In 1819 this was increased to 4ft and it has remained thus ever since. The reason for it being increased to 4ft was simply because the height of the wicket had increased from 22 inches in 1744 to 26 inches in 1819, not in one fell swoop but by two inches on two occasions.

Law 29.2 aims to explain "Which is a batsman's ground" and I feel it does this well, except perhaps section (e), which deals with when an injured striker has a runner, as I feel that it conflicts somewhat with section (c). Should the injured striker be "out of his ground" (his ground is always at the wicketkeeper's end) and he is crossed by the non-striker, it is never the non-striker's ground, even if the non-striker manages to find himself behind the popping crease at that end prior to the wicket being broken. This is what I refer to as "principle 2" when I hold seminars on Law 2, "Substitutes". The seminar and that law are closely allied to Law 29.2.

LAW 30

Bowled

1. Out Bowled

(a) The striker is out Bowled if his wicket is put down by a ball delivered by the bowler, not being a No ball, even if it first touches his bat or person.

(b) Notwithstanding (a) above he shall not be out Bowled if before striking the wicket the ball has been in contact with any other player or with an umpire. He will, however, be subject to Laws 33 (Handled the ball), 37 (Obstructing the field), 38 (Run out) and 39 (Stumped).

2. Bowled to take precedence

The striker is out Bowled if his wicket is put down as in 1 above, even though a decision against him for any other method of dismissal would be justified.

Law 30 contains one minor clarification and came about in response to a question that I had asked. The question was: "If a ball hits the bat or the striker's person, and the ball then goes some distance behind the striker's wicket, can the striker be out bowled if the ball then comes back to break the wicket? I made no mention of the ball striking another fielder. I have seen such an incident at Leicester and indeed described it in *The Wisden Book of Cricket Laws*. When this law is read, I am sure its inclusion may be questioned. Part 1 (b) of the law states that the striker "shall not be out bowled if before striking the wicket the ball has been in contact with any other player or with an umpire". While the meaning is clear, I am still puzzled at its inclusion. Should a situation arise under this new clarification, the umpires would, I am certain, already have taken other action. In the main this would be a call and signal of "dead ball". I have struggled to think of any circumstances, other than the delivery coming back towards the wicket off the wicketkeeper's person, when this might happen and, if it did, I feel sure that umpires know such an incident does not qualify for a decision of bowled. As for making contact with either an umpire or a fielder in front of the wicket, other action most certainly would have been taken by the umpires, with a call of "dead ball" or perhaps "no ball" if a fielder had encroached onto the pitch.

I did uncover some very interesting points in my research into this law. In the very early code of 1744 "the bail definitely had to fall from the top of the stumps for the wicket to be down". This applied until 1924 when the law stated that "the striker would be out under this Law if any part of either bail is struck off the top of the wicket".

For five seasons prior to the publication of the 1947 code, Law 21 carried an amazing note. Note (a) read, "an umpire is justified in giving the striker out bowled when a stump is bowled down, even though the bails by some mischance remain in position". I know that some strange things took place in those latter years of World War II but I would love to have witnessed a dismissal of this nature.

LAW 31
Timed Out

1. Out Timed out
(a) Unless Time has been called, the incoming batsman must be in position to take guard or for his partner to be ready to receive the next ball within 3 minutes of the fall of the previous wicket. If this requirement is not met, the incoming batsman will be out, Timed out.
(b) In the event of protracted delay in which no batsman comes to the wicket, the umpires shall adopt the procedure of Law 21.3 (Umpires awarding a match). For the purposes of that Law the start of the action shall be taken as the expiry of the 3 minutes referred to above.

2. Bowler does not get credit
The bowler does not get credit for the wicket.

One of the purposes of this book is to bring to readers' attention ways in which the laws have been altered, and there are important changes to this law from the previous code that

So, as it is still in existence, there are important changes to the previous code that should be noted. Under Law 31.1 (a) the time allowed for a new batsman to come out to bat has been extended from two minutes to three minutes but that batsman has to cover more ground in that extra minute. Under the 1980 code he had to cover the distance from where he is when the wicket falls to getting himself onto the field of play, i.e. over the boundary line, within two minutes. Under the 2000 code he has to travel from the starting point as previously stated and he will only reach the finishing line when he has arrived at the wicket and taken guard. All of this must take place within three minutes. It would appear that a batsman is now being subjected to a time-trial before being allowed to start his innings.

Part 1 (b) deals with a "protracted delay" and I have covered one aspect of this under Law 21.3. However, if anyone thinks that a match should be awarded simply because one batsman, for whatever reason, takes 3 minutes 30 seconds to arrive at the wicket, I hope I do not have to umpire with him. I have always found this law, and have stated so in the past, ridiculous in the extreme. For those who love the game, they live for the weekend when they can take their place at the wicket and, with bat in hand, reach double figures. Nothing is further from their minds than to delay coming to the wicket. I have never received an appeal under this law and neither do I know an umpire who has.

Law 31.2 simply states that, if a batsman is given out "timed out", the bowler does not get credit for the wicket. Neither should he expect to.

LAW 32

Caught

1. Out Caught
The striker is out Caught if a ball delivered by the bowler, not being a No ball, touches his bat without having previously been in contact with any member of the fielding side and is subsequently held by a fielder as a fair catch before it touches the ground.

2. Caught to take precedence
If the criteria of 1 above are met and the striker is not out Bowled, then he is out Caught, even though a decision against either batsman for another method of dismissal would be justified. Runs completed by the batsmen before the completion of the catch will not be scored. Note also Laws 21.6 (Winning hit or extras) and 42.17(b) (Penalty runs).

3. A fair catch
A catch shall be considered to have been fairly made if
(a) throughout the act of making the catch
    (i)   any fielder in contact with the ball is within the field of play. See 4 below.
    (ii) the ball is at no time in contact with any object grounded beyond the boundary.
The act of making the catch shall start from the time when a fielder first handles the ball and shall end when a fielder obtains complete control both over the ball and over his own movement.
(b) the ball is hugged to the body of the catcher or accidentally lodges in his clothing or, in the case of the wicket-keeper, in his pads. However, it is not a fair catch if the ball lodges in a protective helmet worn by a fielder. See Law 23 (Dead ball).
(c) the ball does not touch the ground, even though the hand holding it does so in effecting the catch.

(d) a fielder catches the ball after it has been lawfully struck more than once by the striker, but only if the ball has not touched the ground since first being struck.

(e) a fielder catches the ball after it has touched an umpire, another fielder or the other batsman. However, it is not a fair catch if the ball has touched a protective helmet worn by a fielder, although the ball remains in play.

(f) a fielder catches the ball in the air after it has crossed the boundary provided that
- (i) he has no part of his person touching, or grounded beyond, the boundary at any time when he is in contact with the ball.
- (ii) the ball has not been grounded beyond the boundary.

See Law 19.3 (Scoring a boundary).

(g) the ball is caught off an obstruction within the boundary, provided it has not previously been decided to regard the obstruction as a boundary.

4. Fielder within the field of play

(a) A fielder is not within the field of play if he touches the boundary or has any part of his person grounded beyond the boundary. See Law 19.3 (Scoring a boundary).

(b) 6 runs shall be scored if a fielder
- (i) has any part of his person touching, or grounded beyond, the boundary when he catches the ball.
- (ii) catches the ball and subsequently touches the boundary or grounds some part of his person over the boundary while carrying the ball but before completing the catch.

See Laws 19.3 (Scoring a boundary) and 19.4 (Runs allowed for boundaries).

5. No runs to be scored

If the striker is dismissed Caught, runs from that delivery completed by the batsmen before the completion of the catch shall not be scored, but any penalties awarded to either side when the ball is dead, if applicable, will stand. Law 18.12(a) (Batsman returning to wicket he has left) shall apply from the instant of the catch.

This law and Law 19, "Boundaries", were the final two to be completed by the working party as they hinged to a great extent upon one another.

From a historical perspective, I could find little detail on the numerous changes to certain parts of this law. However, there are many books that devote chapters to catching feats. The best of these is by Gerald Brodribb in his 1952 edition of "Next Man In". I am proud to say that I have a copy of this, signed by him when I visited him at his home in 1992.

The mere fact that almost half of all wickets taken fall under Law 32 gives licence for much reflection. For many who love the game of cricket, the great catches give great enjoyment. This is certainly true for me as it was in this department of the game that I was most proficient. I can only recall dropping two catches in my career, or at least two that I should have caught.

In 1755 the catching of a striker by a fielder was clearly a hazardous occupation. In the laws of that year there is a reference to the striker which states that "if he runs out of his ground to hinder a catch, it's cut". In the same code it states that "when the ball is hit up either of the strikers may hinder the catch in his running ground; or if it is hit directly across the wickets, the other player may place his body anywhere within the swing of the bat so as to hinder the bowler from catching it". And this was supposed to be a game played by gentlemen?

I take the expression of "his running ground" to mean within his own ground and the expression "directly across the wickets" to mean down the wicket. I would have been in my element, being able to use the "bodycheck" as in my old ice hockey days. Or perhaps the obstruction would have been slightly more refined and the use of the horse racing term "bumping and boring" would have been more appropriate. In view of this I researched the "obstruction" law in relation to a catch. I found that it was first mentioned in 1787 and believe that a revision may have taken place just prior to the first MCC code of laws in 1788.

Law 32.3 is concerned with "A fair catch" and I would ask readers to eliminate from their minds at this juncture catches that are taken in close proximity to any type of boundary demarcation. That having been done, a catch and the methods by which it may be taken are exactly the same as they have been for hundreds of years. As long as the ball is held by a fielder without touching the ground, prior to or after being taken, that is a fair catch. The ball can accidentally lodge in any item of clothing being worn by the catcher and still be a fair catch. The ball can lodge in or between any parts of his anatomy – the mind boggles – and that, too, is a fair catch. A catch will not be valid, however, should the ball lodge in any member of the fielding side's helmet while being worn. Nor will a catch be valid after it has been in contact with any helmet on the field of play, other than those worn by the striker or non-striker.

In many of the books of long ago, there are stories of a ball being caught, thrown into the air and allowed to fall to the ground, the decision being "not out". While I am not able to agree with this, I believe that there was some justification for such a decision by an umpire before the 1980 code came into being. It is only in this code that there is the statement, in relation to the catcher, that he "retains complete control over the further disposal of the ball". My reaction is that, for a catcher to be able to throw the ball into the air, he must have had complete control over the disposal because he actually disposed of it from whence it came.

I wonder if, by the way the law is worded in the 2000 code, we have gone back to the situation that existed in the 1947 code, in cases of a catch being taken and thrown into the air and being allowed to fall to the ground. Yes, we probably have. However, the fact of the fielder being able to throw the ball into the air means that he must have complete control over it.

The law in relation to a fielder catching the ball within the field of play and then being able to ground his person on or over the boundary line has changed back and forth a number of times and is now covered under Law 32.4. For the 1968 season an experimental law came into being which was to the effect that if a fielder caught the ball inside the field of play and carried it over the boundary line, it would not be valid; he had to catch and stay inside the field of play after the catch was completed. This was finally passed as a full law for the 1972 season, my first as a professional umpire.

Now let us consider a ball being caught in close proximity to any boundary of the field of play. This is where a number of alterations to this law are to be found, some of which may not meet with universal approval.

Let us take a line or rope being used to denote a boundary. This part of the law is still as in the 1980 code and should a fielder catch a ball and then with ball in hand make contact with the boundary, the decision will be "not out" and six runs. Previously, though, if the catcher disposed of the ball before he made contact with or crossed the boundary, he would not be allowed to return to the field of play and effect the catch himself. Now he can. If his disposal of the ball sends it so high towards the heavens and he is so fleet of foot and agile that he is able to return to the field of play and catch the ball again before it falls to earth, then the striker is out, caught. While this is most unlikely to happen, I hope that I am present to observe this fine act of agility! Under the 1980 code all the umpire had to be certain of was, during and after the catch being taken, that the catcher was not in contact with or beyond the boundary line. Now, and in addition to this, an umpire has to be certain that the catcher was inside the field of play when he disposed of the ball and that he was back within the field of play when he made the effort to effect the catch. This effort will almost certainly involve a full-length dive to catch the ball and, if he achieves this acrobatic feat, is the catcher entirely inside the field of play as he completes the catch? Has he a foot on the line? If so, "not out" and six runs.

Now to boundary boards. Under the 1980 code a fielder could lean on boundary boards to effect a catch, or after taking the catch fall against the boards. He could take a catch with the ball beyond the boards, using the boards to assist him in not falling beyond them. All of this has changed under the 2000 code. No longer can he touch a boundary board while in contact with the ball in effecting a catch or indeed fielding the ball. In the case of a catch, if he touches the boards while making the catch, as with a line or rope, it is "not out" and six runs. If, of course, he is a superb athlete and can catch the ball, dispose of it, vault the boards going outside the field of play, vault the boards in returning to the field of play and then catch the ball again before it hits the ground, the striker would be "out", as improbable as it sounds. A more realistic way in which a catcher will be able to gain an advantage in regard to boundary boards is, after catching and disposing of the ball, he can run into those boards and use them to arrest his momentum and propel him back to effect the catch. In the case of an act of fielding taking place, prior to the 2000 code, a fielder with ball in hand could bring himself into contact with such a board and it would not be a boundary. Now, if he runs into or slides against such a boundary marker while in contact with the ball, it will be a boundary, usually of four runs.

Law 32.5 confirms that runs completed by the batsmen before the completion of the catch shall not be scored. However, as in other dismissals, any penalties before the catch is taken will be scored, i.e. no ball, wide ball and, under Law 42, penalty runs. There is one exception to this, and it is found in Law 42.17 (b).

LAW 33

HANDLED THE BALL

1. Out Handled the ball
Either batsman is out Handled the ball if he wilfully touches the ball while in play with a hand or hands not holding the bat unless he does so with the consent of the opposing side.

2. Not out Handled the ball
Notwithstanding 1 above, a batsman will not be out under this Law if
(i) he handles the ball in order to avoid injury.
(ii) he uses his hand or hands to return the ball to any member of the fielding side without the consent of that side. Note, however, the provisions of Law 37.4 (Returning the ball to a member of the fielding side).

3. Runs scored
If either batsman is dismissed under this Law, any runs completed before the offence, together with any penalty extras and the penalty for a No ball or Wide, if applicable, shall be scored. See Laws 18.10 (Runs scored when a batsman is dismissed) and 42.17 (Penalty runs).

4. Bowler does not get credit
The bowler does not get credit for the wicket.

Law 33 has been enlarged considerably since the 1980 code to clarify the different situations when a batsman handles the ball. For example, if a batsman returns the ball to any member of the fielding side, by the use of a hand, without permission by word or gesture of any member of that side, it will not now be recorded under this Law but under Law 37, "Obstructing the field". However, all other situations where a batsman handles the ball illegally will still be dealt with under Law 33.

Before 1899 a batsman could be dismissed under this Law if he removed by hand a ball which had become lodged in his clothing or equipment. Some unsightly situations must have occurred before the introduction of that Law, with fielders endeavouring to remove the ball after it had first made contact with the striker's bat. I can well imagine some of the batsmen making efforts to fend off the fielders with their bat.

Another change to this Law, which has taken place more recently, was actually written about in 1874 by a gentleman named James Lillywhite. He commented that a batsman who, while defending himself from a rising ball by putting up a hand to deflect the ball from hitting him in the face, would be most unlucky to be given out. It was not until a 1950s directive, however, that umpires were told that "an involuntary action by the striker in the throwing up of a hand to protect his person will not be regarded as 'handled the ball' should the hand deflect it".

I remember an incident in 1977 when I was umpiring a match between Glamorgan and Gloucestershire at Cardiff. Tony Cordle was bowling to Zaheer Abbas when a ball "took off". Zaheer, who wears glasses, threw up his hand and deflected the ball over the wicketkeeper and it sped down to the boundary. Nobody appealed and a deathly silence descended, with all 13 players looking at me. For a second I was nonplussed and the first thought that passed through my mind was that I would not give him out if there were an appeal. I then noticed that the ball had reached the boundary at the tennis court end of the ground and very slowly and deliberately said: "That's dead ball, gentlemen." I gave this signal to the scorers and still nobody said a word.

At the end of the over, as I walked to my position at square leg, Alan Jones trotted past me and said: "Well done, Don." Those words coming from the Glamorgan captain were praise indeed for Alan was a quiet man. They probably represented about one fifth of the conversation that took place between us during our time together over about ten years. He was a very dedicated batsman and I possibly "stood" more hours watching him bat than any other cricketer.

After the incident I remember thinking for some time whether I had got it completely right. I knew that the "not out" decision, had there been an appeal, would have been correct, but what about the leg byes? There was avoiding action of a sort taken by the striker to stop the ball hitting him, so should I have allowed them? I counted that delivery and saw no need to erase it. Anyway, in conversation with Tony that evening in the pavilion we talked about the unusual incident and I told him that I was not certain if I had been correct in not allowing the leg byes. His final comment to me was: "The action which you took was good for the game." That is what cricketers desire and it is that thought which is always paramount in my mind, both on and off the field.

Finally under Law 33, as in several other laws in the 2000 code, runs that are completed prior to the offence of "handled the ball" will be scored, plus penalty extras and penalty runs awarded under Law 42.

LAW 34

Hit the Ball Twice

1. Out Hit the ball twice
(a) The striker is out Hit the ball twice if, while the ball is in play, it strikes any part of his person or is struck by his bat and, before the ball has been touched by a fielder, he wilfully strikes it again with his bat or person, other than a hand not holding the bat, except for the sole purpose of guarding his wicket. See 3 below and Laws 33 (Handled the ball) and 37 (Obstructing the field).
(b) For the purpose of this Law, 'struck' or 'strike' shall include contact with the person of the striker.

2. Not out Hit the ball twice
Notwithstanding 1(a) above, the striker will not be out under this Law if

    (i) he makes a second or subsequent stroke in order to return the ball to any member of the fielding side. Note, however, the provisions of Law 37.4 (Returning the ball to a member of the fielding side).

    (ii) he wilfully strikes the ball after it has touched a fielder. Note, however, the provisions of Law 37.1 (Out Obstructing the field).

3. Ball lawfully struck more than once
Solely in order to guard his wicket and before the ball has been touched by a fielder, the striker may lawfully strike the ball more than once with his bat or with any part of his person other than a hand not holding the bat.
Notwithstanding this provision, the striker may not prevent the ball from being caught by making more than one stroke in defence of his wicket. See Law 37.3 (Obstructing a ball from being caught).

4. Runs permitted from ball lawfully struck more than once

When the ball is lawfully struck more than once, as permitted in 3 above, only the first strike is to be considered in determining whether runs are to be allowed and how they are to be scored.

(a) If on the first strike the umpire is satisfied that

either   (i)   the ball first struck the bat

or   (ii)   the striker attempted to play the ball with his bat

or   (iii)   the striker tried to avoid being hit by the ball

then any penalties to the batting side that are applicable shall be allowed.

(b) If the conditions in (a) above are met then, if they result from overthrows, and only if they result from overthrows, runs completed by the batsmen or a boundary will be allowed in addition to any penalties that are applicable. They shall be credited to the striker if the first strike was with the bat. If the first strike was on the person of the striker they shall be scored as Leg byes or No ball extras, as appropriate. See Law 26.2 (Leg byes).

(c) If the conditions of (a) above are met and there is no overthrow until after the batsmen have started to run, but before one run is completed,

    (i)   only subsequent completed runs or a boundary shall be allowed. The first run shall count as a completed run for this purpose only if the batsmen have not crossed at the instant of the throw.

    (ii)   if in these circumstances the ball goes to the boundary from the throw then, notwithstanding the provisions of Law 19.6 (Overthrow or wilful act of fielder), only the boundary allowance shall be scored.

    (iii)   if the ball goes to the boundary as the result of a further overthrow, then runs completed by the batsmen after the first throw and before this final throw shall be added to the boundary allowance. The run in progress at the first throw will count only if they have not crossed at that moment; the run in progress at the final throw shall count only if they have crossed at that moment. Law 18.12 (Batsman returning to wicket he has left) shall apply as from the moment of the final throw.

(d) If, in the opinion of the umpire, none of the conditions in (a) above have been met then, whether there is an overthrow or not, the batting side shall not be credited with any runs from that delivery apart from the penalty for a No ball if applicable. Moreover, no other penalties shall be awarded to the batting side when the ball is dead. See Law 42.17 (Penalty runs).

5. Ball lawfully struck more than once – action by the umpire

If no runs are to be allowed, either in the circumstances of 4(d) above, or because there has been no overthrow and

(a) if no run is attempted but the ball reaches the boundary, the umpire shall call and signal Dead ball and disallow the boundary.
(b) if the batsmen run and
   (i) neither batsman is dismissed and the ball does not become dead for any other reason, the umpire shall call and signal Dead ball as soon as one run is completed or the ball reaches the boundary. The batsmen shall return to their original ends. The run or boundary shall be disallowed.
   (ii) a batsman is dismissed, or if for any other reason the ball becomes dead before one run is completed or the ball reaches the boundary, all the provisions of the Laws will apply except that the award of penalties to the batting side shall be as laid down in 4(a) or 4(d) above as appropriate.

6. Bowler does not get credit

The bowler does not get credit for the wicket.

Although it is an unusual occurrence, I expect most of us have seen a batsman hit the ball twice while attempting a big hit at a ball on the leg side. This is a legitimate action as the second hit is quite accidental and merely a result of following through from the first hit. Law 34.1 (a) sets out the action which a striker must not take and if he should do so, he leaves himself in the position of having an appeal made against him for dismissal under this law. The key word here is "wilfully", for it must be remembered that if the second stroke were of an accidental nature, no appeal would be justified or upheld.

This has now spoilt one of the questions I frequently pose in my seminars: "How can a striker be out 'Hit the ball twice', without ever hitting it once?" The answer is that the ball, without making contact with the bat, strikes him in the area of the thigh pad and bounces forward and away from him: one stroke. He then moves forward and kicks the ball some distance into the outfield: second stroke. On appeal, the umpire would be justified, indeed he must do so, in giving the striker out as the second stroke was not in an effort to protect his wicket. The point of law that has spoilt my question is Law 34.1 (b) which makes it clear, unlike previous codes, that a ball making contact with the striker's person will count just as much as a stroke of the bat making contact with the ball.

Law 34.2 (i) explains that there will be no dismissal recorded if the striker returns the ball to the bowler or any member of the field by his second stroke, be it with bat or person. If the return is in this manner and an appeal is made, his dismissal would be recorded under Law 37.1, "Obstructing the field", even though his action was intended to be the converse of such a description. Part (ii) states that neither will the striker be out, should he play the ball a second time after it has been in contact with a fielder. However, he must not obstruct the fielder in any way, by word or action, and should he do so, an appeal under Law 37 would be justified.

Part 3 of this law makes it clear that a striker is only allowed to hit the ball more than once in making an effort to protect his wicket and that he may only use his bat "or any part of his person other than a hand not holding the bat" to do this. Even then he is barred from such action if by it he hinders any member of the fielding side. Should he do so, he will be dismissed under Law 37.

Law 34.4 deals with runs that can be scored from a ball struck lawfully more than once. Under the 1980 code a striker could have runs credited to his score by one of two actions taken by the fielding side: first, by the fielding side committing overthrows in an effort to dismiss either batsmen; and second, by a member of the fielding side illegally fielding the ball after the striker has hit it. Now, should the latter action take place, the five runs to be credited to the batting side will be under Law 41.2, "Fielding the ball", or 41.3, should the ball hit a protective helmet belonging to the fielding side. Those runs will not be credited to the striker, as under the previous code, but will be entered in the new penalty runs column in the scorebook.

It has always been the case that the striker must have played or attempted to play the ball with his bat, or to have taken action to avoid being hit by the ball for any runs to be allowed. Should he not have taken either of these actions, no runs will be allowed in the case of the overthrow situation. If such actions had not taken place during the first stroke, then again no runs will be allowed from any second or subsequent stroke. It is now made abundantly clear that, if a striker hits a ball more than once in the protection of his wicket, only if he has taken the actions set out in Law 34.4 (a) (i) (ii) and (iii) will any runs be allowed from a subsequent overthrow.

Law 34.4 (b) explains how runs are to be credited and by which of the two impacts of the ball coming into contact with the striker's bat or person. Should the striker take action legally a second time, from the same delivery, to prevent the ball from making contact with his wicket and should a member of the fielding side then commit overthrows in an effort to dismiss either batsman, the deciding factor in how the runs are to be recorded is the nature of the first contact. If the ball first made contact with the striker's bat and he then kicked the ball away, the runs scored will be credited to the striker. Conversely, if the first contact was the ball hitting the striker's person and he then hit it away with his bat in defence of his wicket, any overthrows would be credited as leg byes. Obviously, if the striker initially plays the ball with his bat and then hits the ball again in protecting his wicket, any subsequent overthrows will be scored to the striker. Similarly, if the ball had first made contact with his person and he had then kicked the ball away, any overthrows that followed would be recorded as leg byes.

Consider the following sequence of events. A ball is called and signalled a no ball and it then makes contact with the striker's person. Seeing the ball rolling toward his wicket, the striker kicks the ball away, constituting his second stroke. In this situation any subsequent overthrows will be credited as no balls plus, of course, the one run for the delivery of a no ball. By now you may be thinking that he had no need to kick the ball away, for he could not be out bowled from a no ball, and you would be right. However, I am sure that many batsmen, not realising this point in the heat of the moment, would take the action I have described and, should they do so, would not abuse this law. They must, however, accept the consequences of their actions, should they endeavour to take a run and the fielder's throw breaks the wicket.

Law 34.4 (c) explains exactly how runs are scored and credited under this law. The one thing that may appear strange here is that the initial run taken by the batsmen can only be allowed if they have not crossed when the throw is made. If the batsmen have embarked on the first run and the throw takes place before they have crossed, then that run will count. The reason for this is that the run will result from the overthrow; if they had crossed when the throw was made, it would not.

Law 34.5 (a) contains a point that I believe has never been made before. It is that, should the second stroke by the batsman in defence of his wicket be so hard that the ball reaches the boundary, the umpire will not allow the boundary allowance, as it did not ensue from any overthrow. Similarly, section (i) of Law 34.5 (b) states that if no overthrow takes place by a member of the fielding side but the batsmen complete a run, the umpire will call and signal "dead ball" and return the batsmen to their original wickets. Section (ii) says that, should a batsman be dismissed in such an incident or the ball is declared "dead" by the umpires for whatever reason, no-ball penalties or penalty runs, if appropriate, will be scored.

As an umpire, I have figured in few incidents of "hit the ball twice" and I have neither given out, or seen a striker given out, under this law. One of the few, however, was most unusual and I wonder how many umpires would have arrived at the correct decision. For a couple of minutes I wondered if I had.
It was in 1992 and I was umpiring a 2nd XI county match at Horsham between Sussex and Middlesex. The striker went onto his back foot and played a ball down onto the ground, from where it spun back towards his wicket. The striker knocked the ball away to a position of leg slip or leg gully, which was vacant at the time. As the striker looked round to see where the ball had gone, the non-striker from the end at which I was standing ran down the pitch, shouting to his team-mate "run, run".

The wicketkeeper moved over, gathered the ball and threw it at the striker's wicket, breaking it. An appeal rang out. "Not out" was the decision from my colleague as the non-striker had made his ground at that end. The wicketkeeper seeing that the striker had still some distance to go to make the ground at my end retrieved the ball which was lying only a few feet in front of him and threw it. It was another accurate throw and when it hit the stumps a further appeal rang out. "Not out" was my answer to it as the striker had made good his ground at the bowling end.

I then began to walk towards the wicket from my position some 15 to 20 yards away, square with the wicket. Thinking hard, I called and signalled "dead ball" and asked the batsmen to return to their original ends as I began to remake the wicket. Everyone looked a little bemused as I then signalled to the scorers "dead ball" and informed them "no run to count". Later I explained my decision to a fairly large gathering. As the run was gained from neither an overthrow or while an act of illegal fielding was taking place, it would not count. If either of the batsmen had been out of their ground when the wicket was put down, he would have been out under Law 28, "Run out". If the throw at either wicket had missed and runs had been taken, they would have been legitimately scored, but not the one which they had completed. That one did not result from the overthrow as the batsmen had crossed prior to the overthrow taking place. The entire incident must have looked most odd to those who witnessed it, seeing both sets of bails on the ground, both sets of stumps disturbed, both umpires remaking their wickets, both batsmen returning to their original ends and one umpire making various signals and calls to the scorers.

LAW 35
Hit Wicket

1. Out Hit wicket

The striker is out Hit wicket if, while the ball is in play, his wicket is put down either by the striker's bat or person as described in Law 28.1(a)(ii) and (iii) (Wicket put down)

either (i) in the course of any action taken by him in preparing to receive or in receiving a delivery,

or (ii) in setting off for his first run immediately after playing, or playing at, the ball,

or (iii) if he makes no attempt to play the ball, in setting off for his first run, providing that in the opinion of the umpire this is immediately after he has had the opportunity of playing the ball,

or (iv) in lawfully making a second or further stroke for the purpose of guarding his wicket within the provisions of Law 34.3 (Ball lawfully struck more than once).

2. Not out Hit wicket

Notwithstanding 1 above, the batsman is not out under this Law should his wicket be put down in any of the ways referred to in 1 above if

(a) it occurs after he has completed any action in receiving the delivery, other than as in 1(ii), (iii) or (iv) above.

(b) it occurs when he is in the act of running, other than in setting off immediately for his first run.

(c) it occurs when he is trying to avoid being run out or stumped.

(d) it occurs while he is trying to avoid a throw-in at any time.

(e) the bowler after starting his run up, or his bowling action if he has no run up, does not deliver the ball. In this case either umpire shall immediately call and signal Dead ball. See Law 23.3 (Umpire calling and signalling Dead ball).

(f) the delivery is a No ball.

While "hit wicket" was one of the original methods of dismissal, this law disappeared in 1744 and did not return until 1786. Its return was confirmed with a new form of wording in 1788. There was an addition to the law in 1821, that not only the striker's bat but also any part of his dress breaking the wicket would render him liable for dismissal under this law. It remained more or less the same until the 1980 code, when the addition of the wicket being broken by the striker's person when he sets off for his first run, immediately after playing, or playing at, the ball would leave the striker liable to be dismissed.

Thank goodness there is one law that has hardly changed. The one addition is to be found in Law 35.1 (iii). This points out that, even if the striker makes no attempt to play a ball but decides to take a run, should he break his wicket when setting off on this run, he is still liable to be given out under this law. All the umpire has to be sure of is that the breaking of the wicket was immediately after he had the opportunity of playing the ball.

Part 2 of Law 35, "Not out hit wicket", might appear new but is effectively what appeared in the notes section of Law 35 in the 1980 code.

LAW 36

LEG BEFORE WICKET

1. Out LBW
The striker is out LBW in the circumstances set out below.

        (a) The bowler delivers a ball, not being a No ball

and (b) the ball, if it is not intercepted full pitch, pitches in line between wicket and wicket or on the off side of the striker's wicket

and (c) the ball not having previously touched his bat, the striker intercepts the ball, either full-pitch or after pitching, with any part of his person

and (d) the point of impact, even if above the level of the bails,

either (i) is between wicket and wicket

or (ii) is either between wicket and wicket or outside the line of the off stump if the striker has made no genuine attempt to play the ball with his bat

and (e) but for the interception, the ball would have hit the wicket.

2. Interception of the ball
(a) In assessing points (c), (d) and (e) in 1 above only the first interception is to be considered.

(b) In assessing point (e) in 1 above, it is to be assumed that the path of the ball before interception would have continued after interception, irrespective of whether it might have pitched subsequently or not.

3. Off side of wicket
The off side of the striker's wicket shall be determined by the striker's stance at the moment the ball comes into play for that delivery.

This law causes more doubt, disagreement, debate and discussion than all of the other 41 put together. Having said that, it probably has fewer words to explain it than most of the others. I have always felt that this law was well written and the 2000 code endorses that view. Without going to great lengths, a couple of points that have given umpires some concern in the past have been clarified.

The origins of the LBW law are slightly hazy but it is said that even in the laws of 1744 an umpire was allowed to adjudicate on a batsman "standing unfair to strike". It was in the code of 1774 that a law was introduced whereby an umpire could give the striker out should he "put his leg before the wicket with a design to stop the ball and actually prevent the ball hitting the wicket by it". Note the use of the word "leg" rather than "person", which came later. From 1788 to 1937 there were various wordings in regard to the position of the pitching of the ball for an LBW appeal to be upheld. In the main they were that the ball must have pitched in a straight line between wicket and wicket. It was not until 1937 that a ball that pitched on the off side of a striker's wicket could produce a successful appeal, provided that the part of the striker's person which was hit was between wicket and wicket. This is another of the laws that has not changed in its application from the 1980 code.

The next major change came in the 1972 season and read as follows: "Should the umpire be of the opinion that the striker has made no genuine attempt to play the ball with his bat, he shall on appeal give the striker out LBW if he is satisfied that the ball would have hit the stumps, even though the ball pitched outside the off stump and even though any interception was also outside the off stump."

So to the 2000 code. Law 36.1 now sets down the five points that must be satisfied before a striker can be given out LBW. They are the same as in the 1980 code but are laid down in a much clearer style. Part (a) says that the delivery must not be a no ball, something that was not actually stated previously.

Law 36.2 (a) explains that it is only the first interception of the ball by the striker's person that will be considered by the umpire when he assesses any appeal. This, I hope, will stop the barrack-room lawyers from saying: "Ah, but the bat was immediately behind the part of the striker's pad which the ball struck, so it could not have hit the wicket."

I remember an incident at Worksop in 1976 when Nottinghamshire were playing Yorkshire. One of the Yorkshire batsmen played forward and his front pad was hit by a ball that had cut back at him. The part of the pad that was struck by the ball was some three inches outside the line of the off stump. After the initial contact, the ball went on to hit the striker's pad low down on his back leg, which was positioned some 3ft in front of the wicket. I must say that, but for this second interception, the ball most certainly would have hit the wicket. Mike Smedley, the Nottinghamshire captain, was not impressed when I turned down the LBW appeal and he approached me for an explanation at the end of the day's play. I am not sure that he realised until then that it is only the first interception that receives consideration in any appeal for LBW.

Law 36.2 (b) explains a point that has caused confusion for years. Some think that the word "pitch" in this law refers only to a ball alighting on the surface of the ground. That is not so, and never has been. I have heard it said by some that, if a ball hits the striker's pad low down in front of middle stump some 2ft in front of the wicket, they would always give the striker not out. When I have asked why, the answer has invariably been that "it could have deviated if it had pitched". I tell them that it had indeed pitched but had hit the pad "full pitch". They then go on to say: "Well, the bowler has turned the ball six inches every delivery for the last five overs and I assumed that this delivery would have done so as well." I then tell them that any umpire who assumes anything during a cricket match is not worth his salt. When making a decision, an umpire must only consider what has taken place with regard to that delivery which he had observed and no other. I believe that this part of Law 36, as written, will dispel all of those incorrect thoughts.

Law 36.3 has been written because of those batsmen who adopt the reverse sweep shot. There are those in recent years who have been able to change from a left-hand stance to a right-hand stance immediately prior to a bowler delivering the ball. We had to make a decision on these matters for a number of reasons. Firstly, under this law, especially Law 36.1 (b) (ii), the umpires need to know which is the striker's on side and which is his off side. A decision was also required under Law 41.5, "Limitation of on side fielders".

One of the suggestions I made was that consideration might be given to the delivery that is pitched outside the striker's leg stump. There was no chance of progress down that road and I knew there would be none but I did receive more support from the members of the working party than I received from the officers of the TCCB when I returned from New Zealand in 1981. I had just spent a full season umpiring under just such an experimental law and felt then, as I do now, that it should be given a try, as it would be for the good of the game of cricket.

For the time being there is no change to this law in this respect and it is very much a case of steady as you go. However, I do ask readers to study carefully Law 42.6 (b) (i), which will have a bearing upon the LBW decision and possibly an even greater bearing on injury to the striker. I fought very hard and long on this point but failed entirely to have it changed, or should I say, to stop the change.

In recent years this law has worked well in regard to the full-pitched delivery. To some extent it has stopped batsmen being injured and it has been easy for the umpire to interpret. I feel that now we are going backwards as the law will allow, and it states so, the striker to be hit by the ball between chin and waist by a full-pitched delivery. I believe that the law should not allow such contact to be made without penalty against the bowler and certainly he should not be allowed to profit from what was an illegal act under the previous law. We are now supposed to be charged with a "duty of care" to all of those who play the game and I feel that we are failing in our duty in this aspect of law.

When I umpire from now on, I cannot guarantee that the actions I take will be absolutely as written in law but they most certainly will be, as they always have been, in the best interests of the game of cricket.

LAW 37

Obstructing the Field

1. Out Obstructing the field
Either batsman is out Obstructing the field if he wilfully obstructs or distracts the opposing side by word or action. It shall be regarded as obstruction if either batsman wilfully, and without the consent of the fielding side, strikes the ball with his bat or person, other than a hand not holding the bat, after the ball has touched a fielder. See 4 below.

2. Accidental obstruction
It is for either umpire to decide whether any obstruction or distraction is wilful or not. He shall consult the other umpire if he has any doubt.

3. Obstructing a ball from being caught
The striker is out should wilful obstruction or distraction by either batsman prevent a catch being made.
This shall apply even though the striker causes the obstruction in lawfully guarding his wicket under the provisions of Law 34.3 (Ball lawfully struck more than once).

4. Returning the ball to a member of the fielding side
Either batsman is out under this Law if, without the consent of the fielding side and while the ball is in play, he uses his bat or person to return the ball to any member of that side.

5. Runs scored
If a batsman is dismissed under this Law, runs completed by the batsmen before the offence shall be scored, together with the penalty for a No ball or a Wide, if applicable. Other penalties that may be awarded to either side when the ball is dead shall also stand. See Law 42.17(b) (Penalty runs).

If, however, the obstruction prevents a catch from being made, runs completed by the batsmen before the offence shall not be scored, but other penalties that may be awarded to either side when the ball is dead shall stand. See Law 42.17(b) (Penalty runs).

6. Bowler does not get credit
The bowler does not get credit for the wicket.

The first mention of obstruction I have found in the laws was a directive in the code of 1744. It read that "if the fielding side obstructed a run, the umpires could order a 'notch' to be scored as a penalty". Therefore, those who read Law 42 of the 2000 code, and the many situations of how and when penalty runs can accrue, must not think that they are reading something new and revolutionary, for they would be 256 years out of date. In the same code we see the other side of the coin as the law on obstruction states that "if under the pretence of running a 'notch' or otherwise, either of the strikers [batsmen] prevents a ball from being caught, the striker of the ball is out".

In 1844 the law was extended to cover all acts of obstruction and, except for the case of a catch not being taken because of the obstruction, the batsman to be dismissed would be the one who actually committed the act of obstruction. For those unaware, a "notch" was the method by which runs were recorded during the match. The umpires originally, then followed by appointed scorers, took with them onto the field of play a stick and a knife and as each run was scored a notch would be cut into the stick.

Moving swiftly forward to the 2000 code, Law 37.1 explains that it is not only the physical or attempted physical obstruction of a fielder by the batsman that can lead to a decision of "Out obstructing the field". Should the obstruction be of a verbal nature and the umpire considers this type of obstruction deliberate, on appeal he shall give the offending batsman out under this law. The exception is when the obstruction prevents a catch from being taken and then it is always the striker of the ball who is dismissed, no matter which of the batsmen actually commits the act of obstruction.

Law 37.2 deals with "Accidental obstruction". In all cases of obstruction I feel that it is good practice for umpires to call and signal "dead ball" immediately. This may prevent any ill-feeling by either side towards the other at a later stage but will not negate other action which the umpires may take after consultation. Should the obstruction which took place be deemed to be of an accidental nature, then, if an appeal had been made, the "not out" decision would be the correct one. One run would be allowed to the batting side if the batsmen had crossed.

Part 3 of Law 37, "Obstructing a ball from being caught", has been explained above, and part 4, "Returning the ball to a member of the fielding side", was dealt with under Laws 33 and 34. A dismissal of this nature now comes under this law and not, as previously, under "Handled the ball" or "Hit the ball twice".

Some may think that we could have penalty runs scored to each side in certain situations and I cite the following incidents.

A no ball is delivered, which the striker hits. The batsmen run and have crossed on the fourth run when a fielder deliberately trips up one of the batsmen short of his ground. At this instant a total of ten runs will have been scored: one for the no ball, four run by the batsmen and five for the obstruction. Let us take the matter further. The batsman who has been felled then deliberately obstructs the fielder, who is endeavouring to throw the ball to the wicketkeeper to dismiss the striker. Why should the fielding side not receive five penalty runs? This part of Law 37 clearly states that "other penalties that may be awarded to either side when the ball is 'dead' should also stand" and I believe this to be correct. Unfortunately, though sensibly, the umpires would have taken action on the first act of obstruction by calling "dead ball" and therefore any further happenings would be null and void.

My thoughts then turned to parts 13 and 14 of Law 42, which is allied to this law, and I first looked at part 14, "Batsman damaging the pitch". I then realised that there could be a penalty-run situation where a batsman runs down the protected area for the third time and while doing so he is obstructed by a member of the fielding side. It is only when the act of obstruction takes place that the ball can be made "dead" by the umpire's call. Prior to that the umpire has decided that an award of five penalty runs is applicable, under Law 42.14 (c) (ii), but he is not able to make this award until the ball is "dead". So, in this situation, he will be making an award to both sides, and I bet that will test my scorer friends.

I then realised that, under Law 42.13, "Fielder damaging the pitch", it is possible to have two awards of penalty runs to one side off the same incident. Again the culmination of the incident is when an obstruction takes place and an award of five penalty runs is made. Prior to this the umpire has observed that a fielder is committing damage to the pitch. The umpires are not able to make this award until the ball is "dead" and therefore ten penalty runs can be awarded to the batting side from one delivery. I am not really sure that this was a situation we visualised and it all arises because the umpires cannot act until the ball is "dead".

I have made further relevant comments under Law 42.14 but, as all of the above incidents culminate with obstruction, I have discussed them under this law.

LAW 38
Run Out

1. Out Run out
(a) Either batsman is out Run out, except as in 2 below, if at any time while the ball is in play
      (i) he is out of his ground
and (ii) his wicket is fairly put down by the opposing side.
(b) (a) above shall apply even though No ball has been called and whether or not a run is being attempted, except in the circumstances of Law 39.3(b) (Not out Stumped).

2. Batsman not Run out
Notwithstanding 1 above, a batsman is not out Run out if
(a) he has been within his ground and has subsequently left it to avoid injury, when the wicket is put down.
(b) the ball has not subsequently been touched again by a fielder, after the bowler has entered his delivery stride, before the wicket is put down.
(c) the ball, having been played by the striker, or having come off his person, directly strikes a helmet worn by a fielder and without further contact with him or any other fielder rebounds directly on to the wicket. However, the ball remains in play and either batsman may be Run out in the circumstances of 1 above if a wicket is subsequently put down.
(d) he is out Stumped. See Law 39.1(b) (Out Stumped).
(e) he is out of his ground, not attempting a run and his wicket is fairly put down by the wicket-keeper without the intervention of another member of the fielding side, if No ball has been called. See Law 39.3(b) (Not out Stumped).

3. Which batsman is out
The batsman out in the circumstances of 1 above is the one whose

ground is at the end where the wicket is put down. See Laws 2.8 (Transgression of the Laws by a batsman who has a runner) and 29.2 (Which is a batsman's ground).

4. Runs scored

If a batsman is dismissed Run out, the batting side shall score the runs completed before the dismissal, together with the penalty for a No ball or a Wide, if applicable. Other penalties to either side that may be awarded when the ball is dead shall also stand. See Law 42.17 (Penalty runs).

If, however, a striker with a runner is himself dismissed Run out, runs completed by the runner and the other batsman before the dismissal shall not be scored. The penalty for a No ball or a Wide and any other penalties to either side that may be awarded when the ball is dead shall stand. See Laws 2.8 (Transgression of the Laws by a batsman who has a runner) and 42.17(b) (Penalty runs).

5. Bowler does not get credit

The bowler does not get credit for the wicket.

The following incident has been covered for a number of years and has now been inserted into the 2000 code. This is the incident. The striker is taking guard outside of his popping crease when he receives a no ball, which he plays away. The non-striker runs all the way down the pitch, passes the striker and makes the ground at the wicketkeeper's end. Throughout the whole of this action, the striker never moves, either forward or to regain his ground. The wicket at the bowling end is then broken and an appeal made. Is anyone out? If so, which batsman? The answers are "yes" and the striker. How? Run out at the bowling wicket. All of this matter was covered in "green sheet" No 3, published in April 1992, in response to a question that I raised.

Law 38.2 in the 1980 code, "No ball called", said that if a no ball has been called, the striker shall not be given run out unless he attempts to run. However, in the example above it would obviously be farcical not to give him out, whether he runs or not. Since that time the clarification has been made, that by remaining out of his ground the striker had acquiesced in running, even though he is stationary throughout the whole of the action.

The previous matter apart, I feel that this law is easy to understand, particularly the clarifications made to sections (a), (b) and (c) of part 2, "Batsman not run out".

Nonetheless, section (b) may raise a few eyebrows, as well as questions, and I must say that it is one of the changes in the 2000 code with which I do not agree. It must be realised that the bowler enters his delivery stride at the moment his back foot, for the final time, comes into contact with the ground prior to the delivery of the ball. It may not cause problems when the speed merchants are bowling but what about when we have a slow bowler who has a long, slow swing of the bowling arm. A non-striker who is very fast "out of the blocks", such as Derek Randall or Clive Radley of yesteryear, could really make a farce of this clarification. They would legitimately be in their ground as the bowler's back foot landed, six to nine feet in front of the popping crease by the time the bowler released the ball and, by the time the striker was playing the ball, they would have already been halfway down the pitch on their first run, all quite legitimately.

Admittedly, the old law did have a drawback in that an umpire at the bowler's wicket was unable to watch a bowler's feet and his hand about to release the ball simultaneously. A suggestion was put forward that it should be the landing of the bowler's front foot in the delivery stride. The umpire should be watching that anyway, in case he should transgress Law 24, "No ball", by an incorrect foot position. At that point we should also be observing the start and finish of the bowler's delivery stride. Should the bowler not have transgressed with either back or front foot at that time, then the delivery would be a fair one. Should the bowler retain hold of the ball after that time in an effort to dismiss the non-striker, that would be an unfair act and, under Law 42.15, a call of "dead ball" would be made by the umpire. I would prefer that five penalty runs be awarded to the batting side because this action is unfair if taken by the fielding side. However, my recommendation was not accepted. Perhaps it would be simpler if players just played to the spirit of the law. If they do not, we may see another reason, which would make 12 in all, for the award of penalty runs. As the law now stands, by bringing the action as far back in the delivery stride as we have, I believe it will create problems for umpires.

The clarification under Law 38.2 (c) is basically a good one as it explains that a dismissal may not take place if a ball comes directly back onto the wicket from contact with a fieldsman's helmet, after the ball has been played by the striker or after the ball has made contact with the striker's person. However, I do feel that the term "either wicket" should have been used instead of "the wicket", for it is not only the striker who would not be dismissed under such circumstances but also the non-striker.

Law 38.3 deals with "Which batsman is out" and here the old adage "he that be nearer the wicket which is put down" still holds good. The only time there can be an exception to this rule is when a striker is injured and has been granted the concession of a runner, as under Law 2.7.

Of course, in the case of a run-out decision against either batsman, there can still be a considerable number of runs to be credited to the batting side and this is covered under Law 38.4. There could easily be as many as nine, made up of three completed before the dismissal, one for a no ball and, should the fielding side transgress under Law 42, five penalty runs. If, under the same circumstances, an injured striker were using a runner and he himself were dismissed, then all of the runs would be credited except the three completed by the non-striker and the runner, even though their actions were quite legal.

LAW 39

Stumped

1. Out Stumped
(a) The striker is out Stumped if
- (i) he is out of his ground
- and (ii) he is receiving a ball which is not a No ball
- and (iii) he is not attempting a run
- and (iv) his wicket is put down by the wicket-keeper without the intervention of another member of the fielding side. Note Law 40.3 (Position of wicket-keeper).

(b) The striker is out Stumped if all the conditions of (a) above are satisfied, even though a decision of Run out would be justified.

2. Ball rebounding from wicket-keeper's person
(a) If the wicket is put down by the ball, it shall be regarded as having been put down by the wicket-keeper if the ball
- (i) rebounds on to the stumps from any part of his person or equipment, other than a protective helmet
- or (ii) has been kicked or thrown on to the stumps by the wicket-keeper.

(b) If the ball touches a helmet worn by the wicket-keeper, the ball is still in play but the striker shall not be out Stumped. He will, however, be liable to be Run out in these circumstances if there is subsequent contact between the ball and any member of the fielding side. Note, however, 3 below.

3. Not out Stumped
(a) If the striker is not out Stumped, he is liable to be out Run out if the conditions of Law 38 (Run out) apply, except as set out in (b) below.
(b) The striker shall not be out Run out if he is out of his ground, not attempting a run, and his wicket is fairly put down by the wicket-keeper

without the intervention of another member of the fielding side, if No ball has been called.

There are dismissals recorded under this law going back to the 1740s, well over 250 years, and yet throughout all of those years there have been few changes or clarifications to this law, apart from the law number. "Stumped" was one of the original methods of dismissal and it was in 1811 that the law stated that the only way that a striker could be out off a no ball was "run out". This leaves the impression that, prior to that date, a striker could perhaps be stumped off a no ball. In 1912 this law stated that "the striker is not able to be stumped off a no ball but may be run out", thereby endorsing the thought that a stumping could be effected off a no ball before 1811.

The wording of the law in 1912 caused a great deal of confusion for a number of years. If the striker played a no ball and contact with bat or hand holding bat was made with the ball and the striker was out of his ground, should the wicket be put down by the wicketkeeper, the striker would be given out "run out" under Law 28, the number of the run-out law at that time.

It was not until the 1947 code that it was made clear that for a striker to be run out, he must be attempting a run, not merely just standing out of his ground. If he was out of his ground but not attempting to run, he would, of course, be out under this law.

Law 39.2 deals with the "Ball rebounding from wicketkeeper's person" and section (b) gives the ruling that, if the wicketkeeper is wearing a protective helmet, exactly as in the case of a fielder wearing one, no dismissal is allowed, should a ball, after making contact with the striker's bat or person, rebound from the helmet directly onto the stumps, obviously breaking the wicket. Again, as in the previous law, I wish that the term "either wicket" had been used. The law makes it quite clear that the striker is not able to be out "stumped" under these circumstances and I am well aware that a non-striker is never able to be out under this law but neither is the non-striker able to be out "run out" if a ball makes contact with the helmet worn by a wicketkeeper and flies straight back down the pitch to break the wicket at the opposite end with the non-striker out of his ground.

In this part of the law it is made clear that, after contact with a helmet worn by the wicketkeeper, the ball is not "dead". It then states that the striker shall not be out stumped but can be run out if the ball is in subsequent contact with a member of the fielding side. Remember, a wicketkeeper is also a member of the fielding side.

As stated, the ball is not "dead" and should any member of the fielding side come into contact with the ball and effect a dismissal, except as above, this will be allowed. I can think of a number of possible situations that bother me here, even though a dismissal would be quite legal. Take, for instance, a ball making contact with the wicketkeeper's helmet and going a few feet into the air behind him. The non-striker, seeing this and thinking that the ball had carried a distance, calls the striker for a run and they both embark upon it. Unfortunately for the striker, the slip fielder reaches up, catches the ball and throws down the wicket at his end with the striker a couple of paces out of his ground. This is a legitimate dismissal, not under this law but under the previous one, Law 38, "Run out". Although this dismissal could have been considered fortunate, it shows how vigilant the non-striker must be before calling his colleague for a run.

Or take this situation. A wicketkeeper is standing close up to the stumps with a spin bowler operating. The striker is out of his ground when he makes a slight contact with the ball with his bat. The ball flies up and hits the wicketkeeper's helmet, then removes a bail from the wicket before reaching the ground. Seeing this, the striker sets off on the first pace of a run. The wicketkeeper kicks the ball onto the wicket and removes the other bail. Again a decision of "out" is correct, and some may think the striker to be unfortunate.

Should confusion arise concerning this law and Law 38, "Run out", it may have been caused by the last six words of part 3 (b) of this law. Basically, what this states is that "the striker shall not be run out if he is out of his ground, not attempting a run, and his wicket is fairly put down by the wicketkeeper without the intervention of another member of the fielding side, *if no ball has been called*". I say that he most certainly can be, as in the incident which I describe under Law 38. The wicketkeeper can hold the ball until the non-striker has crossed the striker in running and the wicketkeeper can throw the ball and break the wicket at the opposite end. The words "his wicket" are the ones which determine that the decision is correct, because "his wicket", the striker's, is now at the bowling end. He that be nearest the wicket which is put down, running or not.

LAW 40

The Wicket-keeper

1. Protective equipment

The wicket-keeper is the only member of the fielding side permitted to wear gloves and external leg guards. If he does so, these are to be regarded as part of his person for the purposes of Law 41.2 (Fielding the ball). If by his actions and positioning it is apparent to the umpires that he will not be able to discharge his duties as a wicket-keeper, he shall forfeit this right and also the right to be recognised as a wicket-keeper for the purposes of Laws 32.3 (A fair catch), 39 (Stumped), 41.1 (Protective equipment), 41.5 (Limitation of on side fielders) and 41.6 (Fielders not to encroach on the pitch).

2. Gloves

If the wicket-keeper wears gloves as permitted under 1 above, they shall have no webbing between fingers except that a single piece of flat non-stretch material may be inserted between index finger and thumb solely as a means of support. This insert shall not form a pouch when the hand is extended. See Appendix C.

3. Position of wicket-keeper

The wicket-keeper shall remain wholly behind the wicket at the striker's end from the moment the ball comes into play until
(a) a ball delivered by the bowler
either (i)   touches the bat or person of the striker
or   (ii) passes the wicket at the striker's end
or (b) the striker attempts a run.
In the event of the wicket-keeper contravening this Law, the umpire at the striker's end shall call and signal No ball as soon as possible after the delivery of the ball.

4. Movement by wicket-keeper

It is unfair if a wicket-keeper standing back makes a significant movement towards the wicket after the ball comes into play and before it reaches the striker. In the event of such unfair movement by the wicket-keeper, either umpire shall call and signal Dead ball. It will not be considered a significant movement if the wicket-keeper moves a few paces forward for a slower delivery.

5. Restriction on actions of wicket-keeper

If the wicket-keeper interferes with the striker's right to play the ball and to guard his wicket, the striker shall not be out, except under Laws 33 (Handled the ball), 34 (Hit the ball twice), 37 (Obstructing the field) or 38 (Run out).

6. Interference with wicket-keeper by striker

If, in playing at the ball or in the legitimate defence of his wicket, the striker interferes with the wicket-keeper, he shall not be out, except as provided for in Law 37.3 (Obstructing a ball from being caught).

This law has seen considerable change, something that has been brought about by wicketkeepers trying to enhance their own performance as well as those of their side. The working party, along with the members of the redrafting committee, felt that what was taking place was going far beyond the best interests of the game of cricket and have taken steps to redress the balance.

In my first *Wisden Book of Cricket Laws*, I made mention of the point that, in the early days of the game, a wicketkeeper wore no protection whatsoever, not even gloves. Now, under Law 40.1, mention is made of gloves and external leg guards for the first time. It is the gloves that have caused the working party such problems and in the future they may well cause problems for the custodian.

I have mentioned that the wicketkeeper is allowed to wear certain protective apparel while discharging his duties. While wearing such items it now means that, if he is not in a position to discharge his duties as a wicketkeeper, he will in most situations lose all of the rights appertaining to such a position, along with the chance of the dismissal of a batsman under most of the laws. If umpires have to act under this law, all they are able to do is to award five penalty runs, as in Law 42.2, should he take a ball in his gloves while out of position.

There is no call of "dead ball" if he is in a position where the umpires feel that he is not able to discharge his duties. All he relinquishes is the right to effect certain dismissals, i.e. caught and stumped. He will commit his side to penalty runs should he stop the ball with the protective equipment which he may be wearing and a no-ball penalty by illegal positioning under Law 41.5, or should he position himself in front of the striker's wicket. Having stated all of this, it must be remembered that he is always a member of the fielding side. I ask this question: should he be behind the wicket in a gully position and field the ball in a hand not wearing a glove and he then throws the wicket down with the batsman out of his ground and an appeal is made, where in this law can you find reason for a "not out" decision?

Law 40.3, on the "Position of wicketkeeper", clarifies what a wicketkeeper can and cannot do. Where should a wicketkeeper be to assume his correct position, you may ask? Well, as I see things, he must be behind the batting wicket and at a reasonable distance so as to arrest the passage of the ball that has been delivered by the bowler. He, I am sure, along with the lawmakers, will feel that he should be at a distance to endeavour to effect a catch, should the conditions of Law 32 apply, again in a position to the rear of the striker's wicket.

Should a slow bowler be operating, his position should be in close proximity to that wicket so that he can effect a stumping under Law 41. There will, of course, be variations in the distance of the wicketkeeper's position behind the stumps, depending on the ability of the individual. I have observed many amazing dismissals of a batsman by a wicketkeeper while standing very close to the batting wicket, even when bowlers of great pace have been operating.

The whole point of Law 40.1 is that, should the wicketkeeper not be in the position which I have described when the ball is bowled, or at least close to it, he should not be wearing the protective equipment that he is allowed. If he is not in such a position when the ball is bowled, he, and therefore his team, will lose certain rights in regard to the dismissal of a batsman and could also have penalty runs imposed against them. Should he make a catch or a stumping, the decision will be "not out" and five penalty runs will be awarded to the batting side's total. I already hear people saying that he must be behind the stumps and in close proximity to them to effect a stumping. Not so. He could have positioned himself some five yards away from the wicket in a backward short leg position. The delivery by the bowler encounters the striker's person and rolls out to that member of the fielding side, who picks up the ball in the gloved hand and throws down the wicket with the striker out of his ground. The striker is not out stumped, because of the gloved person's position, and five penalty runs go to the batting side.

There may also be abuse of Law 41.5 by the person who wears pads and gloves, should he take up a position well to the leg side of the striker's wicket, since he could be the fielder who makes more than two behind the line of the popping crease on that side.

Also, should he field the ball with either his gloves or external leg guards while he is in any illegal position, this again will be an award to the batting side of five penalty runs. I know that we should not allow this member of the fielding side to wear pads and gloves if he is not in a position to discharge his duties as a wicketkeeper but, if it should happen, that is how I see the penalties applying.

After a study of Law 40.4, "Movement by wicketkeeper", some may think that it places a great imposition on him. I am sure nobody feels that a wicketkeeper should be tied to a stake to perform his duties but there have been instances of a striker being stumped when he had thought and observed that the wicketkeeper was many yards behind the wicket. Indeed, so he was when the bowler began his approach to deliver the ball but, either through collusion or his own initiative, the wicketkeeper had moved surreptitiously and unobserved to a position close enough to effect a stumping by the time the ball passed the striker. This action is now deemed unfair. While the wicketkeeper is allowed to adjust his position a little and move forward a pace or two after the ball comes into play, should there be a "significant" movement forward by him, either umpire is empowered to call and signal "dead ball". Indeed, he must do so. Judging what is "significant" may cause some umpires problems but I feel that it applies to any movement that might give the wicketkeeper even the slightest of unfair advantages.

By reading Law 40.2, "Gloves", and by observing appendix C, it will be seen that the webbing in such items must not form a pouch when thumb and forefinger are extended and spread as wide as an individual's span will allow. When a piece of strap was first inserted and fastened into the aperture that these two digits form, it was for protection of them and to stop the thumb from being bent backwards. Since that time and certainly over the past decade I have seen webbing on wicketkeepers' gloves that corresponded in size to my catching glove when I played for Grimsby Redwings ice hockey team as a netminder. Wicketkeepers are now deliberately catching a ball in the pouch formed by the webbing, and not using palms or fingers at all. I am not qualified to judge whether Mark Boucher, the South Africa wicketkeeper, is good in that position or not but I do know that he rarely drops a catch. With the size of the pouch on his glove, I do not wonder. His gloves now resemble those that the netminders in the National Hockey League use in the United States and Canada. They could easily encapsulate a football, let alone a cricket ball, and possibly both at the same time. By doing this, Mark has not abused any of the laws of the game but he is certainly setting a trend that is not in its best interests. Restrictions have therefore been set down in the 2000 code under Law 40.2 and in doing so we took the advice of some of the greatest wicketkeepers the game has seen, including Alan Knott.

We first felt that a maximum measurement along the top of the piece of webbing would suffice but soon realised that this was impracticable. If we had made it not of any great length it may well have restricted the individual who had a huge hand. Indeed it could have been dangerous for him. Conversely, if we had made the length greater to accommodate the large hand, we would have defeated the object of the exercise and knowingly have abused the law, as it would have immediately formed a pouch for those with a small hand.

Parts 3, 5 and 6 of Law 40 in the 2000 code are the same as parts 1, 2 and 3 of that law in the 1980 code, except for one change of reference number. The other parts of Law 40, parts 1, 2 and 4, are the ones under which we have brought in the many restrictions that are now placed on a wicketkeeper. I have known and still know some brilliant wicketkeepers. They are great guys and gentlemen but they have failed to keep their own house in order, which has caused us to have to do it for them. I do not think that we have been hard on them. There are greater sins in the game at the present time, and the greatest of them a wicketkeeper is certainly unable to undertake with his gloves on.

LAW 41

THE FIELDER

1. Protective equipment
No member of the fielding side other than the wicket-keeper shall be permitted to wear gloves or external leg guards. In addition, protection for the hand or fingers may be worn only with the consent of the umpires.

2. Fielding the ball
A fielder may field the ball with any part of his person but if, while the ball is in play he wilfully fields it otherwise,

(a) the ball shall become dead and 5 penalty runs shall be awarded to the batting side. See Law 42.17 (Penalty runs).

(b) the umpire shall inform the other umpire, the captain of the fielding side, the batsmen and, as soon as practicable, the captain of the batting side of what has occurred.

(c) the umpires together shall report the occurrence as soon as possible to the Executive of the fielding side and any Governing Body responsible for the match who shall take such action as is considered appropriate against the captain and player concerned.

3. Protective helmets belonging to the fielding side
Protective helmets, when not in use by fielders, shall only be placed, if above the surface, on the ground behind the wicket-keeper and in line with both sets of stumps. If a helmet belonging to the fielding side is on the ground within the field of play, and the ball while in play strikes it, the ball shall become dead. 5 penalty runs shall then be awarded to the batting side. See Laws 18.11 (Runs scored when ball becomes dead) and 42.17 (Penalty runs).

4. Penalty runs not to be awarded
Notwithstanding 2 and 3 above, if from the delivery by the bowler, the

ball first struck the person of the striker and if, in the opinion of the umpire, the striker
neither   (i)   attempted to play the ball with his bat,
nor   (ii) tried to avoid being hit by the ball,
then no award of 5 penalty runs shall be made and no other runs or penalties shall be credited to the batting side except the penalty for a No ball if applicable. See Law 26.3 (Leg byes not to be awarded).

5. Limitation of on side fielders
At the instant of the bowler's delivery there shall not be more than two fielders, other than the wicket-keeper, behind the popping crease on the on side. A fielder will be considered to be behind the popping crease unless the whole of his person, whether grounded or in the air, is in front of this line.
In the event of infringement of this Law by the fielding side the umpire at the striker's end shall call and signal No ball.

6. Fielders not to encroach on the pitch
While the ball is in play and until the ball has made contact with the bat or person of the striker, or has passed the striker's bat, no fielder, other than the bowler, may have any part of his person grounded on or extended over the pitch.
In the event of infringement of this Law by any fielder other than the wicket-keeper, the umpire at the bowler's end shall call and signal No ball as soon as possible after the delivery of the ball. Note, however, Law 40.3 (Position of wicket-keeper).

7. Movement by fielders
Any significant movement by any fielder after the ball comes into play and before the ball reaches the striker is unfair. In the event of such unfair movement, either umpire shall call and signal Dead ball. Note also the provisions of Law 42.4 (Deliberate attempt to distract striker).

8. Definition of significant movement
(a) For close fielders anything other than minor adjustments to stance or position in relation to the striker is significant.
(b) In the outfield, fielders are permitted to move in towards the striker

or striker's wicket, provided that 5 above is not contravened. Anything other than slight movement off line or away from the striker is to be considered significant.

(c) For restrictions on movement by the wicket-keeper see Law 40.4 (Movement by wicket-keeper).

There was little written in the early codes in regard to this law. It was a law that did not see the light of day until 1798, when it said that there would be "a penalty of 5 runs if the fieldsman stop a ball with his hat". Top hats were common in those days and must have come in useful for trying to stop the ball. Presumably that is why the law was framed.

No additions were made to this law until 1936 when it was made clear that the penalty of five runs was in addition to any runs already made.

Prior to 1968, when another experimental law was brought in, no more than five fielders could be positioned on the leg side of the striker's wicket. That experimental law was, in effect, what is now stated in Law 41.5 of the 2000 code, that "there shall be not more than two fielders, other than the wicketkeeper, behind the popping crease on the on side". This experimental law was brought into the full code in 1970.

A further experimental law, introduced for the 1975 season, prohibited "any fieldsman standing with any part of his body within the close cut area of the pitch extending five feet either side of the middle stump". This was brought into the full code under Law 41 in 1980 and, while it is now worded slightly differently, it is the essence of Law 41.6 of the 2000 code.

To my mind, Law 40, "The wicketkeeper", and Law 41, "The Fielder", hinge on one another to a very great extent. Law 41 is easy to understand and the small changes that have been made are clearly defined.

Part 1, "Protective equipment", reinforces the point that, except for the wicketkeeper, no member of the fielding side can wear external leg guards or gloves. It fails to point out, however, and I think that it should, that any other protective equipment worn by fielders must not be external, except, of course, a protective helmet. Many items of protective equipment are now worn by close fielders under their cricket clothing. Some of them wear more than I did as an ice-hockey netminder, shoulder harness, chest pad and elbow pads being the norm.

There is an important change of wording to Law 41.2, "Fielding the ball". Whereas the 1980 code stated that "The Fieldsman may *stop* the ball with any part of his person," the 2000 code says that "A fielder may *field* the ball with any part of his person". Because of the word "stop", umpires may not always have taken action under this law when they should have done so. Now with the word "field" replacing it, they have no excuse. Some people will think that both words mean the same but, remember, you can have a misfield.

In New Zealand I recall seeing a player give valiant chase round the boundary in an effort to cut off the ball. He got a foot to the ball and, in running past it, took off his "floppy" in exasperation and deliberately threw it at the ball. The ball encountered the hat and then trickled over the boundary line. My colleague signalled a boundary allowance of four runs, his reasoning being that, in using his "floppy", the fielder had not *stopped* the ball from crossing the boundary line.

You could have a situation much closer to the striker, where he has hit the ball quite hard and a fielder throws his hat, sweater or drying cloth at the ball. The fielder's action slows the ball's progress to the boundary, enabling it to be fielded. While, in taking this action, the fielder neither "stopped" nor "fielded" the ball, it is, to my mind, still illegal. It may be that "field" is not the best choice of word; perhaps "impede" or "arrest" would have been better.

I have been asked the following question and I do hope I am not asked it again: If the bowler is walking back to his mark with the drying cloth in his hand and, when the ball is thrown to him, he catches the ball in the hand holding the cloth, should five penalty runs be awarded against the fielding side? No, No, No. One reason is that he has not "stopped" the ball with the cloth, he has "stopped" the ball with the hand; or, under the new law, he has not "fielded" the ball with the drying cloth but with his hand. But the real reason for not making the award is that the action which the bowler is taking is a help to the game, not a hindrance. Such umpiring might not earn any marks in an ACU&S exam but it would be for the good of the game of cricket and that is what an umpire should remember, as well as the written word.

There have been many instances of illegal fielding, in which the wicketkeeper's glove has been used by another member of the fielding side to catch a ball, when returned from the outfield. I umpired a match at Edgbaston when an 8 was credited to the Warwickshire score for such action being taken by a Northamptonshire fielder.

I have also been told about a match at Chelmsford, where a most unusual case of illegal fielding took place involving the use of a bat. Apparently, one of the batsmen had dropped his bat while taking a run and had continued without it. As the ball was returned from the outfield, one of the Essex fielders picked up the bat and arrested the passage of the ball with it as it was about to cross the pitch. He had "wilfully fielded it otherwise" than with his person and thus had broken Law 41. There was certainly never a dull moment when the Essex boys were in the field.

There was a late clarification, which is laid down under Law 2.6, "Player returning without permission", but I felt that it would be better to point it out under this law. In the situation described under Law 2.6, where a fielder enters the field of play without the umpires' permission and brings himself into contact with the ball, it is clearly an act of illegal fielding. As in all cases of illegal fielding, the award should be five runs. The cross-reference to this is found in Law 42.17, "Penalty runs".

Law 41.3 deals with "Protective helmets belonging to the fielding side". I have been involved on more than one occasion in awarding five runs for a fielder's helmet being struck by the ball while it has been placed on the ground behind the wicketkeeper. In a match at Hinckley between the 2nd XIs of Leicestershire and

Middlesex, it happened twice. The second time was when Peter Hepworth delicately swept a ball so fine that it hit the helmet behind the wicketkeeper. At the end of the over I remarked to him that it was an easy manner in which to obtain five runs to add to his personal score. His reply was: "Yes, and I did it in the last match as well!" However, under the 2000 code, those five runs will not be credited to the striker but will be credited to a side's total as penalty runs in the new column in the scorebook.

The strangest incident in which I have been involved, in regard to a helmet being placed on the ground behind the wicketkeeper, took place in Sri Lanka in 1991. Western Districts were playing Southern Districts in Colombo. The bowler from my end delivered a no ball which was short-pitched and it bounced past the striker and the wicketkeeper. I thought that it was going to land directly on the helmet but it passed over it, bounced again and went on its way towards the boundary. The batsmen were initially not going to run as they thought the ball would reach the boundary but, as an afterthought, they ran through for one when they observed the long-leg fielder closing on the ball.

The fielder's throw was short and landed on the helmet, the ball shooting off towards the square-leg boundary. Seeing this, the batsmen furiously set off on another run. While the impact of the ball on the helmet made it automatically "dead" from that moment, I felt it best to call "dead ball" and to signal this information in order to stop everybody running around in various directions. There was of course much hilarity and, after I had returned the batsmen to the opposite wickets from which they had started, I very deliberately, using a signal and verbal instructions, acquainted the scorers with certain facts. The only signal was a repeat of the "no ball" signal and I shouted "and that is six of them". The reason for relating this story is to show that it is just as much illegal fielding if the ball encounters the helmet on the way back as on the way out.

In this part of the new law, there is a statement in reference to the helmet and where it can be placed, i.e. "on the ground behind the wicketkeeper and in line with both sets of stumps". This is nearly always impossible, for if it were placed in line with both sets of stumps, it very rarely is behind the wicketkeeper. I would have preferred the law to have just stated, "behind the wicketkeeper", for it is usually his intervention that stops the ball from hitting the helmet. How many times do we see a bowler change from over the wicket to around the wicket? And when he changes to this mode of delivery, the first action that the wicketkeeper takes is to move the helmet about three yards to a position which first slip has just vacated, so as the helmet is behind the wicketkeeper when he takes up his new position. The helmet then is most certainly not "in line with both sets of stumps".

Under Law 41.4, "Penalty runs not to be awarded", it is emphasised again that the striker must have made an attempt to play the ball or to have taken some avoiding action from being hit by the ball, before any addition to the score, other than byes, can be made. The exception, of course, is the one run for the penalty of the delivery of a no ball or a wide ball. So the old adage still holds good: no shot, no run.

Parts 5 and 6 of this law detail certain areas of the field of play in which fielders may not be positioned or make restrictions on the number present in a particular area. These are as before, as is the action that should be taken by the umpires should any transgression of these parts of the law take place.

Part 7, "Movement by fielders", and part 8, "Definition of significant movement", have come into being as a direct result of the incident involving Mike Gatting and Shakoor Rana in Faisalabad a few years ago. Individual umpires may have a vastly different interpretation of what constitutes a "significant" movement. Part 8 endeavours to define such movement but, in the end, it will have to be left to each individual umpire.

In regard to section (a) of part 8, I believe that if any movement is a distraction to the striker, an immediate call of "dead ball" must be made. Similarly, under (b), should any movement gain an unfair advantage for the fielding side, a call of "dead ball" would again be appropriate. Finally, section (c) cross-refers to Law 40.4, "Movement by wicketkeeper", and I feel that I have covered this fully under Law 40.

LAW 42

Fair ang Unfair Play

1. Fair and unfair play – responsibility of captains
The responsibility lies with the captains for ensuring that play is conducted within the spirit and traditions of the game, as described in The Preamble – The Spirit of Cricket, as well as within the Laws.

2. Fair and unfair play – responsibility of umpires
The umpires shall be the sole judges of fair and unfair play. If either umpire considers an action, not covered by the Laws, to be unfair, he shall intervene without appeal and, if the ball is in play, shall call and signal Dead ball and implement the procedure as set out in 18 below. Otherwise the umpires shall not interfere with the progress of play, except as required to do so by the Laws.

3. The match ball – changing its condition
(a) Any fielder may
    (i) polish the ball provided that no artificial substance is used and that such polishing wastes no time.
    (ii) remove mud from the ball under the supervision of the umpire.
    (iii) dry a wet ball on a towel.
(b) It is unfair for anyone to rub the ball on the ground for any reason, interfere with any of the seams or the surface of the ball, use any implement, or take any other action whatsoever which is likely to alter the condition of the ball, except as permitted in (a) above.
(c) The umpires shall make frequent and irregular inspections of the ball.
(d) In the event of any fielder changing the condition of the ball unfairly, as set out in (b) above, the umpires after consultation shall
    (i) change the ball forthwith. It shall be for the umpires to decide on the replacement ball, which shall, in their opinion, have

        had wear comparable with that which the previous ball had received immediately prior to the contravention.
- (ii) inform the batsmen that the ball has been changed.
- (iii) award 5 penalty runs to the batting side. See 17 below.
- (iv) inform the captain of the fielding side that the reason for the action was the unfair interference with the ball.
- (v) inform the captain of the batting side as soon as practicable of what has occurred.
- (vi) report the occurrence as soon as possible to the Executive of the fielding side and any Governing Body responsible for the match, who shall take such action as is considered appropriate against the captain and team concerned.

(e) If there is any further instance of unfairly changing the condition of the ball in that innings, the umpires after consultation shall
- (i) repeat the procedure in (d)(i), (ii) and (iii) above.
- (ii) inform the captain of the fielding side of the reason for the action taken and direct him to take off forthwith the bowler who delivered the immediately preceding ball. The bowler thus taken off shall not be allowed to bowl again in that innings.
- (iii) inform the captain of the batting side as soon as practicable of what has occurred.
- (iv) report this further occurrence as soon as possible to the Executive of the fielding side and any Governing Body responsible for the match, who shall take such action as is considered appropriate against the captain and team concerned.

4. Deliberate attempt to distract striker

It is unfair for any member of the fielding side deliberately to attempt to distract the striker while he is preparing to receive or receiving a delivery.
(a) If either umpire considers that any action by a member of the fielding side is such an attempt, at the first instance he shall
- (i) immediately call and signal Dead ball.
- (ii) warn the captain of the fielding side that the action is unfair and indicate that this is a first and final warning.
- (iii) inform the other umpire and the batsmen of what has occurred.

Neither batsman shall be dismissed from that delivery and the ball shall not count as one of the over.

(b) If there is any further such deliberate attempt in that innings, by any member of the fielding side, the procedures, other than warning, as set out in (a) above shall apply. Additionally, the umpire at the bowler's end shall

- (i) award 5 penalty runs to the batting side. See 17 below.
- (ii) inform the captain of the fielding side of the reason for this action and, as soon as practicable, inform the captain of the batting side.
- (iii) report the occurrence, together with the other umpire, as soon as possible to the Executive of the fielding side and any Governing Body responsible for the match, who shall take such action as is considered appropriate against the captain and player or players concerned.

5. Deliberate distraction or obstruction of batsman

In addition to 4 above, it is unfair for any member of the fielding side, by word or action, wilfully to attempt to distract or to obstruct either batsman after the striker has received the ball.

(a) It is for either one of the umpires to decide whether any distraction or obstruction is wilful or not.

(b) If either umpire considers that a member of the fielding side has wilfully caused or attempted to cause such a distraction or obstruction he shall

- (i) immediately call and signal Dead ball.
- (ii) inform the captain of the fielding side and the other umpire of the reason for the call.

Additionally,

- (iii) neither batsman shall be dismissed from that delivery.
- (iv) 5 penalty runs shall be awarded to the batting side. See 17 below. In this instance, the run in progress shall be scored, whether or not the batsmen had crossed at the instant of the call. See Law 18.11 (Runs scored when ball becomes dead).
- (v) the umpire at the bowler's end shall inform the captain of the fielding side of the reason for this action and, as soon as practicable, inform the captain of the batting side.

(vi) the umpires shall report the occurrence as soon as possible to the Executive of the fielding side and any Governing Body responsible for the match, who shall take such action as is considered appropriate against the captain and player or players concerned.

6. Dangerous and unfair bowling
(a) Bowling of fast short pitched balls
 (i) The bowling of fast short pitched balls is dangerous and unfair if the umpire at the bowler's end considers that by their repetition and taking into account their length, height and direction they are likely to inflict physical injury on the striker, irrespective of the protective equipment he may be wearing. The relative skill of the striker shall be taken into consideration.
 (ii) Any delivery which, after pitching, passes or would have passed over head height of the striker standing upright at the crease, although not threatening physical injury, is unfair and shall be considered as part of the repetition sequence in (i) above.
 The umpire shall call and signal No ball for each such delivery.

(b) Bowling of high full pitched balls
 (i) Any delivery, other than a slow paced one, which passes or would have passed on the full above waist height of the striker standing upright at the crease is to be deemed dangerous and unfair, whether or not it is likely to inflict physical injury on the striker.
 (ii) A slow delivery which passes or would have passed on the full above shoulder height of the striker standing upright at the crease is to be deemed dangerous and unfair, whether or not it is likely to inflict physical injury on the striker.

7. Dangerous and unfair bowling – action by the umpire
(a) In the event of dangerous and/or unfair bowling, as defined in 6 above, by any bowler, except as in 8 below, at the first instance the umpire

at the bowler's end shall call and signal No ball and, when the ball is dead, caution the bowler, inform the other umpire, the captain of the fielding side and the batsmen of what has occurred. This caution shall continue to apply throughout the innings.

(b) If there is a second instance of such dangerous and/or unfair bowling by the same bowler in that innings, the umpire at the bowler's end shall repeat the above procedure and indicate to the bowler that this is a final warning.

Both the above caution and final warning shall continue to apply even though the bowler may later change ends.

(c) Should there be a further instance by the same bowler in that innings, the umpire shall

- (i) call and signal No ball.
- (ii) direct the captain, when the ball is dead, to take the bowler off forthwith. The over shall be completed by another bowler, who shall neither have bowled the previous over nor be allowed to bowl the next over.
   The bowler thus taken off shall not be allowed to bowl again in that innings.
- (iii) report the occurrence to the other umpire, the batsmen and, as soon as practicable, the captain of the batting side.
- (iv) report the occurrence, with the other umpire, as soon as possible to the Executive of the fielding side and to any Governing Body responsible for the match, who shall take such action as is considered appropriate against the captain and bowler concerned.

8. Deliberate bowling of high full pitched balls

If the umpire considers that a high full pitch which is deemed to be dangerous and unfair, as defined in 6(b) above, was deliberately bowled, then the caution and warning prescribed in 7 above shall be dispensed with. The umpire shall

(a) call and signal No ball.

(b) direct the captain, when the ball is dead, to take the bowler off forthwith.

(c) implement the remainder of the procedure as laid down in 7(c) above.

9. Time wasting by the fielding side

It is unfair for any member of the fielding side to waste time.

(a) If the captain of the fielding side wastes time, or allows any member of his side to waste time, or if the progress of an over is unnecessarily slow, at the first
instance the umpire shall call and signal Dead ball if necessary and

- (i) warn the captain, and indicate that this is a first and final warning.
- (ii) inform the other umpire and the batsmen of what has occurred.

(b) If there is any further waste of time in that innings, by any member of the fielding side, the umpire shall
either (i) if the waste of time is not during the course of an over, award 5 penalty runs to the batting side. See 17 below.
or (ii) if the waste of time is during the course of an over, when the ball is dead, direct the captain to take the bowler off forthwith. If applicable, the over shall be completed by another bowler, who shall neither have bowled the previous over nor be allowed to bowl the next over.
The bowler thus taken off shall not be allowed to bowl again in that innings.
- (iii) inform the other umpire, the batsmen and, as soon as practicable, the captain of the batting side, of what has occurred.
- (iv) report the occurrence, with the other umpire, as soon as possible to the Executive of the fielding side and to any Governing Body responsible for the match, who shall take such action as is considered appropriate against the captain and team concerned.

10. Batsman wasting time

It is unfair for a batsman to waste time. In normal circumstances the striker should always be ready to take strike when the bowler is ready to start his run up.

(a) Should either batsman waste time by failing to meet this requirement, or in any other way, the following procedure shall be adopted. At the first instance, either before the bowler starts his run up

or when the ball is dead, as appropriate, the umpire shall
- (i) warn the batsman and indicate that this is a first and final warning. This warning shall continue to apply throughout the innings. The umpire shall so inform each incoming batsman.
- (ii) inform the other umpire, the other batsman and the captain of the fielding side of what has occurred.
- (iii) inform the captain of the batting side as soon as practicable.

(b) if there is any further time wasting by any batsman in that innings, the umpire shall, at the appropriate time while the ball is dead
- (i) award 5 penalty runs to the fielding side. See 17 below.
- (ii) inform the other umpire, the other batsman, the captain of the fielding side and, as soon as practicable, the captain of the batting side of what has occurred.
- (iii) report the occurrence, with the other umpire, as soon as possible to the Executive of the batting side and to any Governing Body responsible for the match, who shall take such action as is considered appropriate against the captain and player or players and, if appropriate, the team concerned.

11. Damaging the pitch – area to be protected

(a) It is incumbent on all players to avoid unnecessary damage to the pitch. It is unfair for any player to cause deliberate damage to the pitch.
(b) An area of the pitch, to be referred to as 'the protected area', is defined as that area contained within a rectangle bounded at each end by imaginary lines parallel to the popping creases and 5ft/1.52m in front of each and on the sides by imaginary lines, one each side of the imaginary line joining the centres of the two middle stumps, each parallel to it and 1ft/30.48cm from it.

12. Bowler running on the protected area after delivering the ball

(a) If the bowler, after delivering the ball, runs on the protected area as defined in 11(b) above, the umpire shall at the first instance, and when the ball is dead,
- (i) caution the bowler. This caution shall continue to apply throughout the innings.
- (ii) inform the other umpire, the captain of the fielding side and the batsmen of what has occurred.

(b) If, in that innings, the same bowler runs on the protected area again after delivering the ball, the umpire shall repeat the above procedure, indicating that this is a final warning.

(c) If, in that innings, the same bowler runs on the protected area a third time after delivering the ball, when the ball is dead the umpire shall
- (i) direct the captain of the fielding side to take the bowler off forthwith. If applicable, the over shall be completed by another bowler, who shall neither have bowled the previous over nor be allowed to bowl the next over. The bowler thus taken off shall not be allowed to bowl again in that innings.
- (ii) inform the other umpire, the batsmen and, as soon as practicable, the captain of the batting side, of what has occurred.
- (iii) report the occurrence, with the other umpire, as soon as possible to the Executive of the fielding side and to any Governing Body responsible for the match, who shall take such action as is considered appropriate against the captain and bowler concerned.

13. Fielder damaging the pitch

(a) If any fielder causes avoidable damage to the pitch, other than as in 12(a) above, at the first instance the umpire shall, when the ball is dead,
- (i) caution the captain of the fielding side, indicating that this is a first and final warning. This caution shall continue to apply throughout the innings.
- (ii) inform the other umpire and the batsmen.

(b) If there is any further avoidable damage to the pitch by any fielder in that innings, the umpire shall, when the ball is dead,
- (i) award 5 penalty runs to the batting side. See 17 below.
- (ii) inform the other umpire, the batsmen, the captain of the fielding side and, as soon as practicable, the captain of the batting side of what has occurred.
- (iii) report the occurrence, with the other umpire, as soon as possible to the Executive of the fielding side and any Governing Body responsible for the match, who shall take such action as is considered appropriate against the captain and player or players concerned.

14. Batsman damaging the pitch

(a) If either batsman causes avoidable damage to the pitch, at the first instance the umpire shall, when the ball is dead,

- (i) caution the batsman. This caution shall continue to apply throughout the innings. The umpire shall so inform each incoming batsman.
- (ii) inform the other umpire, the other batsman, the captain of the fielding side and, as soon as practicable, the captain of the batting side.

(b) If there is a second instance of avoidable damage to the pitch by any batsman in that innings

- (i) the umpire shall repeat the above procedure, indicating that this is a final warning.
- (ii) additionally he shall disallow all runs to the batting side from that delivery other than the penalty for a No ball or a Wide, if applicable. The batsmen shall return to their original ends.

(c) If there is any further avoidable damage to the pitch by any batsman in that innings, the umpire shall, when the ball is dead,

- (i) disallow all runs to the batting side from that delivery other than the penalty for a No ball or a Wide, if applicable.
- (ii) additionally award 5 penalty runs to the fielding side. See 17 below.
- (iii) inform the other umpire, the other batsman, the captain of the fielding side and, as soon as practicable, the captain of the batting side of what has occurred.
- (iv) report the occurrence, with the other umpire, as soon as possible to the Executive of the batting side and any Governing Body responsible for the match, who shall take such action as is considered appropriate against the captain and player or players concerned.

15. Bowler attempting to run out non-striker before delivery

The bowler is permitted, before entering his delivery stride, to attempt to run out the non-striker. The ball shall not count in the over.

The umpire shall call and signal Dead ball as soon as possible if the bowler fails in the attempt to run out the non-striker.

16. Batsmen stealing a run

It is unfair for the batsmen to attempt to steal a run during the bowler's run up. Unless the bowler attempts to run out either batsman – see 15 above and Law 24.4 (Bowler throwing towards striker's end before delivery) – the umpire shall

- (i) call and signal Dead ball as soon as the batsmen cross in any such attempt.
- (ii) return the batsmen to their original ends.
- (iii) award 5 penalty runs to the fielding side. See 17 below.
- (iv) inform the other umpire, the batsmen, the captain of the fielding side and, as soon as practicable, the captain of the batting side of the reason for the action taken.
- (v) report the occurrence, with the other umpire, as soon as possible to the Executive of the batting side and any Governing Body responsible for the match, who shall take such action as is considered appropriate against the captain and player or players concerned.

17. Penalty runs

(a) When penalty runs are awarded to either side, when the ball is dead the umpire shall signal the penalty runs to the scorers as laid down in Law 3.14 (Signals).

(b) Notwithstanding any provisions elsewhere in the Laws, penalty runs shall not be awarded once the match is concluded as defined in Law 16.9 (Conclusion of a match).

(c) When 5 penalty runs are awarded to the batting side, under either Law 2.6 (Player returning without permission) or Law 41 (The fielder) or under 3, 4, 5, 9 or 13 above, then

- (i) they shall be scored as penalty extras and shall be in addition to any other penalties.
- (ii) they shall not be regarded as runs scored from either the immediately preceding delivery or the following delivery, and shall be in addition to any runs from those deliveries.
- (iii) the batsmen shall not change ends solely by reason of the 5 run penalty.

(d) When 5 penalty runs are awarded to the fielding side, under Law 18.5(b) (Deliberate short runs), or under 10, 14 or 16 above, they shall be added as penalty extras to that side's total of runs in its most recently completed innings. If the fielding side has not completed an innings, the 5 penalty extras shall be added to its next innings.

18. Players' conduct

If there is any breach of the Spirit of the Game by a player failing to comply with the instructions of an umpire, or criticising his decisions by word or action, or showing dissent, or generally behaving in a manner which might bring the game into disrepute, the umpire concerned shall immediately report the matter to the other umpire.

The umpires together shall

(i) inform the player's captain of the occurrence, instructing the latter to take action.

(ii) warn him of the gravity of the offence, and tell him that it will be reported to higher authority.

(iii) report the occurrence as soon as possible to the Executive of the player's team and any Governing Body responsible for the match, who shall take such action as is considered appropriate against the captain and player or players, and, if appropriate, the team concerned.

In March of 1975 I sat for the first time in the main committee room in the pavilion at Lord's attending my initial meeting of the First-Class Cricket Umpires' Panel. Little did I realise then that I would spend so much time in that room some 25 years later, not only as a member of the full committee but as one of the five member s of the working party assigned to draft the 2000 code of The Laws of Cricket.

That meeting of umpires was chaired by Arthur Fagg, the great former Kent player and a Test match umpire in his own right. Also at that gathering were John Langridge (Sussex), Lloyd Budd (Hampshire), Tommy Spencer (Kent) and Eddie Phillipson (Lancashire), all very good former first-class cricketers and experienced umpires of high repute.

I could not have envisaged then that, some 25 years down the line, I would be part of a committee having to bring forward for consideration a law to penalise players who wished to take so many unfair advantages by going beyond the confines of the laid-down Laws of Cricket. Nor did I expect to have to criticise some of the leading administrators in the game for their utter weakness to uphold the laws that we had in place in the 1980 code. It is their lack of courage that has led to changes under this law having to be made. I could never bring myself to let down all of those great umpires with whom I had sat at that very first meeting of the first-class panel.

My retirement from the first-class panel a season before it was officially due was because of the stance that I took in regard to the upholding of Law 42 of the 1980 code, and in particular to the abuse of Law 42.5, "Changing the condition of the ball", and Law 42.13, "Players' conduct".

In regard to the former, I do not wish to dwell too long upon matters of a decade ago but I will just quote from one or two of my official reports with regard to such matters. In a county match during the 1991 season, my colleague and I reported a side for illegal interference to the ball. This was my third report in 27 days citing the same side and the fact that these reports were countersigned by my colleagues in those three matches made that six reports in all. In my final report of the three, regarding this type of illegal interference, I wrote: "I do intend that this form of cheating will be eradicated from the game and will take all steps required to ensure I succeed." My efforts were unsuccessful as no action was taken in regard to any of those reports. The following season I was present in an official position at two high-profile matches where Law 42.5 was again abused. With no action being taken by the administrators to remedy this situation, I knew that my days were numbered.

You may wonder what all the foregoing has to do with the new 2000 code but those who know the law will realise that the only action that could be taken by umpires in these situations under the 1980 code was that they could change the match ball. It will now be seen that this law has changed so that much more drastic action is available to umpires when the condition of the ball has been altered. Law 42.3, "The match ball – changing its condition", now allows for penalty runs to be awarded against the fielding side, with the bowler being removed from the attack and not allowed to bowl again in that innings. With these dramatic changes, we are now getting closer to the punishment fitting the crime and that is no bad thing.

Over some 250 years, those who have had the good of the game of cricket foremost in their minds, have been those within the membership of MCC. They have given much time in the setting down of the various codes of the Laws of Cricket and while they had the responsibility for administering those same laws, the game remained upon an even keel. It was only when the responsibility of upholding those laws passed into a third party's hands that the game began to deteriorate and the bad conduct of the players was allowed to pass unpunished by the administrators. The third party was perhaps not so bad but the fourth has shown a complete disregard for the very qualities that lovers of the game hold most sacred, sportsmanship and impeccable conduct.

Over the past four years, I have held an official position with the European Cricket Council and in the past 12 months I have found the same reluctance to punish those who abuse the laws of cricket, particularly in regard to those same parts of Law 42. Again, readers may wonder what this has to do with the 2000 code of The Laws of Cricket. I would ask you to scrutinise Law 42.13 of the 1980 code and Law 42.18 of the 2000 code, which deal with players' conduct, and also to look at "The Preamble – The Spirit of Cricket", which was instigated by Lord Cowdrey, at the beginning of this book.

To those who think that any member of the working party had the remotest desire to see penalty runs imposed for the various misdemeanours by the players, I say this: for at least a decade administrators at the professional level have shown no support for those who have set down the 1980 code of The Laws of Cricket; nor have they supported my umpiring colleagues. In short, they have turned their backs upon their responsibilities to the game. The lawmakers, of which I am proud to be one, have had to frame laws that give umpires immediate and severe sanction against those who abuse Law 42. I do hope that this will suffice, and that the introduction of penalty runs will act as a deterrent. If this were to be the case, I am sure that the game would once again give credence to the expression "it is not cricket", and would return to its former glory.

I am not certain that it was the original intention of the members of the working party to set down penalties for so many misdemeanours by the players under Law 42, but as we had gone some way down that road, it was suggested that we went the whole way. If the game of cricket were always played in the manner in which we all know that it should be played, there would never have been a need to visit this law. Unfortunately, most of the misdemeanours have originated and are magnified at the professional level of the game by media coverage, and the antics and actions are aped by those who observe them.

In the main, the parts of this law that are major sources of abuse number about four. Many have felt for years that it is unfair for a law to deprive a side of a bowler, after two warnings, for the act of damaging the pitch, while a batsman could run up and down those same areas with total impunity and receive no reprimand. The progression of this law was that originally an umpire could chastise a bowler and do nothing else. Then a warning procedure was brought in, which did not appear to have any effect whatsoever, for the most severe punishment the perpetrator could receive was to be reported to the authorities. This action was akin to allowing one comedian to use another's banned jokes. Even the players realised that this action was useless and, as far as I am aware, that was the ultimate destination of any report.

As a cop-out, a regulation was framed and was implemented by myself and a number of my colleagues, wherein we could instruct offenders to leave the field of play and remove spiked footwear. They could then return in footwear with rubber or crepe soles. It soon became obvious to those of us who have seen a batsman slide in such attire that the damage which could be inflicted on the surface by them was just as great as by studded or spiked footwear. There was also the fear of the legal aspect of our actions. If the umpire had issued such instructions and the player had carried them out, should that player slip and break an ankle or worse, could the official be held legally responsible for the injury sustained?

Abuse by players of the fielding side of the match ball, the raising of the seam, has been covered in law for almost 60 years, so obviously this is not new. However, all the law stated was the obvious "it is unfair", without any action being laid down. The law was then framed to allow the ball "to be changed for one which had similar wear or use as that of the one discarded" but under Law 42, only the word "wear" was included. This was felt at a later time to be inadequate and the wording was altered to read "change the ball for one of similar condition to that in use prior to the contravention". The law did not mention a reporting procedure, let alone any action that could be taken against the bowler.

In some competitions at first-class level, amazing regulations have been introduced from time to time, ranging from the umpires being allowed to change a ball for the oldest and most worn one which could be found to allowing the batsmen to select one that they desired from a box of spare balls. I can only describe these actions as like using a mousetrap to catch an elephant. No administrator had the strength to take any action and, from what I hear, they are afraid to implement the new law laid down.

Those who study the laws will see that the working party have addressed this matter and have certainly taken appropriate action in Law 42 to penalise those who abuse it.

The whole aspect of time-wasting, so that a loss is not incurred or overs are not bowled, is a problem which was covered many years ago, from 1967 in fact. This was through the introduction of a regulation relating to the final hour of play and, to my mind, it was a great step forward. Unfortunately, this did not punish players for time-wasting at other times during a match. The new law takes this into account and punishment can be administered.

I, like many others, deplore the conduct we see from time to time, but I must say that the number of players who abuse umpires do not make up one quarter of one per cent of those who play the game. While many would wish for an immediate and severe punishment to be available to be taken against such individuals, the working party were of the opinion that laws could only be framed that allowed for punishment of fact and not opinion.

These are, in the main, the areas that I feel had to be tightened up and the ones that cause the most concern. Of course, there are others but, I state again, if players play to the Spirit of Cricket, no actions need ever be taken under any part of Law 42.

One further point before I begin to explain this law and its 18 parts. I have no axe to grind with match referees. I have met only a few of them, and then only briefly, but I do talk with many of my former colleagues on the first-class umpires' panel and get a fair opinion of those who are firm and those who are not. I know that the match referees have a difficult position to fill but I wonder if the right men have been selected for such an important position. When this scheme first saw the light of day, and I was one of those there at the instigation of this panel, my thought expressed to the then Sir Colin Cowdrey was that "if they are there to support the umpires, then that is great". I can tell you that, between July 1992 and April 1995, less than three years, there were 41 incidents of players having to appear at disciplinary meetings before match referees. In only three instances was a player suspended and then for only one match. In one case it was the same player putting in a repeat appearance. In another case the same player appeared twice in 12 months and on the second occasion he was fined only 10 per cent of his match fee for, and I quote, "dissent and attempted intimidation of the umpire after appeal turned down". In my book, that is almost a hanging offence. The weakest action concerns the same player, who again appeared twice in 60 days. The first time, for "showing dissent to umpire and abusive language", his punishment was 10 per cent of his match fee, and 60 days later, for violations of sections 3 and 5 of the ICC code of conduct he was "severely reprimanded". I wonder what would have happened if he had committed the same offences again? He would probably have had one of the administrators kiss him on both cheeks and present him with the man-of-the-match award. Whether Lord Cowdrey's document, "The Spirit of Cricket", will have any effect on conduct of that nature, I am not sure, but at least he, along with all of the members of the working party, have endeavoured to do something for the good of the game of cricket.

And so on to a detailed look at the 18 parts of Law 42, the first of which deals with "Fair and unfair play – responsibility of captains". When I hold my seminars on the Laws of Cricket, I stress, and will continue to do so, that the responsibility lies with the captains to ensure that he and all of his players observe the spirit as well as the laws of the game. When I act as a tournament referee, I emphasise to captains and players at a meeting before the tournament that good conduct is expected of all of them. I also inform them that I am no lover of fines and suspended sentences. For excessive abuse of Law 42.18, as it is in the 2000 code, I will endeavour to make the punishment fit the crime. More on this under Law 42.3.

Part 2 of Law 42 deals with "Fair and unfair play – responsibility of umpires". All umpires, myself included, are most reluctant to take drastic action against players. When umpires have complained to me about a player's conduct, and I have asked them whether they reported the incident, their reply has usually been: "No." I then tell them that they have no grounds for complaint. If they are not man enough to carry out their duties, how can they expect the administrators to carry out theirs? The same individuals then come back at me with: "Well, what use is it?" and I have some sympathy with that sentiment. A couple of seasons ago, after a league match close to my home, two umpires reported a player for verbal abuse directed towards them during a match. The player was suspended by the local league committee but the decision was immediately rescinded by the county league. If this sort of thing goes on, it is no wonder that there is a shortage of league umpires in many parts of the country. I expect stories of this nature can be told from many areas.

There are clearly some actions by players that are not specifically covered by this law yet still can be deemed unfair by the umpires. In these situations a call of "dead ball" will suffice to ensure that the actions do not lead to the dismissal of a batsman, and neither will there be an award of penalty runs. I am thinking of instances such as Allan Lamb putting exploding caps in the hole made by the bowler's front foot in his delivery stride and then covering them with sawdust so that, when the unsuspecting bowler bangs down his foot into the sawdust, they explode. Or David Ward, of Surrey, fielding at forward short leg with all his protective equipment on, when suddenly the striker looks through the grill of David's helmet and spots him wearing a false nose, causing him to reel away with tears in his eyes as the bowler is pounding in to deliver the ball. In the main, such incidents are good for the game and indeed often enlighten a dull day's cricket. In such situations, I have had to call "dead ball", for the simple reason that everyone was laughing so much, myself included.

Law 42.3 covers "The match ball – changing its condition" and this is a matter upon which I could write a book in itself. Indeed, one day I may do just that. I have in my possession cricket balls that have had their condition changed illegally from Test matches, county championship matches, European Nations Trophy matches and one-day games. I also have photographs of others that have been used in certain high-profile matches, with interference to them there for all to see. They have all been documented and deposited in a safe place, should I ever have to produce them. However, these artefacts and photographs are not the subjects of this book. What is relevant here is that reports are available on how these balls came to be in that condition, reports upon which no action has ever been taken. Some of these reports can be read in the book I co-wrote with Jack Bannister, "Tampering with Cricket", in the chapter "The Surrey Factor".

After my professional career had come to a close with the TCCB in 1993, by the terms of my contract I was able in 1996 to write about what had happened in 1991 and 1992 regarding abuse of Law 42.5, although not everything of course.

When I had completed my part of "Tampering with Cricket", I felt relief that such matters for me were now closed, but I think that it was clear how the three officers of the TCCB had, in my opinion, all let down the great game of cricket. Never again would I find myself in a position to have to answer to any of them for actions that I would take to uphold the laws of cricket.

Since 1994 I have been a member of MCC, and my efforts for cricket have been channelled through that organisation. Listed among those efforts was to be the acceptance of a position of tournament referee within European cricket. I am delighted to say that I have seen the game prosper in all of the member countries.

Quite recently I am afraid that Law 42.5 and the one remaining official of the gang of three have come back to haunt me. I had the misfortune to have to administer a one-match ban to a player of one of the European sides for abuse of Law 42.5 and, despite various pleas and then threats from officials of the player's side, there was no way I would alter my decision. Imagine my surprise when, within two hours of my decision, this one official, who still holds a very prominent position in the game worldwide, flew in and called me to a meeting.

He had been met at the airport by those same officials and conveyed to the hotel post haste. After he, the two officials and I had met, he then stated that he desired to speak with me on my own. After what I can only describe as a character assassination, he instructed me to rescind my decision in regard to the one-match ban. Those who know me will also know that I was unable to take that decision. He tried several avenues, ranging from, "why do you get so involved in such a tin-pot tournament?" to " why do you always puff your chest out when making a statement?"

The answer to both questions is easy. To the first, "I love the game and wish to uphold its dignity." To the second, and a little more to the point, "my chest is always that shape because it contains a big, brave beating heart, which allows me to make and take decisions without fear or favour. Unlike one administrator, whose chest contains only a wet sponge and that individual has not the strength to make it even drip."

The outcome of the acrimonious meeting was that I was told that if I did not rescind my decision, he would and he would make a statement to that effect. I replied: "If that is your decision, as tournament referee I will inform the officials of the offending player's team, but it certainly is not mine."

David Lloyd, the former Lancashire professional, umpire, coach and England manager, has said recently that he found some officials "gutless". I found that to be the case in 1992 and again in 1999. Little did I think that the reluctance to take any action in 1992 would be compounded, for abuse of the same law, by rescinding actions that I had been strong enough to take in 1999. Needless to say, my duties as a tournament referee have now ceased.

Returning to Law 42 in the 2000 code, section (a) of part 3 lists the actions that can be taken by players quite legally during a match to enhance the condition of the ball. These actions are always allowed and are reasonable and sensible. Section (b) details the actions that are not allowed and never have been, except in regard to the action by a bowler of scrubbing the ball on the ground. This is not allowed now but it was only outlawed in the 1950s and I am certain that bowlers before this date used this practice to remove the lacquer from the surface of the ball. I once saw a bowler take this action right in front of me prior to an innings starting. Not only did I chastise him but I had to delay the start of the innings to fetch another new ball. It was a good job I was fit, as the ground was the old one at Swansea, with "the steps". Up and down them twice in a ten-minute interval between innings was plenty.

More recently, I have seen a bowler prior to the start of an innings take the ball and run a fingernail around the row of stitches farthest away from the seam of the ball. This action was to free this row of stitches from the final covering of lacquer which is put on the surface of the ball before it leaves the manufacturers, or so I am told. There was no raising of the stitches and I expect that this action is taken by the bowler so as to obtain a better grip. Some bowlers dislike a new ball and prefer it a few overs later when this top lacquer surface has been removed, either from contact with the bat or the surface of the pitch. The attempts by players to cause damage to the surface of the ball, other than by legal means, have become so sophisticated in recent years that a regulation has been brought in that forbids players to deliberately skim the ball over the surface of the ground in returning it to the wicketkeeper. This was always done when the ball was thrown down onto the worn bowling ends of recently used pitches. I had departed the professional game when this regulation was brought in but I feel that it must be very hard to prove.

Section (d) details the actions now available to umpires, and at last my endeavours over the past decade are seen to be coming to fruition. The ball is changed and five penalty runs are awarded to the batting side. After such actions by the umpires, the information that this has taken place is then passed on to the respective parties. The batsmen, the fielding captain and the captain of the batting side, unless he was one of the two batsmen when the decision to change the ball was made, are informed and a reporting procedure put into operation, as it is in all incidents when an award of penalty runs has been made. There are seven specific abuses of Law 42 when such an award can be made to the batting side and four specific abuses of the same law when the award can be made to the fielding side.

Should the umpires feel that there has been further abuse of Law 42, they will repeat the above procedures and furthermore they will instruct the captain of the fielding side to take off the bowler who last delivered the ball. It will therefore be seen that, prior to a bowler beginning an over, it is prudent for both the umpire and players to scrutinise the ball. Should they not do so until one ball of an over has been delivered and it is then found that the condition of the ball has been altered, it will be the bowler who has made that one delivery who is taken off. The action to alter the condition of the ball may have taken place during the previous over or indeed after it had finished. If it is after a bowler has completed his over but prior to the following one being started that the umpires find illegal damage to the ball – and it is generally between overs that this takes place – I do not think that the bowler who has just finished an over will be very pleased. It is he who is suspended from the attack for the remainder of that innings. At last we are beginning to punish a team as well as the players, not only for their own misdemeanours but for an illegal action that may have been committed by other members of the side.

Law 42.4, headed "Deliberate attempt to distract striker", addresses any possible incidents of this nature that may occur before the striker receives the ball but after it has come into play. Note (i) of section (a) tells the umpire to call and signal "dead ball". This immediately stops everything and may prevent ill-feeling later in the match. Note (ii) instructs the umpire to give the captain of the fielding side a "first and final warning", while (iii) says that the umpire must inform his colleague and the other batsman what has taken place. I feel that such a deliberate act of unfair play by a member of the fielding side should not even allow for one warning but that is what was decided by the working party and that is how this part of the law will be applied. In such a situation, there will be no dismissal of either batsman and neither will the ball count in the over, received or not.

Should the umpires have to intervene again for a similar action by any member of the fielding side, the action taken by the umpire will be similar to that above but there will be no further warnings and five penalty runs will be awarded to the batting side. Both captains will be informed of what has taken place, the fielding captain immediately and the batting captain at the earliest opportunity. The umpires are then left with putting the reporting procedure into practice again.

Law 42.5, "Deliberate distraction or obstruction of batsman", deals with such actions taken by members of the fielding side after the striker has received the ball. Sections (a) and (b) emphasise that any action of this nature must be of a wilful or deliberate nature. Note (i) of section (b) details the first action to be taken by either umpire, i.e. to call and signal "dead ball". In (ii) the captain is informed of the reason for the call. Unlike Law 42.4, however, no warning shall be given, although to my mind both matters are equally against the "Spirit of Cricket" and should be penalised immediately. No dismissal can be made if an umpire intervenes, an immediate award of five penalty runs is made to the batting side and the reporting procedure is again implemented. Under note (v) the captain is again informed, even though we will already have taken this action under note (ii). If umpires do not follow this laid-down procedure, though, it gives an opportunity for weak administrators to abort their duty.

Part 6 of Law 42 covers "Dangerous and unfair bowling", with section (a) addressing the "Bowling of fast short-pitched balls". Note (i) is exactly as laid down in the 1980 code while (ii) makes the point that deliveries bowled in such a way and which rise to such a height when passing the striker that they would pass over even the tallest of strikers are still to be considered unfair in respect of this part of the law. All deliveries in (i) and (ii) will be called and signalled as no balls.

Section (b) of Law 42.6, "Bowling of high full-pitched balls", is where I feel that I have failed in my efforts to make the game safer. I was one of the umpires responsible for the introduction in May 1998 of the part of law that penalises any delivery of any pace being bowled full pitch, if it passes or would have passed the striker above waist height. Indeed, I was calling such deliveries as long ago as the 1992 season. I stated in Law 36, "Leg before wicket", my thoughts in regard to parts of this law but I feel that it is worth reiterating them here. A few years ago, when the law mentioned "a fast full-pitched delivery", there was an inconsistency among umpires' interpretations of what was "fast". An umpire had no problem with the other part of the law, in deciding if the delivery had passed above the height of the striker's waist, because they were observing a fact. But pace is a matter of opinion and this, as I say, caused problems. In addition, I and many others consider that a slow or slower delivery is just as dangerous as a fast one. It may not injure as much but there is no denying the pain, should it contact the striker's person. Very often the striker has gone through with his stroke before the ball has arrived when the ball approaches him at the slower pace. I am not against this type of delivery if it passes or would have passed the striker, or indeed if it makes contact with him, below the waist, as there is a reasonable chance of a dismissal. I ask one question: how many umpires have given an LBW decision where the ball has hit the striker's person above the waist? Not many, I would wager. I believe that there are far fewer players given out in this way than there are injuries sustained by players from such a delivery.

When I umpire, I shall only allow a delivery a little faster than stationary. If quicker, I shall call and signal "no ball", should it pass or would have passed above waist height of the striker.

Law 42.7 details the action that umpires must take when they see bowling that is an abuse of Law 42.6 (a) (i) or (ii) or (b) (ii), and also (b) (i), should the delivery be other than slow-paced. A call and signal of no ball is made and a caution is issued to the bowler in the first instance and the relevant parties are informed, i.e. the other umpire, the captain of the fielding side and the batsmen. This caution will remain in force for the remainder of that innings. If there is a repetition by the same bowler in that innings, the procedures will be repeated and a second and final warning will be issued. If the bowler abuses this law a third time, the umpire shall again call and signal "no ball" but when the ball is "dead" he must direct the captain to take the bowler off and advise him that he will not be allowed to bowl again during that innings. It will be noted that this is exactly the same action as in the 1980 code. I feel that if such dangerous bowling is to be stamped out, an award of five penalty runs should have applied in addition to the warnings for the second and third offences.

If an umpire feels that a high, full-pitched ball, as described in Law 42.6 (b), has been bowled "deliberately", he must act immediately under Law 42.8. There will still be a call and signal of "no ball" but no warnings will be given. The umpire will direct the captain of the fielding side to remove the bowler from the attack forthwith and he will not be allowed to bowl again during that innings. Of course, the reporting procedure will be applied. There is no award of penalty runs. If it is against the "Spirit of Cricket", then a penalty should be applied in addition to the bowler being dismissed from the attack. Some people say that the side has suffered the ultimate sanction by having one of their bowlers withdrawn from the attack but, in my opinion, the ultimate sanction would be a five-run penalty award as well.

Law 42.9, "Time-wasting by the fielding side", is one I really like. It is punishment of a side and of an individual of that side, even if he is not the culprit. There is also an award of penalty runs to the batting side and, in addition, the side could lose the services of one of its bowlers. In this case the punishment certainly fits the crime and my only wish is that this punishment could have been applied to other aspects of this law. It must be realised that there is only one warning issued to the captain of the fielding side, "a first and final warning". This will be issued for a waste of time by any member of his team, for whatever reason. I do not see a great need for a call of "dead ball" but the law states that this action can be taken "if necessary". As before, the umpire must inform his colleague and the batsmen of his actions.

Should there be a further waste of time, either by the same member or another member of the fielding side, and this action takes place during the course of an over, the umpire will instruct the captain to take off the bowler forthwith, once the ball is "dead". Even if the bowler is ready to bowl and it is another member of his side who is deliberately wasting time, this is the penalty that will be imposed. He will not be allowed to bowl again during that innings and I imagine the bowler will not be too pleased about any of this. If the waste of time occurs between overs or at some time other than during those six legal deliveries, then there will be an award of five penalty runs to the batting side. The other umpire, the batsmen and the captain of the batting side must be informed of what has occurred "as soon as practicable". I thought that this was only necessary when five penalty runs were to be awarded but in Law 42.9 (b) (ii) we do not make this award.

It is, of course, also unfair for a batsman to waste time and this is dealt with under Law 42.10, where, once again, I think that the punishment fits the crime. Many times over the years I have had to give batsmen a gentle reminder with the words: "Come along, gentlemen, the bowler is ready." Now, under section (a) of Law 42.10, a warning will be issued to the batsman either before the bowler starts on his approach to deliver the ball, or after a delivery and when the ball is "dead". Again, there will be only a first and final warning. What I like about this part of the law is that the warning applies to all incoming batsmen and they will not receive a further warning of their own. As each fresh batsman takes his place at the wicket, the umpire will inform him that a warning has already been issued to one of his predecessors. They must realise that they are carrying the can for a transgression of this law by a previous batsman of their side. The usual parties are also made aware that this procedure is in place.

Under section (b), should any of the remaining batsmen in that innings be the cause of a waste of time, the umpire will award five penalty runs to the fielding side once the ball is "dead". Again, the respective parties shall be informed and the reporting procedure completed.

Law 42.11 is headed "Damaging the pitch – area to be protected" and explains exactly what "the protected area", previously known as "the danger area", is. It is slightly smaller than before, by some 4 square feet, and the reason for this is that the distance between the popping crease and the start of the protected area is increased from 4ft to 5ft. For the mathematicians among you, it was 100 sq ft, now it is 96 sq ft – 48ft long by 2ft wide. No player of either side must cause damage to this area and should they do so, be they fielder, bowler or batsman, action will be taken against them. In the case of batsmen or fielders, penalty runs may be awarded.

Part 12, "Bowler running on the protected area after delivering the ball", is exactly as written in the 1980 code, so there is little to say in regard to its application and action which is taken against the bowler. What I would like to impress upon umpires is that the new distance of 5ft in front of the popping crease should be strictly adhered to. In the past, when the distance in front of the popping crease only extended to 4ft before the protected area began, umpires tended to allow some leeway and it was only used as a guide. Some umpires felt that if the damage was only 4ft 3in forward, that the striker could cover this with his reach, or hit the ball away. Other umpires may well have allowed a bowler to cause damage to a distance of 4ft 6in in front of the popping crease and a deal of inconsistency crept in. Now the distance has been extended to 5ft, a move made to help the bowlers, a batsman will encounter more difficulty in playing a ball alighting on this area of the pitch. Therefore, no latitude whatsoever should be allowed. Any bowler landing beyond that mark must be cautioned as soon as the ball is "dead". As it has been felt prudent to move another 12 inches forward, I am not happy that we still allow an initial warning, then a second and final warning, and then he may damage the protected area again before he is banned from bowling. In other matters that are far less of an encumbrance to the playing of the game of cricket, only one warning is given. We must be consistent, not only with warnings but also in the award of penalty runs, as in the following.

Section (a) of Law 42.13, "Fielder damaging the pitch", specifically states, other than as in 12 (a), which enforces the point, that this part of the law refers to any member of the fielding side other than the bowler.

Under note (i), the captain of the fielding side is issued with only one warning, a first and final. The other umpire and the batsmen are informed of this caution. While it is the captain who receives this warning, it is implicit that the fielder who committed the act of damage should also be informed of the warning, probably by his captain. If it had been left to me, I would have issued only one warning in the case of a bowler who damages the protected area, before he is relieved of his bowling duties for the remainder of that innings.

We can also see that, by collusion, a bowler can damage the protected area twice and then get his team-mate in the following over to damage the same area, making three efforts to enlarge the pit some 5ft 6in in front of the popping crease, with still no action, other than warnings, having been taken against the side or the individuals who caused the damage. The fielder in this case could well be the spin bowler who is about to bowl into the area that has been damaged three times. Before we get ourselves into a bigger hole than we can now find in the pitch, let us return to Law 42.13. After one warning in the case of damage by a fielder, any further damage by any member of the fielding side will incur an award of five penalty runs to the batting side. The usual parties must be acquainted of this action and the reporting procedure carried out.

And so to the offence that started it all and Law 42.14, which deals with "Batsman damaging the pitch" and how he should be punished.

As long ago as 1986, in a match at Oxford, I took action to remedy a situation of batsmen running down the length of the protected area. Since then I have taken similar action on ten occasions and this practice has ceased immediately each time. Bowlers have been stopped from bowling for transgression of Law 42.12 for many years but batsmen have been able to damage the same area with impunity. In two or three instances I have even required batsmen to repair damage that they had inflicted on the surface of the pitch when they have run down the protected area. In one case, in a second XI match between Middlesex and Essex at Chelmsford, justice was really seen to be done. Jason Pooley, playing for Middlesex, ran down the centre of the pitch and slipped, gouging a piece of turf out of the pitch about 7ft in front of the popping crease. After a good ticking-off from me and after extensive repairs had been carried out by him, the game continued. Some 30 minutes later, with Jason batting at that end, a ball flew off the scarred area, caught the edge of his bat and he was caught at gully. As he left, he looked down at the pitch, and then up at me, and I was unable to suppress a smile.

Now, a batsman who runs on the protected area will receive a caution. Even if no damage is sustained to the pitch, umpires must act to prevent damage as, once it has taken place, it really is too late. Each incoming batsman will be acquainted that a warning has been issued and the caution will apply throughout the innings.

Section (b) (i) of Law 42.14 says that, should any batsman damage the pitch again, the umpire has to issue a further caution, which is to be a final warning.

Note (ii) details another action that must be taken by the umpire if the batsmen take no notice of the warnings that have been issued. It is exactly the action that I took at Oxford in 1986 and have repeated a number of times since. All runs obtained from the delivery will be disallowed and the only credit to the batting side will be in the case of a no ball or wide ball having been bowled.

The umpires could have a dilemma with the batsman damaging the pitch and the timing of their intervention with a call of dead ball. The umpires have a duty to prevent damage to the pitch, but on the other hand an early call of dead ball could result in a striker not being given out under Law 32, "Caught". This is not an easy question to answer, however, and umpires must consider each incident on its merit and act accordingly. The first sentence of Law 42.14 (a) finishes with the words "when the ball is dead". Except in the case of a likely catch being taken, I state categorically that I shall be calling "dead ball" immediately, as soon as I observe a striker running down the centre of the pitch in the protected area, as I did at Oxford. We would be foolish indeed if we allowed the batsmen to cause damage before the ball was made "dead". This ludicrous instruction to the umpires is repeated in section (b) (i) and again in section (c). Imagine this situation. The striker hits the ball way into the outfield and the batsmen take three runs before the return is made dead by the wicketkeeper catching the fielder's throw. By this time the batsmen will have completed three sprints up and down the protected area before we are able to act. We really have missed something here. Should the striker be unfortunate enough to have hit the ball into the air, I would not call "dead ball" until the catch is taken or otherwise. I would then give him out and make the award of five runs, the ultimate sanction.

I would like to relate the action I took in that match at Oxford. After numerous friendly warnings to a batsman who thought that the only place he should run after hitting the ball was directly down the protected area, I said to him: "If you do that again I will give you out." His reply was: "You are not able to do that." I said: "No, but I can stop you running down the middle." He hit the very next ball and set off straight down the middle. I immediately called "dead ball", which stopped both batsmen running, and I sent them back to the wickets they had left. The ball reached the boundary and when he asked why I had not signalled the four-run allowance, I replied: "Because I had made the ball 'dead' before it had reached the boundary." He kept himself well off the pitch after that. Colleagues said to me after that incident: "You cannot take that action, Don. You know the laws do not allow you to do so." I simply told them: "Read Law 42.3, you will see that I can." When it is understood by batsmen that they will neither have runs credited to their own individual score or to that of their team, this practice soon ceases.

Should any batsman transgress again, they will get no runs from the delivery and furthermore they will, by their actions, be the cause of an award of five penalty runs to the fielding side. In the extreme case of a striker running down the pitch in the protected area, as he watches his big hit sail over the boundary, he will not get the six runs he was expecting. He will also be instrumental in five penalty runs being awarded to the fielding side, making a debit of 11 runs. I bet he will not do that twice. The usual individuals are made aware and, of course, the same reporting procedure carried out.

I would like to relate one final story in respect of this part of the law. It is a story that causes me great concern and makes me lose faith in this great game of ours. A short time after a match in which I had to remind a batsman a number of times that he was not allowed to run on the protected area, I found myself umpiring the same side in another important one-day fixture. Just after the match started, I asked the same batsman to ensure that he did not run again on the protected area and he did not. After the game was suspended for the day because of rain I found myself in discussion with that same batsman and I enquired why he had managed to keep off the pitch today, when last week he appeared to be able only to run down the middle. This is what he told me. In the match the previous week, he had been told by his captain during the tea interval that "we require about another 50 runs and I want you to get up and down the middle". That is an exact quote. His reply to his captain was: "If I run down the middle of the pitch, Don Oslear will chew my ears off." The captain then told him: "If Don Oslear has not chewed your ears off by the time you get back, I will." A captain of great ability and of high repute, but not so high after I was told that story.

In considering Law 42.15, "Bowler attempting to run out non-striker before delivery", I would ask readers to remember what I have written under Law 38, "Run out", about the bowler's position when the delivery stride starts. The bowler is permitted to run out the non-striker if, before the start of the delivery stride, he is out of his ground. If such an attempt fails, a call and signal of "dead ball" will close the matter and the ball will not count in the over. What about the situation where the bowler attempts to run out the non-striker after he enters his delivery stride? Remember what has been decided in regard to the start of the delivery stride. The decision will obviously be not out from such an attempt but I can see a considerable increase in the efforts by bowlers to dismiss non-strikers under this law which are not legal. It may be best to consider this action by the bowler another case of where five penalty runs should be awarded to the batting side. Looking back at what I wrote in Law 38, I can already see conflict between Law 42.15 and Law 38.1.

Part 16 addresses "Batsmen stealing a run", which is obviously an unfair action and has been so for over 100 years. If the batsmen try to do this, the bowler can try to run out either batsman, the non-striker before the start of his delivery stride and the striker by throwing the ball at his wicket or to the wicketkeeper for the same purpose. I do, though, advise him not to take this action should the scores be level in the match, because the award of a no-ball penalty is an instant one. If action is taken to dismiss either batsman and it fails, then, as the law reads, the batsmen are allowed to gain whatever runs they can. Without doubt, the best action to be taken by the bowler, unless he can be certain of a dismissal, is to take no action. The umpires will not allow a run and when the batsmen cross in their effort to gain one, "dead ball" will be called and the batsmen returned to their original wickets. Five penalty runs will be awarded to the fielding side, all parties informed and the reporting procedure observed. There is no intimation in this part of the law as to the award, or not, of the five penalty runs if the run-out attempt is successful but, as the batsmen were embarking upon an illegal action, to my mind this award should be made.

While there is nothing written under Law 42, there is another case of a penalty-run award to the batting side and it arises under Law 2.6, "Player returning without permission". I have described it more fully under that law but, briefly, if a member of the fielding side returns to the field of play without the permission of the umpire and he brings himself into the game by making contact with the ball in any way, either by fielding or catching it, this will be considered illegal fielding. Some wished for such an incident to yield an allowance of four runs, in the same way that it does if spectator enters the field of play and interferes with the progress of the ball. However, the working party, after much discussion, felt that the fielder's actions constituted an illegal act, just as much as if he had thrown a sweater over the ball. He is a member of the fielding side and must suffer the penalty of illegal fielding for what is an illegal act.

Under Law 3.14 I discussed the many signals that are part of the umpires' duty and by which he acquaints the scorers with the reasons for runs in certain situations. In connection with Law 42, there are two new signals, penalty runs to be awarded to the batting side and penalty runs to be awarded to the fielding side. These signals are easy but I do hope that we get a little practice of putting them into operation. Section (c) of Law 42.17 gives information on how penalty runs are to be credited and, with a little scrutiny of this part of the law, I feel that scorers will soon handle such matters with their usual correctness.

To try to put matters in a nutshell, when penalty runs are awarded to the batting side, they shall be in addition to any other penalties which are to be awarded. If a no ball is bowled and any act that will incur penalty runs takes place, the five penalty runs will be added to the no ball. In this case, it would be one to debit against the bowler and five in the new column in the scorebook; six to the total of the batting side, none of them to the individual batsman. In addition, any runs made and extras gained will be scored. So, should the no ball have been hit and the batsmen complete three runs, and then a situation arise by which penalty runs are awarded, four runs would be debited against the bowler, five marked in the new column in the scorebook, three credited to the striker and nine added to the total. I think that 12 is the maximum which can be credited to the batting side from one ball, as described earlier under Law 42.14, but in this case the hit would have been from a "no ball".

Should the award of penalty runs be made to the fielding side, then these will be added to the score of that side in its most recently completed innings. Of course, much of the cricket in this country is of the one-innings per side variety and, if penalty runs are awarded to the side who is fielding first, they as yet do not have an innings to which those runs can be added. In that instance, prior to them starting their innings, they will already have scored however many runs the batting side were penalised. From this it can be seen that a side could win a match without ever having to bat.

And finally to Law 42.18, "Players' conduct", which will be of great disappointment to many of my umpiring colleagues who deplore the conduct of a small percentage of those who play cricket. The first paragraph sets down what players must not do but unfortunately it is still seen week after week, with players showing dissent to the game, dissent to umpires' decisions and abusing umpires in an appalling manner.

The working party felt that we would be going beyond our brief to lay down laws to enforce what is written in the "Spirit of Cricket" and that it should be left to "higher authority", as stated in Law 42.18 (ii), to uphold the dignity and sportsmanship of the game. Let us pray that we find some administrators who are prepared to do just that.

But as I sat watching the final innings of the recent Test match between England and the West Indies at Lords, an innings in which England had to achieve a score of 188 runs if they were to win, I have to admit to a feeling of both embarrassment and guilt as I watched not only the efforts of the English batsmen but also the magnificent bowling of two of the greats of the game.

Curtley Ambrose and Courtney Walsh almost denied England those runs, and despite some ill fortune they never once wavered, in either skill or conduct, and always with a smile on their faces. They bowled as if their lives depended on the result being gained for their side, but never once did they allow themselves to be seen in any other way than as the best of sportsmen.

It has been my privilege to have both of them run past me in my position as an umpire, and to observe them at close quarters in the heat of battle. At no time have I ever had to admonish them. There are many other West Indian bowlers who I am pleased to say have set these same high standards, going way back to Wayne Daniel of Middlesex, Joel Garner of Somerset, Ian Bishop and Michael Holding of Derbyshire, and in more recent years Malcolm Marshall of Hampshire.

The reason for my embarrassment and guilt is this: I, along with the four other members of the working party, had sat for many hours and days discussing the ramifications of Law 42, "Fair and Unfair Play". We had set down the penalties which would apply to all the various misdemeanours by players who wished to make a spectacle of themselves during a match. But on Saturday, 1 July, I sat and watched players on both sides, and particularly Ambrose and Walsh, show how the game can and should be played. Those two bowlers may have finished on the losing side, but they can most certainly be proud – not only of their own efforts but of having restored to the game that level of conduct which is cherished by all of us who love cricket. If only this had been the norm over the past decade, there would have been no need for us to have re-visited Law 42.

If this is now to be Test cricket, it will do for me.

APPENDICES

Appendix A

Law 8 (The Wickets)

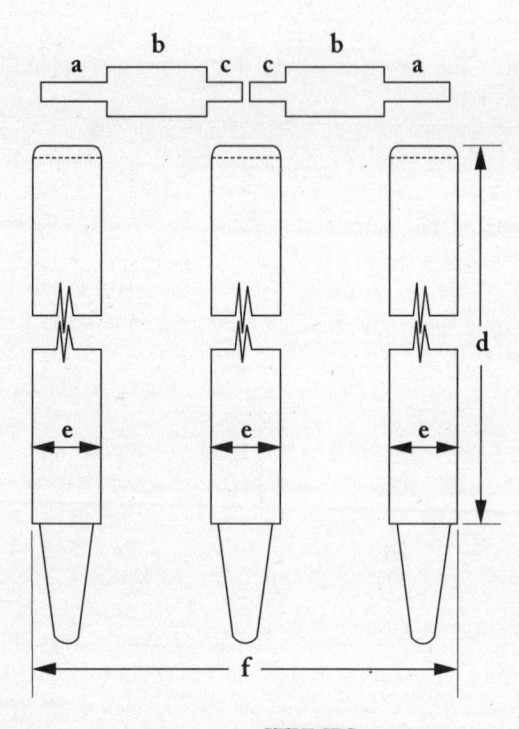

BAILS

	Senior	Junior
Overall	4 5/16 in/10.95cm	3 13/16 in/9.68cm
a=	1 3/8 in/3.49cm	1 1/4 in/3.18cm
b=	2 1/8 in/5,40cm	1 13/16 in/4.60cm
c=	13/16 in/2.06	3/4 in/1.91cm

STUMPS

	Senior	Junior
Height (d)	28 in/71.1cm	27in/68.58cm
Diameter (e)		
max.	1 1/2 in/3.81cm	1 3/8 in/3.49cm
min.	1 3/8 in/3.49cm	1 1/4 in/3.18cm
Overall width of wicket (f)	9in/22.86cm	8in/20.32cm

Appendix B

Law 7 (The Pitch) and Law 9 (The Bowling, Popping and Return Creases)

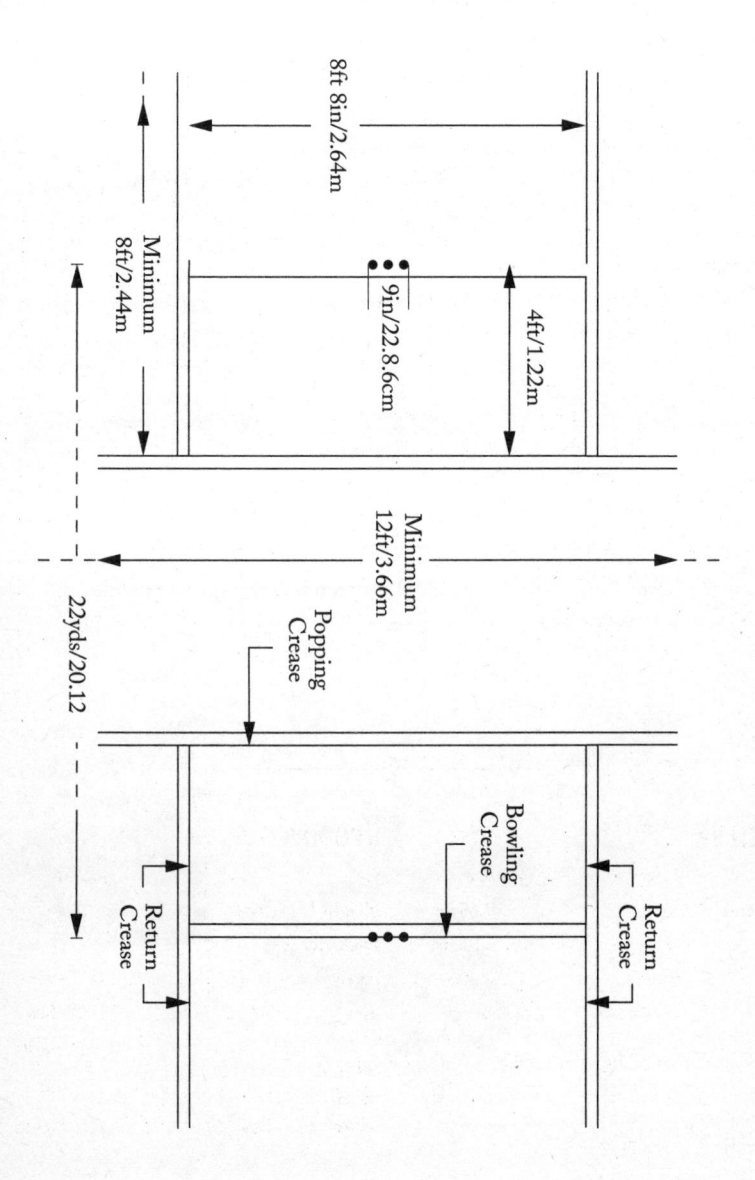

Appendix C

Law 40.2 Gloves

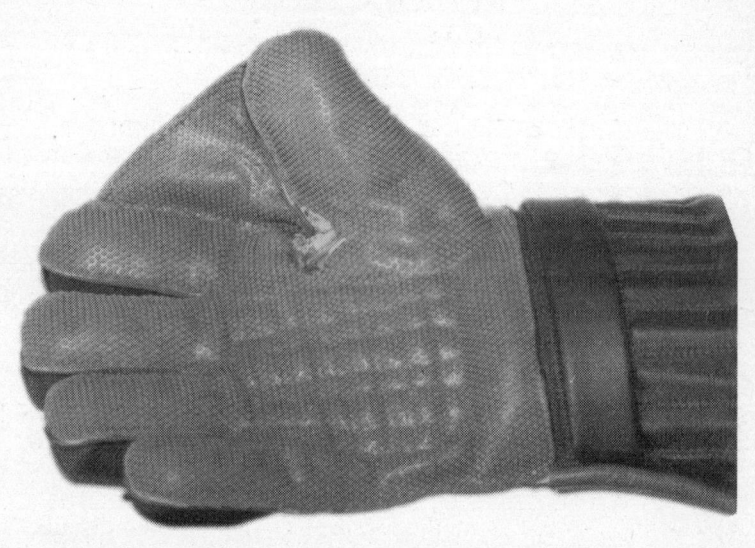

These diagrams show what is meant by:
- no webbing between fingers
- single piece of flat non-stretch material between index finger and thumb, solely as means of support
- not forming a pouch when hand is extended

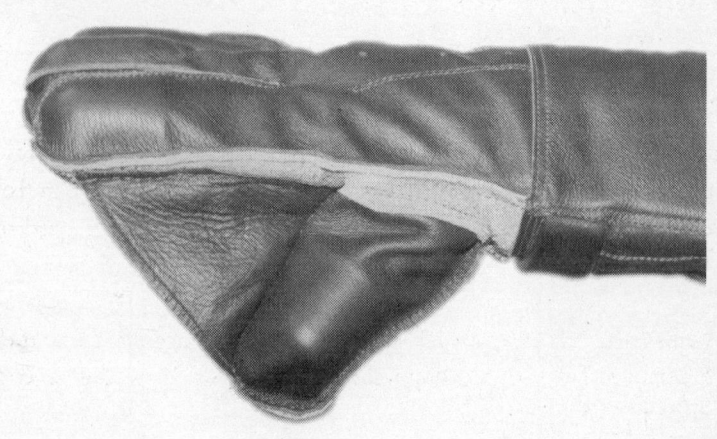

Appendix D

Definitions and explanations of words or phrases not defined in the text

The Toss is the toss for choice of innings.

Before the toss is at any time before the toss on the day the match is expected to start or, in the case of a one day match, on the day that match is due to take place.

Before the match is at any time before the toss, not restricted to the day on which the toss is to take place.

During the match is at any time after the toss until the conclusion of the match, whether play is in progress or not.

Implements of the game are the bat, the ball, the stumps and bails.

The field of play is the area contained within the boundary edge.

The square is a specially prepared area of the field of play within which the match pitch is situated.

Inside edge is the edge on the same side as the nearer wicket.

Behind in relation to stumps and creases, is on the side further from the stumps and creases at the other end of the pitch. Conversely, **in front of** is on the side nearer to the stumps and creases at the other end of the pitch.

A batsman's ground – at each end of the pitch, the whole area of the field of play behind the popping crease is the ground at that end for a batsman.

In front of the line of the striker's wicket is in the area of the field of play in front of the imaginary line joining the fronts of the stumps at one end; this line to be considered extended in both directions to the boundary.

Behind the wicket is in the area of the field of play behind the imaginary line joining the backs of the stumps at one end; this line to be considered extended in both directions to the boundary.

Behind the wicket-keeper is behind the wicket at the striker's end, as defined above, but in line with both sets of stumps, and further from the stumps than the wicket-keeper.

Off side/on side – see diagram below.

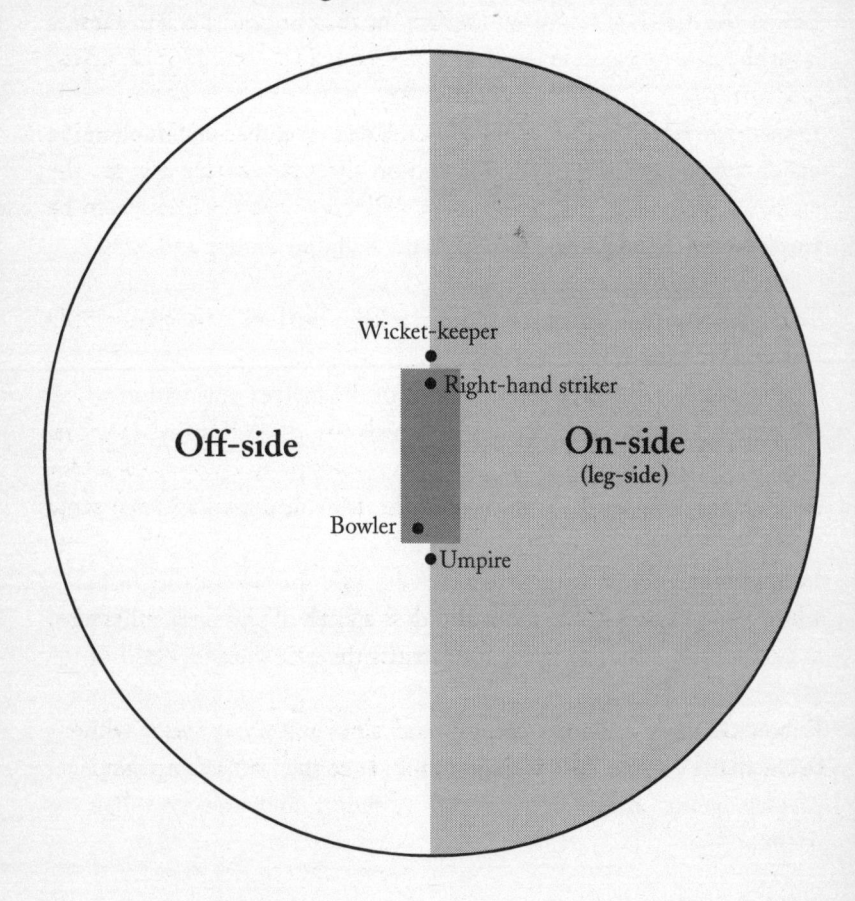

Off-side

On-side
(leg-side)

Wicket-keeper
Right-hand striker
Bowler
Umpire

Umpire – where the word 'umpire' is used on its own, it always means 'the umpire at the bowler's end', though this full description is sometimes used for emphasis or clarity. Otherwise, the phrases **the umpire concerned, the umpire at the striker's end, either umpire** indicate which umpire is intended.

Umpires together agree applies to decisions which the umpires are to make jointly, independently of the players.

Fielder is any one of those 11 or fewer players currently on the field of play who together compose the fielding side. This definition includes not only both the bowler and the wicket-keeper but also any legitimate substitute fielding instead of a nominated player. It excludes any nominated player absent from the field of play, or who has been absent from the field of play and who has not obtained the umpire's permission to return.

A player going briefly outside the boundary in the course of discharging his duties as a fielder is not absent from the field of play nor, for the purposes of Law 2.5 (Fielder absent or leaving the field), is he to be regarded as having left the field of play.

Delivery swing is the motion of the bowler's arm during which normally he releases the ball for a delivery.

Delivery stride is the stride during which the delivery swing is made, whether the ball is released or not. It starts when the bowler's back foot lands for that stride and ends when the front foot lands in the same stride.

The ball is struck/strikes the ball unless specifically defined otherwise, mean 'the ball is struck by the bat'/'strikes the ball with the bat'.

Rebounds directly/strikes directly and similar phrases mean without contact with any fielder but do not exclude contact with the ground.

External protective equipment is any visible item of apparel worn for protection against external blows.

For a batsman, items permitted are a helmet, external leg guards (batting pads), batting gloves and, if visible, fore-arm guards.

For a fielder, only a helmet is permitted, except in the case of a wicket-keeper, for whom wicket-keeping pads and gloves are also permitted.

Clothing – anything that a player is wearing that is not classed as external protective equipment, including such items as spectacles or jewellery, is classed as clothing, even though he may be wearing some items of apparel, which are not visible, for protection. A bat being carried by a batsman does not come within this definition of clothing.

The bat – the following are to be considered as part of the bat
- the whole of the bat itself.
- the whole of a glove (or gloves) worn on a hand (or hands) holding the bat.
- the hand (or hands) holding the bat, if the batsman is not wearing a glove on that hand or on those hands.

Equipment – a batsman's equipment is his bat, as defined above, together with any external protective equipment that he is wearing.

A fielder's equipment is any external protective equipment that he is wearing.

Person – a player's person is his physical person (flesh and blood) together with any clothing or legitimate external protective equipment that he is wearing except, in the case of a batsman, his bat.

A hand, whether gloved or not, that is not holding the bat is part of the batsman's person.

No item of clothing or equipment is part of the player's person unless it is attached to him.

For a batsman, a glove being held but not worn is part of his person.

For a fielder, an item of clothing or equipment he is holding in his hand or hands is not part of his person.